Guide to Library and Information Agency Management

Charles Curran
Lewis Miller

The Scarecrow Press, Inc.
Lanham, Maryland • Toronto • Oxford
2005

SCARECROW PRESS, INC.

Published in the United States of America
by Scarecrow Press, Inc.
A wholly owned subsidiary of
The Rowman & Littlefield Publishing Group, Inc.
4501 Forbes Boulevard, Suite 200, Lanham, Maryland 20706
www.scarecrowpress.com

PO Box 317
Oxford
OX2 9RU, UK

British Library Cataloguing in Publication Information Available

Library of Congress Cataloging-in-Publication Data

Curran, Charles, 1938–
  Guide to library and information agency management / Charles Curran, Lewis
Miller.
    p. cm.
  Includes bibliographical references and index.
  ISBN 0-8108-5115-6 (pbk. : alk. paper)
  1. Library administration. 2. Information services—Management. I. Miller,
Lewis, 1942– II. Title.

Z678.C87 2005
025.1—dc22   2005013271

♾™ The paper used in this publication meets the minimum requirements of
American National Standard for Information Sciences—Permanence of
Paper for Printed Library Materials, ANSI/NISO Z39.48-1992.
Manufactured in the United States of America.

Contents

Contents

Acknowledgments

Charles Curran and Lewis Miller gratefully acknowledge those who helped them with this project, some of whom, because of the sensitivity of their responses, asked not to be identified. The authors appreciate every contribution from every respondent.

Colleagues Robert V. Williams and Robert Molyneux read and critiqued chapters, as did information technology administrator Lisa R. Curran. Encouragement and many useful suggestions were gratefully received from Kathleen Miller. IT manager Larry Miller provided inspiration and motivation by writing and publishing two books on IT security during the time his dad was working on this project. Bosses Fred W. Roper, Daniel Barron, and Gwen Fountain supported this venture. Graduate assistants Cristi Bade, Sarah Nagel, Amanda LeBlanc, and Cara McDaniel provided tireless assistance. Thanks to paralegal Alicia O'Kelley for her encouragement. Marine biologist Mary Carla Curran provided a critical review of the concept of *field guide*.

Practicing information professionals answered numerous requests for input, and the authors are indebted to many others who influenced their thinking about things managerial. Among them are anonymous, Richard Band, Todd Barrett, Brian Beattie, Ralph Blasingame, Dennis Bruce, Marilyn Coe, Trudy Craven, Salley Davidson, Ernest R. DeProspo, Pat Feehan, Henry Hall, Diane Harms, Stephen Hinkley, Jim Johnson, Lisa Kling, Michael Lambert, John Landrum, Helen R. Long, Sarah McMaster, Daniel McNeill, John Olsgaard, Joseph Pukl, Mary Salony, Eileen Saner, Betty Schild, Donna M. Shannon, Carl Stone, J. D. Waggoner, and Susan Williams. A special thank you is owed to the librarians and staff of the Butler University Libraries, who exemplify the best qualities any manager could desire from a library staff.

A special wave goes to Charles, to Catherine, and to Bob Davidson . . . and to Carlisa.

Foreword

The profession has long needed a work that serves to interpret research into practice and at the same time inform the theory class about the derived wisdom of practice. Granted this is not an easy task, which may be why no such work exists. Curran and Miller appear to have made a major step in that direction. The book is a solid, comprehensive, and useful overview of the field. As one would expect in a field guide, the coverage here is one of breadth rather than depth.

The book is written in a style which can fairly be called "Fat-Free Scholarly." Documentation is well done, and there is clearly reliance upon recent work, except in discussing historical matters. It is to the author's credit that they draw fully from the literature of administration and management, not relying solely on LIS writing. The authors cited are certainly tops in their fields, with the exception of the undersigned. There is humor, which recognizes that in healthy organizations life is not solely real and earnest but often puzzling and sometimes humorous. At the same time, the issues and problems presented are treated with the sobriety that their importance merits.

Another strength is that the work is not limited to a type of library organization but indicates application across the breadth of what the authors refer to as "information places," a useful concept that provides bridges to and from many organizations in the field. A very useful feature is that at many points there is a section labeled, "Your Turn," where the reader is invited to consider a practical problem or issue in the light of the immediately preceding section. These sections are helpful to those who might use the book as a text or in training sessions.

On the other hand, this is not a "how-to-do-it cookbook." It won't tell you how to fill out the new budget forms from the county manager's office. It will help you to know what is known and thought about budgets and how they work, and how to work them. It is thus a distillation and not a procedure guide.

Some reviewers, especially those who believe that only that which is known from RESEARCH has validity, and who tend to be over-represented in the reviewing community, will find fault with parts of this work. Those who recognize that things which work in practice are often good theory will find it very valuable.

As with all works in the field guide genre, this one will depend heavily upon the strength of the index which was not seen in the pre-print sheets examined. Many will find favorite quotes in the work which they will reflect and draw upon from time to time. For this reader, the favorite was "the parlor game of separating leadership from management and management from administration can result in the creation of symmetrical lines and boxes on sheets of paper; in the trenches the lines blur and the boxes bleed."

The LIS profession should be pleased to receive this book, and the authors deserve recognition. It will find application in many venues including LIS education and training programs and be useful to many people as they deal with the increasingly complex problems of decision making in information organizations.

F. William Summers
Dean and Professor Emeritus
Florida State University

Introduction

We hope that we have provided a different kind of textbook/guidebook to help new managers, managers-to-be, and veteran managers too. By "different" we mean several things:

1. The authors of this book neither claim exclusive ownership of all managerial truths nor pontificate about what they think they do know; instead they take some stands and invite discussion. We will have achieved our purpose if this book prompts readers to think about information place management and to talk about management with their teachers, mentors, mentees, supervisors, and staff.
2. We know some teachers and managers will disagree with some of our positions.
3. We often provide "Your Turn." We think managers make better decisions when they challenge and evaluate conventional wisdom about things managerial. We invite discussion. We are strong advocates for "the answer may be in the room."
4. The tone is often purposefully conversational and sometimes a bit irreverent. Our use of the term "information place" to refer to the locus, concrete or cyber, of information provision and sharing is a respectful generic reference.
5. This book aims not at providing what other excellent management texts already do very well but at filling in the   cracks between information about managerial principles and the processes required to carry them out. For example, while we display a line-item budget for inspection, we emphasize the processes, political and managerial, which decision makers employ to secure and manage a budget. Of course we care about the differences, structural budget. Of course we care about the differences, structural and conceptual, between line-item and zero-base

budgets. We care, too, about what goes on line 13 of a line-item budget, but what we care most about is the ability to influence the budget process. How does one get the ear of a budget officer? Whom should one court? Who knows what? What if all of a sudden one had to cut a budget that was already bare bones? These are the kinds of questions this book pursues.

6. We have not accepted the singular *they* or *them*. So when a client comes into our information agency, we help *him*. Or we help *her*. Or we help *him or her*. The PC crowd is offended by masculine references to describe personkind and argue that *him or her* is awkward. Perhaps we have already provoked the first discussion about the book!

7. We know there are important differences between administration and management, but we think it makes more sense to talk about how these functions blend than how they separate.

8. Like other management texts, this one pays homage to Planning, Organizing, Staffing, Directing, Coordinating, Reporting, Budgeting, Representing, and Communicating (POSDCORB-RC), but it is not organized around or driven by these key practices. Instead it represents what we think managers, veteran and novice, ought to consider when they set about doing what it is they do. What they do is decide.

But Why a Guide?

Why would an information place manager require a field guide? What is it about being a manager in an information place that requires him or her to do the kinds of things field guides help people do? Well, sometimes field guides answer questions that managers should ask in the heat of battle when they are most distracted. They are in the field. There's a search or a struggle going on. It would be good to have some guidance.

Do information workers have to be able to tell the difference between a deadly tsunami and the benign wake of a water skier? Do information workers need a field guide to take with them to staff meetings so they can identify and avoid disgruntled coworkers and their poisonous fangs? Must they consult a text in order to avoid rubbing a CEO the wrong way and, as a consequence, developing a rash? Is it the male or female board member who devours the significant other? In the midst of problem solving or opportunity seeking, managers sometimes forget to ask important questions. Field guides can help them remember. Field guides do four specific things:

They define and explain
They help people identify opportunity
They help people avoid danger
They help people plan responses

This field guide aims at doing for library and information place managers what other field guides do for beach erosion experts, herpetologists, botanists, and entomologists. It identifies issues and opportunities. It considers problems and ways to deal with them. It supplies concrete examples of ways to achieve success and avoid mistakes. It pays homage to the experts who address the issues contained herein, but it does not aim merely to repeat what they have already offered.

"Red and yellow can hurt a fellow." That advice is often given in field guides to reptiles. Harmless California king snakes have bands of yellow, black, and red. Deadly coral snakes, cousins to our friend the cobra, have similar markings, but they display adjacent bands of red and yellow. So if you spot yellow and red touching, scram. That is a good plan. The problem with this plan is one has to be perilously close to a coral snake to make the identification and solve the problem. So it is with the management of the information place. Managers deal with issues not in the abstract, but up close and personal, and often on the run. Opportunities and problems frequently appear unannounced and without warning.

That is why it is good to have a guidebook handy—a guidebook that helps a manager develop and pursue a mission, make a presentation, supervise, decide, deal with people, nurture a budget, cooperate or go it alone, avoid mistakes, and deal with daily contradictions. That statement describes the conceptual framework for this book. *Conceptual framework* is a favorite expression of people who think about conceptual frameworks. Here, in a little more detail, is what this book is about:

Chapter 1 sets the stage. It describes "the nature of the information place," and it offers examples such as the information services at schools, public libraries, corporate agencies, and knowledge management operations. It asserts three key propositions:

1. Managers of information places must compose lucid mission statements that communicate what business they are in, and

they should save outrageous promises like "create lifelong learners" for the greeting card industry.

2. The people who practice library and information science (LIS) must be able to define it: otherwise that practice will be flawed.

3. Information places exist for the purpose of addressing community information needs. All other purposes are subsidiary.

Chapter 2 emphasizes the importance of communication to the management process and presents a step-by-step guide for managers who want to make good presentations. Its early placement in this text results from our conviction that good communication skills underpin the management process.

Chapter 3 discusses key issues of leadership and management and explores important relationships between these functions. The responsibilities to influence, to decide, and to oversee are major managerial tasks.

Chapter 4 observes that even those who study history are bound to repeat the mistakes of the past. Maybe one can cut down on the number and seriousness of those errors. One can do so if one more fully understands how today's views about managing people in the workplace have taken hold. So we display a few of those views, some from the Garden of Eden and some from a twenty-first century fish market, and some from in between.

Chapter 5 emphasizes the role of the trained staff and offers tips on how to select, train, supervise, and reward them. Sometimes treating valuable employees to lunch may be a more effective boost than the checks on a formal traits-based evaluation form. Firing them! Getting fired oneself! These formidable events are also covered.

Chapter 6 is about people and the way they behave in organizations. What happens when self-interest and altruism collide? Should managers go uninformed, and therefore unarmed, into such environments? This chapter identifies some inappropriate political behaviors, some good ones, and offers some suggestions for building a healthy political climate.

Chapter 7 is unlike many budget sections in other texts which address primarily the types of budgets and the advantages and disadvantages of each type. We take a different path because we believe few managers get to select the type of budget they will employ. Instead they inherit a type, just as they often inherit a staff. So the real question is "How do I best manage the budget I must work with?" Some real answers to this question are provided in this chapter, which is about planning, developing, presenting, and spending a budget.

Chapter 8 is about learning to be a manager. Deciding is the pivotal managerial act, so it presents several opportunities for managers to make decisions in a laboratory setting that offers enough realism to make the event meaningful to the participant and enough safety net so the manager will not fall from grace as the result of a poor decision. The lemon exercise can demonstrate even to the severest skeptic that experiential exercises can work. The second exercise will offer the participant numerous opportunities to employ principles and suggestions from the previous seven chapters. While this exercise is at one level a budget-cutting exercise, it also introduces political behaviors, management styles, personnel issues, communication issues, leadership concerns, and tells us a lot about the nature of the information place.

"You can't have everything; anyhow, where would you put it?" Chapter 9 addresses this problem/truism suggested by comedian Steven Wright. Clients are impatient with the explanation that an information place can neither afford nor house all the information materials they demand. Information managers often attempt to solve this problem by seeking external support and by joining with other information agencies to cooperatively purchase, catalog, store, and make available to all members what no one agency could possibly afford. *Cooperation* is a lovely word and a good thing to do. Cooperative ventures can be fraught with peril too. Cooperative ventures often require separate management. Loyalties can divide. Publishers can bundle their wares and force agencies to purchase items they neither want nor need in order to obtain what they must. Chapter 8 targets the decisions to join, participate in, and withdraw from consortiums.

Chapter 10 is about mistakes, about doing wrong things and not doing right things. Because one's own experience is usually a very severe teacher, we suggest learning from the experiences of others—managers whom we polled to get examples of mistakes for this chapter. We present them in venerable POSDCORB-RC order. The chapter also considers why we make mistakes and offers a series of do and do not couplets for inspection and discussion.

Chapter 11 acknowledges that managers often deal with contradictions and demonstrates why formula approaches may not work. Censorship and intellectual freedom often collide. "Free libraries" are not free. In a very real and important way, the Internet places the selection of some of what an information place acquires squarely in the hands of clients, not staff. Bureaucracies are by nature rigid; communities they serve are often fluid, even turbulent. Managers make their decisions in environments where these kinds of paradoxes intrude.

Chapter 12 is about information policy—those guidelines that cover the management of information from its inception through use and retirement. The term may sound remote and less meaningful to the manager in the trenches. Yet information policy has global, national, and local implications for all information managers. Do you allow your expensive new encyclopedias to circulate overnight? Why not? Is it because there is an "R" above the call number on the spine, and "R" means Reference, and reference books do not circulate? Will that circular argument appease a client who notes that the information place closes at 10:00 P M, thus rendering that expensive information unavailable to the person whose tax dollars purchased it? All politics is local? So are many information policies. There is nothing "remote" about serious challenges to the manager's rule.

Chapter 13 is about knowledge management (KM). The two elements that most clearly distinguish a knowledge management approach from the more traditional approaches to library and information agency management are these:

1.   The knowledge resource that knowledge managers deal with is called intellectual capital, and it often resides in the minds of people, not in books, journals, or reports.
2.   The knowledge manager's chief function is to engineer the sharing of valuable, coveted, often secret intellectual capital among a work force not used to or inclined to share.

Chapter 14 addresses, among other questions that standard texts infrequently tackle, whether it is okay for the boss, the manager, to have sex with his or her secretary. While this may well be an issue of sexual harassment, Chapter 14 is not about sexual harassment; it is about sexual stupidity. It is also about cliques, trust, enemies of information places, crazy ideas, and what to do when nothing works. You will find nothing remotely close to this chapter in any other management text.

Chapter 1

The Nature of the Information Place

This Term: *Information Place*

The term *information place* is used here to describe the location, electronic or concrete, of an information resource. It is a catch-all term intended for use as a descriptor for library, media center, learning resource center, information agency, knowledge center, locus of knowledge management, or archive. Its purpose as a term is neither to mask differences nor to suggest similarities but to accommodate the widest assortment of information acquisition, management, and dissemination functions. It is an umbrella term. It is the beginning of an explanation, not the explanation itself.

Managers and Administrators

Managers and administrators make decisions in information places about the deployment of scarce resources like time, money, people, and equipment and facilities. Managers operate close to the day-to-day action. They provide tactical support. They supervise and evaluate. Even when they manage no other people, just their own time and equipment, they usually function close to the action. Everybody is a manager, actually. Administrators may be a few steps removed from everyday management. They establish priorities, oversee strategic and long range planning, and set organizational goals, as a committee of one or participatively. They have bigger offices. They make higher salaries.

1

Decisions

Decisions are choices. Ideally, one makes a choice from an array of alternatives, ranked according to doability, advantages and disadvantages, and likely outcomes. If the manager's job is to make decisions in organizations, then it would be a good idea for the manager to have a firm understanding of what the organization is supposed to do so that he or she can make decisions that help the cause.

What the Organization Is Supposed to Do

Most thinkers about things organizational assert that knowing "what business the organization is in" is the essential requirement for good management. Years ago Peter Drucker admonished us to state in clear, precise terms what it is we are supposed to be doing (Drucker 1974, 75). Some of us cannot do this. Look at the mission statements we compose. Many of them are packed with metaphors and fancy figures of speech. Many of them communicate very little about "the business we are in." Staff, clients, and funding agencies really must know our specific mission if they are to understand and support that mission. We do not tell them. Instead, we load up with "meet their needs," "produce lifelong learners," "make self-reliant inquirers," and "broaden horizons." These pious pronouncements crowd out references to acquiring and classifying information, retrieving and disseminating it, interpreting it, and helping people use it, which is the business we are in!

Mission Statements

The mission statement and the nature of the information place are topics that intertwine. Mission statements announce purposes; they anchor the organization; they identify the enterprise and announce to one and all how the organization serves its constituents. The very best way to describe an information place is in terms of its mission. We suggest to readers that they use the following checklist to help them construct a new mission statement or to critique an existing one.

  1. Mission statements should make brief, succinct statements about purpose. Two paragraphs should do it. Save the more elaborate declarations for the vision statement or some other document. Mission statements should be readable, quickly, by anybody

who needs or wants to know what the information place is about.

2. Mission statements should tell what the people who manage the information place do. Those people select, purchase, create, acquire, classify, store, retrieve, interpret, and help people use and enjoy information. That is the business. That is what goes on in information places.

3. Mission statements should tell by whom the business is conducted. We believe the statement, "Graduate professional librarians and trained support staff manage . . ." announces the need for educated, degreed, and qualified staff to run an information place, for example. Too many people think anybody can run a library—stamp books out. The assertion about education and training puts the community on notice that the business of the information place requires professional management. Not all information places are libraries, obviously, so composers of mission statements for other kinds of information agencies should find an acceptable alternative to "graduate professional librarians."

4. The mission statement must state for whom the business is conducted. A public library serves all citizens of a given city or county, and maybe others too; a special library serves employees and clients of the firm; an academic library or a school library media center serves the students, faculty, and staff of the college, university, or school; an entrepreneur serves the information interests of anyone who will pay for information products.

5. Where possible, the mission statement should employ the active voice, especially when describing what the business does and who does it. Passive voice is excellent for stylistic purposes and it can provide nice variety and balance, but it is flabby and weak when it diverts attention from doers of actions—the persons accountable.

6. Include the word "purchase" in the mission statement. Lunches are not free; neither are libraries. We must communicate the truism that information places require money to operate. As marvelous as the new technology is, connecting Podunk with the British Library, it is not free. Attic drives often supply missing copies of National Geographic or multiple copies of quaint vanity press volumes of Aunt Hortense's almost publishable poetry, but libraries need money to function. Print, microprint, film, and electronic information is costly and so is the equipment to deliver and store it. "Acquire" is not an acceptable synonym for "purchase." "Acquire." That is how the information place added the Aunt Hortense collection, remember?

7. A very important reason for composing a lucid mission statement, and getting it approved by the powers that be, is to obtain

permission to move in certain directions and to take advantage
of opportunities to expand upon the legitimate functions of the
information place. This is extremely important. Conversely, the
mission statement must not confine the information place to
some lockstep or routine-bound position. That is why the language, "such as but not limited to," with respect to the kinds of
resources an agency collects is so important.

The Martian Example

Suppose a Martian named Zeldar came for a brief visit to earth,
spotted a Wal-Mart, but had no time to visit the business. He asked a
citizen to describe the enterprise. The citizen told the Martian,

> Wal-Mart is a place where dreams come true, where everyday citi-
> zens can come and find what they want. Wal-Mart people greet cus-
> tomers warmly and provide them with mobile metal baskets, cus-
> tomer assistance, and an ironclad guarantee of satisfaction or money
> back. Moreover, Wal-Mart emphasizes American products to meet
> the widest assortment of family needs.

What will Zeldar tell his/her/its friends back at the spacecraft? Has
the "mission statement" told to Zeldar described Wal-Mart and stated
what business Wal-Mart is in? No! It was silent about the purpose of
the store. Neither Zeldar nor Zeldar's friends have the slightest idea
about what goes on at Wal-Mart, not an iota of a clue as to the business
Wal-Mart is in.

Read the mission statement for your information place. Does it
sound like the description provided by the earthling; is it laced with
feel-good figures of speech, or does it announce the purposes and activities of the organization?

A Mission Statement: Westview Public Library

What do you think of this one?

> At the Westview Public Library the staff strives constantly to help
> citizens reach their full potential by providing the means for them to
> grow intellectually and to pursue interests in a wide variety of fields.
> The library staff offer this opportunity in a friendly, nonjudgmental
> manner, and they encourage all patrons to take full advantage of pro-
> grams carefully designed to help them become lifelong learners, re-

energized users of leisure time, and informed consumers of the library's many products and services.

How does this statement match up with the seven criteria in the checklist? Not well, we suggest. If Zeldar asked what earthling libraries were about, how would this mission statement help? We acknowledge the inclusion of the flowery language, such as "broaden horizons" and "lifelong learners," and we have no objection to its use as a descriptive adjunct to a clear explanation of the business. Our number one aim, however, is to describe the business of the information place, and we assert that the business of the information place is to select, buy, classify, store, retrieve, and help people use information. Above all else, this is what the mission statement should communicate.

A Better Mission Statement: Westview Public Library

At the Westview Public Library, graduate professional librarians and trained support staff manage the selection, purchase, acquisition, classification, organization, retrieval, and interpretation of information. The staff acquires a variety of information formats such as but not limited to books, magazines, tapes, electronic hardware and software, maps, pamphlets, and art prints. In order to address the educational, inspirational, and recreational information needs of all county citizens, the library acquires materials on a variety of topics and points of view. The staff are committed to observe the principles of intellectual freedom as expressed in the American Library Association's "Code of Ethics," and they are equally determined to provide advice and help to clients who require assistance in the use of any library materials.

We submit the above mission statement as an example of one that more clearly explains both the reasons why an information place exists and the functions which advance those purposes. It tells what business the library is in. It does so clearly. It avoids making pledges the library could never verify, such as making a lifelong learner out of someone who heretofore may have decided to spend his life doing something other than learning. Having one's horizons broadened is not a bad thing; it may be quite painless. What library has the resources to do the longitudinal studies required to verify claims such as these? None, we claim. Better the library should tell citizens and funders exactly what it is it can do, which is quite a bit indeed!

> **Your Turn:** You may agree that a mission statement is an important document, but you may not agree with the recommendation to include "purchase," and you may strongly believe in telling people in the mission statement that the information place can help them cope, provide leisure time enjoyment, and even change their lives. Argue this case. Compose a mission statement you think tells the story better.

A Context for the Mission Statement

Every information place will pursue a different variety of sub-purposes in accordance with its chief purposes. The chief purpose of the entrepreneur is to market information products that clients will pay for. Academic and school information workers support curricula and help their chief clients, students and teachers, make use of information products acquired and accessed. Knowledge managers in information centers create, acquire, massage, package, and distribute information products needed in their corporate or governmental environments. Though they differ in type and function, all information places, actual and virtual, concrete and cybercraft, share one common purpose: They exist to serve the information needs of people who own rightful access to their products and services.

Agencies thrive when they maintain a focus upon this central, specific purpose and invent innovative ways to accomplish it. They falter when, moved by a self-conscious drive to do good, they depart from it or undertake purposes that exceed their missions and capabilities. Witness the crisis-counseling experiments in libraries. Some would argue that free breakfasts, values clarification, and condoms in schools fall into the *beyond the mission of the schools* category. Administration and management must constantly monitor such decisions to see whether they fit the mission, or if they do not, whether the mission must be amended to accommodate the changes.

The Inner-Outer Environment Model (IOEM) offers a graphic representation of the information place's purpose (figure 1.1).

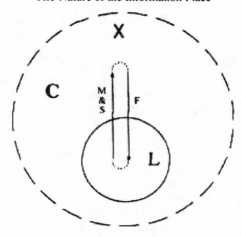

Figure 1.1. The Inner-Outer Environment Model

In the IOEM, I stands for inner and O stands for outer. E stands for environment. So we have two environments in which we operate, an inner and an outer. The inner environment is the information place, labeled L (for library). The outer environment is labeled C for community.

In the inner environment of the library, the staff performs a trio of major functions: administrative, interpretive, and systems. Administration includes planning, budgeting, and organizing. Interpretation includes acquiring, classifying, interpreting, and instructing. Systems people coordinate and maintain the information place's electronic enterprises.

In the outer environment (C) of the library reside all those persons who have rightful access to the information place's materials and services. While C has geographical properties—boundaries and tax districts—the community is defined conceptually rather than geographically because the locus of clients can vary. Consider the archive. The majority of its clients may be historians and genealogists who live mere blocks away, but a substantial minority of clients may live thousands of miles away, in other continents, even. Communities are sometimes amorphous; clients come and go. People living outside geographical tax boundaries sometimes purchase nonresident privileges. Sometimes libraries federate or provide reciprocal borrowing privileges to residents in one or more additional jurisdictions, thus expanding their "communities." By contrast, in some corporate or government settings, the community may be a strictly defined core group of employees and/or clients whose access to highly sensitive organizational intelligence is tightly managed.

The 'definition" of community may vary from information place to information place, but the chief purpose of the information place, four walls or electronic, Carnegie or cyberhighway, is to serve the information needs of the community. That is a universal, a generic. All other purposes or functions—literacy, coffee shoppes in the reading rooms, lamination and deacidification, story hour, *homeworker helper,* collecting the cultural heritage, and summer reading fairs—are related to the one central mission: to serve the information needs of the community.

In the IOEM model an arrow extends from the inner environment, or library, to a target group X in the outer environment, or community. The arrow from the library represents materials and services. The arrow from the target group to the library represents the feedback from the target group to the information place. Managers must engineer this flow and feed it into the decision apparatus of the inner environment. By basing their products and services upon needs analysis and other feedback generators, managers "close the loop" and form a communications loop between agency and customer. Making the loop work can provide valuable answers to the question, *How are we doing?*

The model displayed shows only one X. Actually, there are many Xes dispersed throughout the community. There are multiple targets of opportunity, therefore, with a variety of information needs and a number of different ways of dealing with them, some of which can involve the information place.

What People Do in These Information Places

The IOEM is an abstraction that has to be managed into being. People who work in information agencies earn their keep by knowing about and acting upon:

The Origin of Information

How do knowledge managers, and librarians too, discover where information begins, where it resides, and how to access it in its earliest stages? Sometimes these origins can be found in lab reports, journals, or even books. Often they reside in the minds of people and constitute a major part of an organization's intellectual capital.

The Dissemination of Information

How is information spread? What are the mechanisms of disbursal? Once on hand, how do managers make sure it flows to whoever needs it? How do the invisible college and the back-fence college work?

The Acquisition of Information

Who provides information? How do managers deal with vendors and publishers? How do managers set up an acquisitions department and coordinate with the collection development and cataloging departments. When does it make financial sense to participate in an approval plan with a supplier? What reporting systems best inform the organization about how the budget is being spent?

The Properties of Information

What does the acquired information look like with respect to format, subject, language, audience level, type (fiction/nonfiction), and form (verse/prose)? Is it a music disc, an art print, electronic, or microprint?

The Classification of Information

Based upon these properties, how do managers catalog and classify the information? What subject headings and classification numbers apply? How do they process the information for client use, and what access instruments do they create?

The Organization of information

What architectures do managers select for the arrangement of electronic information so they and clients can access it? Where, physically, do they display print sources in the information place? How do factors such as format, currency, and usage affect placement? What decisions do they make about dated or little-used information?

The Storage of Information

What are the best ways to present and store information: print, electronic, or micro? Should little-used but potentially useful documents be stored off-site? The decision to acquire electronic information necessitates the acquisition and maintenance of what additional equipment and climate control capability? Shall storage be open or closed to clients?

The Retrieval of Information

Once managers have acquired, classified, organized, and stored information, how do they call it back for themselves and their clients? Do they retrieve it for clients, or do they permit clients to do the searching? If clients search, which managers teach them retrieval techniques? How do factors like speed and accuracy affect document deliverability?

The Interpretation of Information

Whose responsibility is it to determine what the information *means*? Is the dynamic neutrality once practiced by library managers an obsolete value in the information age? Whose responsibility is it to interpret, evaluate, synthesize, and organize retrieved information? Who teaches these information literacy skills? Do the answers to these questions vary according to the type of information place?

The Use of Information

Who uses information and who appears not to? Are there ways to encourage use? What kinds of information appear to have the most appeal or utility? How does one study user behavior, and what does one do with the results of such study? How should what managers learn about user behavior affect information system architectures and public service provisions?

By the way, a useful pneumonic device for remembering this assortment of responsibilities with respect to managing information provision is ODAPCOSRIU. You can say it, O-DAP-COS-RI-U. It rhymes with "What do information managers do?" They "ODAPCOSRIU" (Curran 2001).

Your Turn: "What is the best way to market hand soap in the Southwestern United States?" Considering the mission statements that would apply and the manager's responsibilities with respect to retrieval, use, and interpretation, how would you respond to this question in a high school where your client is a student writing a term paper? How about in a special library where your client is the CEO of the soap company? Hint: In scenario one curriculum support is your chief concern; in scenario two it is the bottom line.

The Organization of the Information Place

Any attempt to provide a graphic representation of the organizational structure of the information place always draws several immediate reactions. One is I am a school library media specialist, or I am in a one-person operation, and that pyramid does not apply to me. Another is the hierarchical pyramid no longer describes my situation. Organizations are flattening, and there is less up-down structure and more lateral linkage.

To those who observe that they function in smaller operations, with too few people to fill the slots depicted in a standard model of organization, we offer the suggestion that it is the functional aspect of the model that applies in their cases. They may not have an acquisitions librarian on staff, but someone must perform the function of acquisitions. That acquisitions function exists in a context that includes selection, classification, organization, and interpretation. In the case of a one-person information place, one person performs all those functions, and how the manager coordinates those functions is extremely important. The pyramid may not describe every staff, but it does identify key functions in every information place.

The second favorite indoor sport among many observers of organizational structure and behavior is to predict the demise of the bureaucracy. They speak about dated hierarchical concepts, the supremacy and insurgency of collegial models, the flattening of traditional bureaucracies, task force approaches, and other surefire evidence that bureaucracies are dying animals. They cite red tape, impersonality, delay, maintenance of the status quo, and the Peter Principle as bureaucratic ills and predict that the end is nigh. Such forecasters win approving nods from ivory tower types, but the fact of the matter is that the vast majority of employed people work in bureaucracies, and the vast majority of people who are about to become employed will join a bureaucracy.

Why Is This?

We think it is because bureaucracies work. People in bureaucracies eventually manage to get the job done. People in bureaucracies usually know what their jobs are and what their jobs aren't. This sometimes infuriates the customers in line or the people on hold who have to listen to music they normally would not choose. Bureaucracies divide chores manageably. People in bureaucracies usually know whom to report to. They can access numerous written procedures and regulations.

And, wonder of wonders, bureaucracies can coexist with, even accommodate, just about every new quick-fix managerial orthodoxy, which is why task forces work in bureaucracies, and so do management by objectives, total quality management, quality circles, empowerment teams, and job enrichment schemes. Collegial models, once thought to be the very antithesis of bureaucratic ones, thrive within hierarchies, as the success of research and development teams within corporations and the durability of colleges within universities clearly indicate.

So we display the bureaucratic model for inspection, fully aware that the pyramidal structure looks less glamorous than the glitzy concentric circles that describe collegial models or the symmetrical geometrics that portray bureaucracy's competitors. We know that bureaucracies are slow, resist change just for the sake of resisting it, sometimes coddle the incompetent, often employ burnt-out citizens, and seek to perpetuate themselves. They are all around us, however, so let us know them and make them better (figure 1.2).

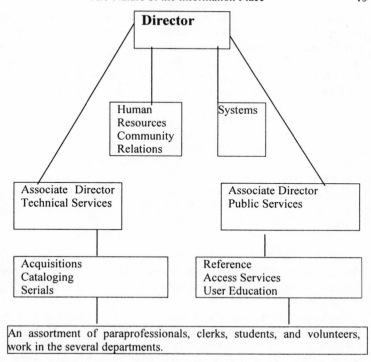

Figure 1.2. The Typical Bureaucratic Hierarchy of a Typical
Information Place

What Drives the Information Place to Do What It Is Supposed to Do?

As important as it is to know what business it is that the information place conducts, it is equally important to know the values that drive the organization to accomplish its business. "Core values" is a term that applies here. A value is a belief that someone or an organization holds dear. Values drive behavior. They supply the why which influences the what. We suggest earlier in this chapter that the IOEM, the Inner Outer Environment Model, displays the single most important value—service to a community—that should drive the information place to pursue its business.

That certain values should drive practice is in itself a value statement which has drawn fire from advocates of special interests, political correctness, and various kinds of information service providers. Witness the attempts of the ALA's Core Values Task Force. Their posted list of core values never got past the language police (DeCandido 2001, n.p.). Here are the core values the task force suggested:

- The connection of people to ideas
- Unfettered access to ideas
- Learning in all its contexts
- Freedom for all people to form, to hold, and to express their own beliefs
- Respect for the individual person
- Preservation of the human record
- Professionalism in service to these values
- Interdependence among information professionals and agencies

The task force offered that the *core* core value was the connection of people to ideas. "All others flow from that" (DeCandido 2001, n.p.; see also DeCandido 2000).

Perhaps if those who found conceptual and semantic fault with the Task Force's list were to digest Michael Gorman's excellent *Our Enduring Values* (Gorman 2000), they would have more tolerance for the list, or perhaps even less. In any case, Gorman holds that "those of us who believe in real libraries serving real people need, now more that ever, to reaffirm our values and value" (Gorman 2000, 4).

We invite anyone who is considering the administration and management of an information place, and everyone who is considering visiting or using an information place, to consult Gorman's book and see his explanations of central values, both for librarianship and for libraries. For librarianship,

- Stewardship
- Service
- Intellectual Freedom
- Rationalism (for management and procedures)
- Literacy and Learning
- Equity of access to recorded knowledge and information
- Privacy
- Democracy

For libraries,

- A focal point of a community
- The heart of the university
- The one good place in a city
- The collective memory of a research institution
- The place remembered fondly by children when grown
- The solace of the lonely and the lost
- The place in which all are welcome
- A source of power through knowledge

(Gorman 2000, 26-27, 30).

We would add here a variation of the venerable "right book" statement. At the very heart of our reason for being is the responsibility to provide the right information product or service, in a timely fashion, to people who need it, and at a cost which they can afford. In some kinds of information places, notably knowledge management operations and entrepreneurial ones, this may involve creating and distributing interpreted data in response to specific needs and requests. Special librarians in a variety of information places anticipate interest from user profiles and offer programmed responses to clients.

Some Types of Information Places: A Managerial Perspective

At a very early stage in one's study or employment, an information manager may develop a target fix on a given kind of information work, even on a specific job in a specific building. We think this limits options and closes the door to opportunity too quickly. We also believe it is useful to understand the various kinds of issues which confront managers in the several varieties of information places.

Students also hear conflicting views about management itself. Some authorities claim, "Management is management." They assert that a good course on management in business administration, in education, or in social work will cover the same general issues. Other authorities insist just as strongly that media center management requires a unique set of skills which are available to students only in special school library media center management courses. State certification administrators agree.

As is the case with many pronouncements, each of the above two points of view is valid to a degree. Management is management, and there are many common truisms that cross type lines. Yet the fact that client groups differ from type to type matters to managers. Children are different from scientists. Both of these groups differ from research staffs and parents, and they differ from school teachers and nurses.

Why should managers in training know about managing various kinds of information places? This knowledge may

1. Help identify career options and opportunities
2. Help identify course options
3. Be of great value should they ever change jobs
4. Influence their choosing to join a consortium
5. Enable them to interact with other managers at professional meetings
6. Help them share a kinship

Public Libraries

Tax-supported public libraries have existed in the United States since the early 1800s, and their main job is to serve everybody. Not everybody accepts this service, but today public libraries exist to serve all citizens who earn this service as a condition of their residence within the political boundaries from which the libraries' tax support comes. Forward-looking administrators and managers who understand the political process can successfully influence the politicians who set funding levels. They do this by demonstrating their accountability and vigorously delivering this message to the public and to the funders. By law, most public librarians do this through boards of trustees and friends groups who can be the official spokespersons for the library, and by accepting every opportunity they can to represent the library to community groups.

Public library management performs a tough job. While many of their clients are part of the captive audience of students with assignments, half or more of their business comes from people who are not required to visit the library but do so of their own choosing. Managers try to influence that choice, that client decision to trade his or her valuable time for whatever it is that the public library can offer. Public library managers must market. They must find out what people want, acquire it, and deliver it. Public library managers must plan strategies and tactics to accomplish this purpose and they must conduct evaluation procedures that reveal how successfully they planned. They must recruit and train employees who can participate in this endeavor, and they must retrain, discipline, or fire the employees who cannot.

Public library managers deal with budget crunches, soaring costs, demanding clients, the electronic revolution, censorship, latchkey children left unattended, street people, problem behaviors, and the mounting necessity to train staff.

Academic Libraries

In the United States academic libraries serve institutions enrolling students above the twelfth grade. These are technical schools, junior colleges, colleges, and universities. Some are private, some are public, and some are a mixture of both, as in state related.

Like those serving elementary and secondary schools, the academic libraries perform an educational function related to the mission of their parent organizations and in specific support of the school's curriculum. The faculty is supposed to teach to that mission and the library is supposed to support instruction with resources for study and research.

Insofar as management is concerned, the chief clients of the information place are the faculty who make the assignments which require their students to visit the library, virtually or in person. Therefore management has to recruit, train, and supervise a staff of professionals, support personnel, and student workers who will serve the faculty and the students who pursue research interests, assignments, and personal interests.

User education is a major function of academic libraries, many of which offer courses in research methods. In many of these libraries it is a common sight to see information service personnel patrolling the computer areas and looking for opportunities to help users with their computer searches.

In the case of large university libraries where research is the main interest of the faculty, the library staff often caters to the interests of those researchers. Most often the curriculum of the school will drive acquisitions, but faculty interests also influence purchases. Ideally, curriculum and personal interests of faculty dovetail or at least peacefully coexist.

Academic library managers face the usual organizational problems: budget, staffing issues, and the ever present requirement to demonstrate accountability. There are some problems peculiar to this type: a sometimes unreasonably uncooperative faculty group who are impatient with the details of running an agency, and a significant cadre of work-study student staff who come and go and who require frequent training sessions.

Most academic librarians are spared the censorship woes suffered by their cousins in school and public libraries. Generally they weed their collections less often and much less brutally than school or public librarians do. Whereas public and school librarians sometimes operate with tiny budgets, the librarians at large university libraries may spend hundreds of thousands of dollars per year on acquisitions. Many of the large libraries establish a curriculum-related profile of need and then work with vendors who automatically supply newly published items which match the profile. This is a partial outsourcing of the collection development function, without which the information place could not spend its materials budget. *Spend it or lose it to the general fund of the university* is a mighty motivator.

Major concerns surface in the electronic age to confront academic library managers, chief among which are the intricacies of licensing arrangements accompanying the purchase of electronic products, copyright issues, intellectual property rights, and keeping up with the latest technologies. A problem with the latter is the enormous training requirement the new electronic media demand both for the training of information personnel and for the training of users. Academic library managers quickly learn that teaching is one of their chief responsibilities, in addition to planning, deciding, deploying, supervising, and evaluating.

Managing in the academic library has many rewards, not the least of which is contributing measurably to the learning process, both by partnering with teaching faculty and by participating in cooperative arrangements (like the consortiums considered in chapter 9) to help facilitate that learning.

School Libraries

School libraries, or school library media centers, serve teachers and children in schools which enroll preschoolers, kindergarteners, and children in grades one through twelve in elementary schools, middle schools, junior high schools, high schools, and certain vocational schools.

"When I earn the proper credentials and take over a school library, media center, or learning resource center, will I be a manager? Will I decide how to run the media center, or shall someone else make those decisions for me? Shall I manage a program in which the centerpieces are electronic skills, computer and information literacy, and the joys of reading, or shall I be the "sitter" for the classes of students whom teachers have sent to me while they enjoy their planning periods?"

We begin this section with these questions because experience teaches us that when school library media specialists enjoy decision-making prerogatives, support from building-level supervision, and the cooperation of teachers, they can manage superior programs. Managers of successful media programs enjoy enormous psychic rewards. Experience also provides us with examples of media specialists who struggle to put to use the skills and techniques learned in their LIS educations, so challenged are they by administrative interference and indifferent teachers. Rewards are harder to achieve under these circumstances.

An applicant for a school library media center position can discover during the interview process what specific challenges the new manager will face. We propose, therefore, that at the job interview an applicant should ask some key questions. The prospective new hire will want to avoid creating an adversarial relationship during the information gathering, so he or she may wish to soften these questions somewhat. We believe the following questions get at issues the candidate will want to know about before, not after, signing on board.

1. Is there a budget for the media center and who sets the allocation amount? How may I influence this process?
2. Will my acquisitions requests be honored?
3. Will I have the opportunity to demonstrate that the media center staff performs essential functions so that when teachers are absent, media aides will stay on duty and not be routinely withdrawn as substitutes for the classrooms?
4. What is the scheduling arrangement? Is it fixed, requiring teachers to send students to the library at designated times? Or is it flexible, permitting me to schedule teachers and classes as needs and opportunities are discovered and developed? Or is it a mixture of these?
5. Will I have the opportunity to meet with teachers and instructional teams in order to help integrate electronic skills and information literacy with the goals of classroom instruction?
6. Are non-media center functions scheduled in the media center during school hours (standardized testing, for example)?
7. Does the faculty observe a policy which governs the use of entertainment videos during class time?

8. If a teacher or a parent complains about a book and/or demands its removal from the library, what policy does this
school observe?

The answers to these questions should help the job applicant determine
whether he or she will be a manager or will be managed by situations
and by others.

A manager needs to know that there will be a budget and that he or
she may submit a budget request, not merely spend the dollar figure
granted by some authority. Knowing that someone is not going to red-
pencil acquisitions decisions is also important, as is understanding that
one's aide is not going to be commandeered to fill in for an absent math
or language arts teacher. If scheduling procedures allow for opportunities for teachers and media specialists to meet and plan together, this is
a definite managerial plus. The media specialist who knows that the
program will not be disrupted by non-media activities can plan with
more assurance. After-school teacher meetings or parent visits, if
scheduled in the media center, offer the media specialist valuable public relations opportunities. If there is a school policy in place which
regulates the showing of entertainment videos in the classroom, this can
spare the media manager from having to deal with unreasonable requests. If the media manager has the support of approved policy and the
principal when the censor calls, this is a great comfort.

Ideally, principals, teachers, and students will consider the media
center as the heart of the school's academic program and the hub of its
information function. Unless the principals, teachers, and students are
especially anointed, however, this will not just happen. The media specialist will have to engineer it.

To do this, the media specialist must write and win administrative
and board approval for collection, selection, weeding, and challenge
(censorious complaints about books or other materials) policy.

The media specialist must win administrative support by convincing principals that the media center should play a central role in the
school's instructional program. The media specialist should seek to be a
full member of the school's curriculum committee.

By aggressively marketing the media center program to the teachers, the media specialist may win them one by one to the realization
that wise use of the center contributes to student accomplishment and
helps the teachers teach well.

In years past, we have personally conducted informal investiga-
tions of the curricula and textbooks studied by educators who seek certification as school administrators. We found references to the school

library or media center, in the syllabi of courses and in the texts, conspicuously absent. This means that if the building-level supervisors are ever to become "media minded," the job of making that happen falls squarely to the media specialist. No one else will do this marketing job. The media specialist must educate the principal and also many of the teachers about the role the information place, real and virtual, can play in the life of the school and its students and teachers.

The manager of the media center must market: discover needs, develop products and services which address those needs, and publicize and deliver those products and services to teachers and students. Winning teacher support, incrementally rather than en masse, is key here, for the teachers have the greatest influence on the students. Student use of the media center rises and falls in direct relationship to teacher recommendations and assignments.

To be successful, school library managers must earn administrative support, develop sound policies, educate faculty and students, keep up to date, market the information place, train staff, recruit and supervise volunteers, encourage parent support, and provide hospitable surroundings. Otherwise the job manages the manager.

In offering services to children and young adults, school library media specialists and also the children's services librarians and young adult librarians in public libraries, give assistance to children and teens in very special ways. By providing story times for children and their parents, too, and places where teens can congregate in nonjudgmental surroundings to read and talk about the things that matter to them, librarians spark imaginations, encourage inventive problem solving, and enlist interest in the spoken and printed word—an essential precondition for information literacy and for cultural literacy.

Special Libraries

The term *special library* is very difficult to define because there are several different types of special libraries and some that are part special and part something else, usually academic. There are special libraries attached to government agencies, corporate entities, and academic institutions. The library of a state judiciary is a government library, the one at the corporate headquarters of a textile firm is an industrial or corporate one, and the law library at a university law school is part special, part academic, whereas the law library at a private law firm is a "purer" form of corporate special library. Some large urban libraries have technology divisions which serve local industry. These information places are part special and part public.

Special libraries are called special for three special reasons. First, they usually collect in special, even narrow, areas. Their subject collections mirror the specific interests of the parent group. For example, special librarians in a public utilities special library may collect materials on electric power management: the acquisition, storage, disbursal, and costs of electric power. They may place particular emphases on research and development, marketing, and alternative (competitive) power sources. They might collect print, micro, and electronic products. They may not have any interest in popular nonfiction or novels.

Second, special libraries serve a very special clientele, usually the employees of the sponsoring company, and sometimes no one not so connected. Often the pursuits of the sponsoring company are secret and subject to competitive intelligence raids, even espionage; hence the need for strict controls.

Third, special libraries offer a very special brand of service. It is demand driven, aggressive, and liberal. Special library managers focus upon the interests of their clients, often developing user profiles which guide acquisition and alerting/delivery activities. Special librarians do not always wait for demands to surface. Rather than merely react, they often assertively seek opportunities to serve clients. Service in a special library is of the liberal type. Special librarians search, analyze, package, and deliver information to clients. Their primary job is to find information and provide it. They do provide instruction on occasion, especially in the use of electronic resources. Where their purposes are substantially educative, as in the case of a music library at a university, they may provide more traditional, less liberal, services to the students who are supposed to be learning how to navigate. To the faculty they may provide fuller, liberal service, such as assembling items or providing annotated subject lists on request.

The significance of all of this for special library managers is considerable. In the corporate environment, the existence of the special library is tied directly to the bottom line. Special library managers continually demonstrate their contribution to the corporate welfare, or they go away. No law says a chemical company must have a library. No state ordinance requires every corporation to have a certified librarian the way some states mandate that every school employ a media specialist. Very few corporate types intone librarianship's favorite metaphor: "The library is the heart of the institution." An underperforming corporate library is subject to reduction in force or elimination. Corporate special librarians keep their jobs by demonstrating that they make money for the company and that without the library the company would lose money. This is a pressure-packed situation for the library manager, but the rewards are greater in that special librarians are paid better than their public, academic, or school cousins.

Special library managers must market successfully. They have to be resourceful searchers and keen analysts of retrieved information. They have to be able to plug into information flow at its earliest stages, so crucial is current information to corporate pursuits. They must possess superior interpersonal skills. Like other managers, they plan, budget, recruit, hire, train, supervise, discipline, reward, and fire.

Entrepreneur

A successful entrepreneur is a person with information skills who prefers the freedom and challenge of the marketplace and decides to strike out on his or her own rather than work a rigid schedule, for a boss, in a building. Instead of providing information for free in a library, the entrepreneur provides it for a fee to people willing to pay for it. Interestingly, some entrepreneurs do research for free in the public library and then charge their clients for information public librarians provided. Some people, mostly the public librarians, have questioned the ethics of this practice; the entrepreneurs seem at peace with the process.

Information broker is another term for entrepreneur, and sometimes these brokers find companies who sell information for a living. Some entrepreneurs work for a consulting firm, and in a building, for a boss, after all. So the real entrepreneur in this example is the company, but many people with retrieving, sorting, and analytical skills get into the business of selling information to people who need it and will pay for the convenience of having it delivered.

In the mid-1970s when electronic searching established a foothold, some information pioneers opted to try to sell their searching and retrieval skills. Many of them failed. They failed because their marketing skills were underdeveloped. They had thought that their searching skills were all that they needed to thrive. Entrepreneurs do not enjoy the benefits of captive audience syndrome. Teachers do not deliver twenty-five clients to the entrepreneur the way they do to the school library media specialist. So the entrepreneurs survive only if they convince others to buy what they have to sell, and they do not survive if they cannot generate a customer base willing to pay for information. The message here for entrepreneurial management is that the business of the entrepreneur is business. Information skills alone will not feed the bulldog. Entrepreneurs must develop the interpersonal and marketing skills to convince customers that they have something worth purchasing. Entrepreneurs must buy computer hardware and software. They must secure a location, advertise, pay for supplies, maybe even hire staff who must be trained and supervised. Entrepreneurs have to keep books (business records) and establish billing procedures. Knowing what to charge is seldom a problem for the public librarian; it is a key managerial function for the entrepreneur. Entrepreneurs often deliver their findings to groups which hired them, so they have to possess excellent presentation skills also.

Information Resource Management

The information resources management (IRM) movement "arose in the 1970s" (Srikantaiah and Koenig 2000, 546), and the idea received a boost by the U.S. Government's Paperwork Reduction Act of 1980. More recently a number of managers of information resource management functions have guided their programs toward knowledge management. IRM continues to exist in corporate, government, and university environments, however, and IRM associations, such as the Information Resources Management Association and the Information Resources Management Commission, flourish.

While IRM is more aptly described as an information function, rather than as an information place, there are corporate, government, and university places at which people manage IRM.

Managers of IRM make decisions about how best to serve "all the major data creators and users" (Kansas n.d., 1) in a given organization. Who are these creators and users? In his teachings and writings, a veteran educator and information manager identifies "islands" of information management as:

- The Library and technical information center
- Research and statistical information management
- Telecommunications
- Data processing
- Information services/public information offices
- Office systems

* Paperwork/records management

(Marchand 1982, 2000)

On each of those islands reside some important nitty-gritty functions and issues such as e-mail, information architecture, information collection, Internet and Intranet configurations and usages, privacy, departmental records management, systems security, and telecommunications management. Managers dealing with all of this also wrestle with rapid change, increasing demand for information products and services, and legislation which governs applications (Departmental 2002, 1).

The single most important concept with which the IRM manager operates is this: Information is a commodity. It is a resource that has value to the organization. This means that "the responsibilities of management [are] extended to the information itself, as well as the technology, equipment, personnel, and funds" (Fletcher 1997, 313) required to create, evaluate, classify, store, and distribute it.

While information as a resource is IRM's central concept, its central function is control, and it is interesting to note that the notion of bibliographic control is also librarianship's core concern. The question bibliographic control poses is, How can we gain access to the ideas of mankind? IRM managers ask, How can we control all the data produced by and important to this organization, and how can we achieve a convenient sharing of the data?

IRM managers apply this question in their dealings with Marchand's islands. For example, they help ensure that agency information architectures will permit the data processing island to cooperate with the research and statistical information management island to enable the library island to serve its clients' needs. In fact, they work to integrate the islands so that they become less separated from each other and from the organization as a whole.

Team concepts apply as the IRM manager handles information from generation to dissemination; prepares access tools to information; and analyzes, digests, and repackages information to meet the needs of the organization—all of this in direct pursuit of the goals of that organization (Williams 2002, n.p.).

Oversight of information resources is a special function of the manager. The National Aeronautics and Space Administration (NASA) has developed an IRM program that places special emphasis "on consolidation, sharing, and reuse of information resources." One of their "Best Practices" statements with respect to investment oversight strikes a chord in light of disasters experienced over time: "2. Perform IR investment planning by balancing risks and benefits" (National 1996, 10).

Shuttle disaster investigation seeks to discover what happened and, just as important, who knew what, and what could have been done by whom to avoid the catastrophe.

IRM managers write policy and coordinate requests for telecommunications services, online training, and software orders. They involve themselves in\the oversight of management information systems (MIS), information technology (IT) security, and e-mail architecture and usage. They come very close to performing knowledge management.

Knowledge Management

Chapter 12 of our book is devoted to knowledge management (KM) and contains a section on the management of KM on pages 316-17. Like IRM, knowledge management is more a function than a type of information place. Nevertheless, in many corporate settings one finds the KM function operating in libraries, information agencies, computer centers, systems departments, and in combinations of these sub-agencies.

The KM manager engineers the identification, acquisition, description, storage, and sharing of intellectual capital. Intellectual capital is what the organization knows. Most of what it knows resides in the heads of people, while some of it resides in traditional information sources like books, periodicals, e-mails, websites, and technical reports—electronic and print. In KM operations the users may also be the resources. That, along with the absolute necessity for sharing, are what distinguish KM operations from other information places.

So what exactly is knowledge management? Can an intangible be managed? How does the KM manager accomplish this feat in an environment where not sharing and competitive instincts are more ingrained in the corporate culture than sharing and cooperating? KM has to do with assembling and disseminating what the organization knows and what it needs to know. How one does this is the subject of chapter 12.

Information Types and Services, Their Clients, Purposes, and Accountability

Table 1.1 on the next two pages displays in a very general way some differences and similarities between and among the several types of information places/services.

Table 1.1 Information Types and Services

TYPE OF INFORMATION PLACE OR SERVICE	CLIENTS	PURPOSE	ACCOUNTABLE TO	DEMONSTRATES ACCOUNTABILITY BY

Public	Students
	Children & Parents
	Independent Learners
	Business Persons
		Study materials
		Leisure reading
		Personal growth
			Boards
			Political bodies
			The public
				Attracting registrants
				Counting
				  Visitors
				  Attendees
				  Circulation
				Delivery on requests

School	Students Faculty Staff Parents	Curriculum support Reading interests Information Literacy	Building Level Supervision Teachers	Supporting teachers Counting circulation Supplying requests Reporting regularly

Academic	Students
	Faculty
	Staff
		Curriculum support
		Research interests
		support
			Academic administration
			Faculty committees
			Student government
				Getting what faculty
				  needs
				Supplying student needs
				Outcomes assessment
				  measures

Table 1.1 Information Types and Services Continued

TYPE OF INFORMATION PLACE OR SERVICE	CLIENTS	PURPOSE	ACCOUNTABLE TO	DEMONSTRATES ACCOUNTABILITY BY
Special	Employees Clients Persons with special interests	Interests of parent governmental or corporate agency	Chief Executive Officer (CEO) Chief Information Officer Department Chief	Measured value to parent organization Demonstrating document deliverability
Entrepreneur	Anyone willing to pay	The needs of clients for consultation or information	To oneself if self-employed One's creditors A parent corporation	Making a profit Achieving customer satisfaction
Information Resource Management	Employees of corporation	Database management Records management Paperwork reduction Statistics Information sharing/disclosure	CEO CIO Department Chief	Formulating strategic plans for information technology Satisfying users Managing information from a business perspective
Knowledge Management	Employees of corporation Consulting clients	Identifying sources of knowledge both internal and external	CEO CIO Department Chief Knowledge Manager	Organizing and disseminating knowledge on demand; effecting sharing of knowledge

References

Curran, Charles. 2001. What do librarians and information scientists do? They ODAPCOSRIU in the I&OEM. *American Libraries* 32 (January): 56-59.

DeCandido, GraceAnne. 2000. Core values task force report. www. ala.org/congress/corevalues/draft5.html (accessed 10 February 2003).

———. 2001. E-mail to JESSE Listserv.

Department of Transportation. 2002. Departmental information resource management manual (DIRMM). cio.ost.dot.gov/policy/dirmm.html (accessed 10 February 2003).

Drucker, Peter. 1974. *Management: Tasks, responsibilities, practices.* New York: Harper & Row.

Fletcher, Patricia D. 1997. Local governments and IRM: Policy emerging from practice. *Government Information Quarterly* 14:313.

Gorman, Michael. 2000. *Our enduring values: Librarianship in the 21st Century.* Chicago: American Library Association.

Kansas State University. Information resource management council (IRMC). www.ksu.edu/committees/irmc/ (accessed 10 February 2003).

Marchand, Donald. 1982. *Information management in public administration: An introduction and resource guide to government in the information age.* Arlington, VA: Information Resources Press.

———. 2000. *Mastering information management.* New York: Financial Times/Prentice Hall.

National Aeronautics and Space Administration. 1996. Information resources self-review process guide. www/sti.nasa.gov/SelfReview (accessed 11 February 2003).

Srikantaiah, T. Kanti, and Michael E. D. Koenig, eds. 2000. *Knowledge management for the information professional.* Medford, NJ: Information Today, Inc.

Williams, Robert V. 2002. CLIS 724 Special libraries class lecture notes. Columbia: School of Library and Information Science, University of South Carolina.

Chapter 2

Managing Communication and Representation

> *If you think your interpersonal and public communication habits*
> *are in need of improvement, you are probably correct. We think this*
> *chapter will help you improve if you have the will to practice some*
> *new behaviors.*

Interpersonal Communication

Interpersonal communication is the exchange of ideas between or among two or more persons. The participants are senders who select word symbols to represent what they are thinking and want to communicate orally or in writing, and receivers who get the sent communications and attach meaning to them. Among the most helpful and lucid descriptions of the "Essentials of Clear Communication" is Nicole Chovil's construct of the sender, content, receiver, and context. Of special interest is her treatment of context—the environmental circumstances—that have an impact on meaning (Chovil 1999). How a message is delivered, and through what channels—electronic, print, or personal oral, and where—the manager's office, the break room, or a worker's desk, matters. Whether the sender smiles or frowns matters. Whether that smile, or frown, or indifferent demeanor is masked or unavailable, as is the case with most electronic communications, matters.

When one considers all the things that can go wrong with the process, one reaches the conclusion that every successful communication event is a minor miracle. Osmo Wiio has applied a Murphy's Law-type

31

spin on this: "If communication can fail, it will. If a message can be understood in different ways, it will be understood in just that way which does the most harm" (King 2000). For more pithy advice, consult King's excellent piece on interpersonal communication, available at www.2.pstcc.cc.tn.us/-dking/interpr.htm.

Here are some additional factors to consider:

- For communication to occur, there has to be transfer. No transfer or exchange means no communication. Miscommunication is a faulty exchange. Merely sending a message is not "communicating." For exchange to happen, a receiver has to actually receive and interpret.
- A sender may ineffectively encode the message by choosing vague or faulty symbols to express thoughts.
- A sender may select an inappropriate channel to deliver the message. Examples are employing a pink memo slip when a letter is preferable or using a letter when face-to-face would be better.
- When decoding a message, receivers filter contents through their own arsenals of characteristics and backgrounds, which include gender, age, attitudes, opinions, education, culture, previous experience with this communicator, and language skills. These characteristics form one's psychological set, the characteristics that determine the shades of meaning one applies to a message.
- Because the receiver is, therefore, in charge of applying the meaning to the communication, there is a chance the meaning applied is not the one intended by the sender. Insofar as exchange is concerned, and exchange is the essential ingredient in the process, there is no meaning to a message until the receiver attaches it.

Why Managers Should Be Interested

The two most important responsibilities of managers of information places are deciding and communicating. Managers spend most of their time in meetings where they and others communicate. Managers manage by communicating to their staffs and to the agency officers to whom they report. If managers spend so much of their time communicating, would it be good if they were very able communicators? If they did not enjoy the process and if they were poor communicators, might that not interfere with their managerial practice?

Experts in their respective fields have told us for years that good communication forms the basis of productive human interaction, and that poor communication or miscommunication is the chief cause of conflict, the bad kind, on the job. If how we get along together depends upon good communication and if we are to manage productive workplaces as free of distress as human groups can be, then we must communicate effectively. The record shows that managers who are well spoken advance their careers more quickly. For these reasons in particular, managers will be interested in acquiring and improving communication skills. This chapter aims at defining interpersonal communication, examining its components, and presenting practical advice for honing interpersonal and group communication skills. We place special emphasis upon feedback, body language, listening, shyness, managing a meeting, making presentations, stage fright, and mistakes to avoid. We will conclude this chapter with some observations about communication mythology and we will share some good news with you.

Feedback

Whether the meaning received is the one that the sender intended must be verified through feedback, giving it and getting it. Sometimes feedback is delayed and senders find out after some mistake has been made that the message was not understood. Communicators benefit from feedback delivered in real time—in time to verify an understanding or fix a misunderstanding. Personal feedback about sensitive issues can strain relationships, especially when it is unsolicited, and sometimes even when it is requested. Feedback invites frustration and distress when it is delivered after the fact—after a mistake in understanding has led to a costly error.

With feedback, the "it all depends" motto applies. Traditional views about timeliness hold that managers should deliver feedback immediately. Researchers have reported findings which demonstrate that "processes which require conscious, effortful deliberation and pre-planning are best managed through postperformance feedback," whereas immediate feedback works best with rote or repetitive performance (King, Young, and Behnke 2000, 367).

When communicators engage in feedback, their roles shift back and forth. Senders become receiver/decoders, and receivers become sender/ encoders.

Feedback denied is costly. Feedback delivered in real time can promote success; feedback delivered after the fact, after some error in coding or decoding, or in the form of dysfunctional activity that could have been avoided had communicators processed their messages, is frustrating.

Feedback affects the delicate procedure that is human communication. Unasked for, it can provoke dissention. Delivered clumsily, it can destroy relationships. Denied, it can lead to disaster. As crucial as it is—it is necessary to verify transactions—it can be explosive. Negative, even constructively negative, criticism may offend if delivered poorly or in the wrong setting.

Language is imprecise. Some of it is so charged with meaning that terms conjure up emotions or antipathies that short-circuit the exchange process.

Body Language

Body language intrudes. We communicate mightily with gestures, behaviors, dress, posture, and demeanor. When body language contradicts spoken language, receivers "read" the body language and decode it their way, usually by applying a negative meaning. The manager who yawns, looks at a watch, and shuffles papers while "listening" to an employee negates her orally delivered "tell me what's on your mind" message. Conversely, when skillful managers employ body language to complement and support spoken language, they clarify messages. Facial displays are among the most important components of body language. They serve a linguistic function, and they "contribute semantic information to the content of the conversation" (Chovil 1991/92, 164). By the way, we only gesture when we are speaking or thinking about speaking (McNeill 1985).

We invite managers who wish to learn more about this fascinating and important component of human communication to consult the Center for Nonverbal Studies, the home of *The Nonverbal Dictionary* at http://members.aol.com/nonverbal2/adajum.htm and to access entries in the dictionary itself online. Beware, however! Experts argue that while there is no universal language of gestures, expressions, and behaviors, there is the undeniable fact that receivers decode and interpret these signals. Take the Adam's-apple-jump, for example, described as "an unconscious sign of emotional anxiety, embarrassment, or stress" (Nonverbal 2001). Shall we not swallow, or gulp, when communicating? Good question perhaps, but a better one is this: What steps shall I take to make sure the message I intend to send has been received in the manner intended? Adapting the concept of executive position and applying it to the sender's role can help. Executive position describes an important function for communicators. It involves taking charge of one's communication behavior and assuming the responsibility for managing it. Knowing that one has the option of responding positively or negatively, angrily or happily, warmly or coldly, directly or obliquely, with reason or with emotion, as a feeling child or as a scolding parent, and with or without specific gestures or expressions does empower one to select on the basis of context and purpose. Getting and giving feedback can help senders make sure that messages have been received as intended. Authentic feedback can be an excellent antidote for contaminated or faulty communication.

It is okay to be skeptical about this body language business. Each communicator/speaker must study his or her own style and make personal adjustments based upon comfort and perceived results. It is not very useful to deny the impact of nonverbal communication, for nonverbal communication definitely plays a major role in the communication act. Attitudes, for example, are communicated through body, voice, and words, and study after study reinforces this fact. Moreover, they confirm that body and voice account for 90 percent of the communication of attitudes; the words one uses account for only 10 percent (Fallon 1981, 147). How we use our bodies matters.

Listening

Listening, the process that makes the communication happen, is the least studied, least understood, and least practiced communication skill. Many experts claim listening is the most important communication skill. Listening enables the decoder to give the message its meaning. By demonstrating that they are listening, receivers send powerful messages to senders.

For years experts have been explaining that of all the activities managers perform, communicating is by far the one most frequently performed. They observe that listening behaviors comprise over 60 percent of managers' communication time, but that little formal training in listening is offered, and that very few managers have sampled that training (Nichols and Stevens 1957; 7, Nelson and Economy 1996, 170). Today's middle managers and frontline staff participate in the running of information organizations; they do not just accept orders and perform routines. Administration and upper level management require the understanding and cooperation of the entire staff in order to accomplish the purposes of the information agency. They do not simply issue orders to be passed without challenge to the lower echelons; they de-

pend on the goodwill and competence of staff who must feel that they
have a voice if participatory methods are to succeed. Staff who risk
advancing their own ideas depend upon managers who listen. Managers
who risk the consequences of asking people for suggestions know that
they create expectations among the volunteers, expectations that managers hear and that they care about what they hear. Modern managers
who manage well, listen well. This enables them to gather intelligence
to support their most important activity—deciding.

We find it next to impossible to overstate the importance of listening. When receivers accept information, they advance the process of
communication launched by senders. "Listening has occurred when a
human organism receives data aurally," and "You can not listen to anything without paying attention to it" (Weaver 1972, 4-5, 30). Neither
can we pay attention to everything! Fortunately, we do not have to. To
be good listeners, and good communicators, however, we have to acknowledge this limitation, in ourselves and in our audiences, when we
prepare to speak. Acknowledging is step one. Step two involves doing
something. Here is a list of some of the things that good listeners do:

1. Good listeners consciously decide that they are going to adopt
    openness to ideas and a respect for the people who are assigned
    to contribute ideas or who volunteer to do so.
2. Good listeners decide in advance that they might learn some-
    thing, so they listen.
3. Good listeners strive for patience, a kind of serenity that enables
    them to pay attention to what another person is saying.
4. Good listeners work to master two disciplines: They resist think-
    ing, at midsentence during an argument advanced by another,
    about the counter arguments they will employ (Thus they stop
    listening!). They resist temptations to interrupt.
5. Good listeners remember to breathe, and they do it, deeply.
6. Good listeners practice giving their full attention to communica-
    tion partners. They maintain eye contact. They strive for an open
    face. They smile, if it is appropriate. They may nod, which is the
    body language equivalent of the empathetic grunt. They may in-
    cline toward the speaker. These activities encourage and com-
    municate engagement, an agreement to listen. All of these prac-
    ticable, learnable behaviors enhance the communication act be-
    cause they send positive signals to the partner. The signal is:
    You have my attention; I care about what you have to say.
7. Good listeners also demonstrate attention by focusing on the
    partners, not on wristwatches, papers that require shuffling, e-
    mail that requires processing during the conversation, or hero

sandwiches. They may even curtail interruptions by limiting calls or by seeking an environment free of distraction.

8. Good listeners relax enough so they can listen without anticipating what the partners will say. Of course they think while listening, but they think about what the partner is saying, not about what they anticipate the partner is *going* to say. Consider this: we think at 500 words per minute, but we speak at about 150 words per minute (Nelson and Economy 1996, 180). The mind will get way ahead of the tongue if listeners permit their minds to wander. They will occasionally, of course. Bring them back!

9. Good listeners sometimes ask questions.

10. Good listeners occasionally paraphrase or repeat a communication partner's offering, and they also practice summarizing content. This verifies understandings and provides structure; it also sends the signal that one is listening and interested.

11. Good listeners prepare for tears, anger, fear, antagonism, or stubbornness—their partner's or their own. They prepare to steady the scene; they prepare not to be thrown off balance. They provide tissues, a mint, or coffee, maybe. Good listeners understand the value of hospitality.

12. Good listeners listen to complaints carefully but control the urge to decide until checking other sides to the story. This is especially important at the beginning of conflict management activity.

There is an old joke about time management and time management workshops, and the punch line is, "Well, I certainly needed to go to the time management workshop, and I wanted to go, but I could not work it into my schedule." It is old, not necessarily a knee-slapper, but like many jokes, it speaks some truth. What is truly odd about many time management workshops is that they often provide such a monster list of time management tricks and strategies that harried time-challenged participants are overwhelmed and do not know where to begin. So they regress.

We have just presented a dozen listening "tricks." What superperson could master all twelve tactics at once from scratch? Pray there is no one for whom all twelve are completely new notions. Who has already mastered eight and needs only to practice four new ones? The fact of the matter is that all new behaviors are best considered incrementally. Communicators wishing to improve their listening skills ought to select one or two "biggies" and work on them first. Master them, and then move on to others as needed.

Here is another tip. There is absolutely no way on earth for people to successfully monitor their own behaviors unless they have the luxury of hiring a film crew and a team of experts and surrogate listeners to review communications episodes. So many of our antilistening behaviors are inadvertent or unconsciously performed. We commit them out of habit in both formal and informal surroundings. Annoying audible pauses fly under the radar. We are oblivious to them; they torment our audiences. There is a simpler way to get some practice at securing and reacting to feedback. For practice, supply a little bell, a clicker, or maybe some maracas to partners who agree to help you. Instruct them to briefly but firmly work their instruments every time you look away, interrupt, or drift off when you are supposed to be listening, or whatever listening faux pas you want to correct, even if they, not you, identify it. You might well videotape a couple of these episodes. When you play the tape back, you might hear what sounds like a middle school percussion orchestra gone mad. Eventually, however, you will improve. Why? This method complements your intention, and your will, to improve because it supplies you with precious, real-time, problem-specific feedback, feedback totally unavailable to you unless and until you find a way to identify and monitor listening problems. Do this. Practice. Soon the silence of the bells, clickers, and maracas will signal newfound mastery, and the insane percussion will go away for good.

Another observation is in order here. Every single one of those twelve is a practicable, learnable behavior! While there are identifiable behaviors that good listeners master, the most important prerequisite to becoming a good listener is deciding to listen. One makes a conscious decision: I will listen to this conversation. I will free up my mind and accept the words I hear as the authentic message delivered. I will practice patience, strive to understand, and engage the topic, not just wait my turn to enter the discussion.

Your Turn: Think of a time when you were speaking about something of extreme personal importance to a supervisor who was not listening to you. What does it feel like not to be listened to? What steps will you take to make sure you do not create these feelings among those you manage? Talk about this.

Shyness

Some people prefer not to communicate often. They do not like it. Some think they are poor at it and that nature has cast them in the role of a quiet, retiring, and even shy person. They are convinced they cannot emerge or improve, and they choose not to try. They may actually embrace shyness.

A modest but sizeable industry has sprung up to address the shyness issue. Its teachings, study materials, and work sessions aim at easing the pain of shyness, and they are based upon behaviorist theories which posit that shy behaviors can be unlearned. First, though, the automatic thoughts and beliefs in the shy person's arsenal of defenses must be challenged and replaced. Managers who consult the Shyness Home Page at www.shyness.com/ will get a good picture of the kinds of materials, forums, and clinics that are available.

Let us not mistake glibness and vocabulary for wisdom, however. There is a considerable range between mild discomfort and terrifying paralysis, between slight withdrawal and social phobia. If people's anxiousness prevents them from conducting their lives, there is a real problem. The problem may be treated by counseling, therapy, or medication, or by some of each. Jonathon Davidson of Duke University has developed a seventeen-question inventory and a three-item miniversion, which he claims can correctly diagnose social phobia with 93% accuracy.

The questions are

1. Does fear of embarrassment cause you to avoid doing things or speaking to people?
2. Do you avoid activities in which you are the center of attention?
3. Are being embarrassed or looking stupid among your worst fears?

If people answer yes to at least two of these questions . . . , they are probably phobic (Davidson, Is Shyness 2001, 1-2).

A most convincing methodology for helping to deal with shyness is Morita therapy, an intervention designed by Japanese psychiatrist Shoma Morita. Not surprisingly, there is a distinct Zen flavor to his therapy. For example, accepting, not fighting, one's feelings is recommended, and conquering a fear is never suggested as a prerequisite for dealing with it. In other words, we can take action without obliterating fear. We can speak before a group without having to defeat stage fright, and, surprisingly, just doing so may assuage the fear. We can learn to focus less upon ourselves and the labels which we think define us. We can liberate ourselves from preoccupation with perceived limitations. Morita therapy aims at loosening our chains, not at obliterating them

(ToDo 1999), and it fits nicely with our thesis here: Stage fright is a natural, useful, and manageable phenomenon.

As gently as possible while still maintaining our passion about this issue, we invite managers who may engage in negative self-appraisal to discontinue that practice for the few minutes it takes to read and absorb this chapter. The awful truth is that negative self-talk results in negative goal setting. Put another way, "Argue for your limitations and sure enough they're yours" (Quotes 2001,7).

Managing a Meeting

Managers spend most of their time in meetings. The next time a manager contemplates calling a meeting, he or she ought to stop and ask, "Do we really need to have one?" If there is a real need for one; if plans have to be suggested, formulated, and discussed; if information has to be collected and distributed; if the face-to-face meeting is the best way to conduct this business; and if the manager is not calling the meeting merely because it is Tuesday and Tuesday is meeting day; and if the manager will prepare and distribute an agenda; then the manager should go ahead and call the meeting.

People often complain about poorly run meetings that waste their valuable time by keeping them from their other responsibilities. Conversely, they often appreciate a well-run meeting where something happens, decisions are made, closure established, and the meeting adjourned promptly upon the completion of business.
Some tips include

- Determine a solid reason for meeting—the need for information exchange, for example—or do not call a meeting. Cancel one that does not need to happen.
- Compose an agenda for distribution.
- Determine who should be there and notify them.
- Inform people of the expected length of the meeting and stick as much as possible to that estimate.
- Manage the meeting. Take charge. Rotate the chair if that is useful. Delegate if you choose. Above all, make sure everyone understands and observes the rules of engagement.
- These rules may change, depending upon the purpose of the meeting. Some meetings are called to distribute information, some involve making decisions, some require heavy discussion and exchange, and others may include all of these. In any case, the manager must manage.

Making Presentations

Sometimes We Go Public with Our Public Speaking! Public speaking experts and corporate experts agree: People who speak well in public not only get their messages across, they advance their careers. We think Paul Gruhn is correct when he asserts that being a better speaker "will increase the effectiveness of your presentations, increase the likelihood of your recommendations being acted on, increase your self-confidence, and get you where you want to go" (Gruhn 2001, 1). Readers may be amused by his reverse recommendations, which really serve as an excellent list of don'ts. He tells us to shoot from the hip instead of preparing, to begin with a bad joke so the audience will cringe, and to read to them from our slides. Practicing the opposite of his recommendations will help speakers prepare and eventually deliver the presentation.

"If you want to lead, first learn to speak," advises *Success* in its review of Bret Filson's book, *Executive Speeches* (If you 1992, 42). This piece is one of many which lay out strategies that work for speakers who wish to improve. Its value lies partly in the list itself, but lists like this are repeated over and over in the literature. What is important here is the message that one can improve, and the rewards for doing so are great indeed.

When we speak in public, we unveil our communication skills to groups. Many of the proven interpersonal skills apply in public too. Maintaining eye contact, including the audience, demonstrating interest and concern, and listening well all enhance one's public communication.

As with most ventures of import, planning to plan is a requirement. The opportunity to represent an information agency to its public should trigger the manager's *make ready* (as in make ready-do-put away, a manager's code for preparing, executing, and recovering) mechanism.

1. First figure out what the assignment is
2. Then consider who will be hearing this
3. Go to work gathering material
4. Interpret, evaluate, and organize collected information
5. Write the presentation
6. Practice the presentation; get some preliminary feedback, especially about visuals employed; make sure the talk conforms to time restrictions
7. Present

How does one improve chances for making a good presentation? Practice! Okay, just how does one do this? After accomplishing the first five steps listed above, the speaker is ready to do some dry runs, get comfortable with the content and sequence, and begin the process of owning the presentation so he or she can *present* it, not read it.

We think Arch Lustberg has created the best cluster of simple, doable instructions (Lustberg 1992). We have interpreted them, modified them, and shaped them into a set of practical tactics we call the Lustbergian Principles. We have taught them, and we have observed speakers use them to their great advantage. They reinforce the message. Their mastery inspires confidence in listeners. They mask and eventually subdue anxiety. We know these principles work. They are

1. Sweep the audience
2. Speak only to animate objects
3. Present—do not read
4. Pause silently, if you must pause
5. Make intellectual *like* to your audience
6. Move

Sweep the Audience

This means include the audience. Direct your attention to them. Draw as many of them as you can into the presentation. Look at them as individual people, not as a mass of humanity. If you sweep by rotating your gaze from side to side, make sure you avoid robotic monotony. Vary the sequence occasionally. If you start out left-center-right, on the next pass go center-right-left. Above all, establish eye contact as you sweep. This means lingering with a target a bit. You banish the vacant stare when you engage your audience, and it helps you avoid a mechanical swivel. There is only one way you can be sure you have observed this principle—tape yourself before a live audience and get some feedback.

Speak Only to Animate Objects

When you speak, speak only to people. Speak only after you have made eye contact. Avoid speaking to your notes, the wall screen, the exit signs, the empty space above the heads of your audience, or your shoes. It is the people you are trying to convince, not the walls. There is only one way you can be sure you have observed this principle—tape yourself before a live audience and get some feedback.

Present—Do Not Read

An audience who goes to hear a poet or an author may expect to be read to. An audience attending a political rally may tolerate being read to and even applaud on cue. An audience who has come to be entertained, informed, convinced, or challenged will resent being read to. They will mutter to themselves, "I could have read this at home myself," or worse, "A person who has to read to us why library service is so important and in need of funding cannot really believe in the cause all that strongly."

Tell a message if you want others to believe with you that your message is righteous, crucial, or important. Read that message if you want others to believe you could just have easily mailed it in, and probably should have.

Use your notes productively. To present, rather than read, the speaker must practice. The speaker must know the talk. This raises the issue of how, if at all, to prepare notes and how to manage them. We think you should not type out your entire presentation, whether you triple-space it, use all caps, or even if you restrict yourself to two or three items per page. If you have a word-for-word cheat sheet, you will most likely recite it verbatim. Your talk will sound memorized and canned. You might as well read. There is divided opinion about this. Some believe that unless everything is there in the notes, the speaker will forget or overlook some key item.

Our advice is to put key words on note cards. Sheets become unwieldy and they rattle annoyingly if held in nervous hands. If you must refer to your note cards, carry them at about waist level so you can conveniently raise them for viewing and manage/shuffle them as you proceed from point to point. Carry them at downward arm's length and you will get an annoying up/down swivel going when you repeatedly raise them for viewing and then lower them.

You may instead create a personal poster of post-it notes arranged in sequence for the presentation. Use the poster in the same consult-and-speak way you would use notes stationed at the podium; for example, the sequence would flow from addressing the audience, to moving to the podium, to consulting the poster, and to returning to the audience. Again, this makes movement purposeful, not random, and it establishes the speaker in the role of communicator to people in the audience.

Several factors have to be considered here. Many experts warn against using a podium because it becomes a crutch, acts as a barrier between speaker and audience, and can even hide a speaker from view.

Yet we have seen advice to the nervous speaker that encourages leaning on the podium, embracing it almost, for support.

Your hands should complement. What to do with one's hands? The most comfortable-*looking* posture is hands at the sides. The most un-comfortable-*feeling* posture is hands at the sides. Practice can help with the discomfort. Men should know that the once popular fig leaf maneu-ver—hands protecting genital area—should be avoided. It has become a caricature of itself. Folded arms can send unwanted messages also.

The podium is not a crutch. One can use a podium without leaning on it, and one can have copious if orderly notes, if one will station those notes at the podium. The speaker walks to the notes, consults them, and then returns to the audience. The podium becomes a station, not a support. By going to one's notes, checking them, and returning attention to the audience, one punctuates the engagement with them. A drama unfolds. Speak from the heart. Stop. Move. Consult. Come back to the people. The audience begins to expect and appreciate being summoned again and again to the matter at hand by a speaker who ad-dresses them, not a stack of papers.

Pause Silently, If You Must Pause

Our *ers*, *uhms*, and *ahs* are so inadvertent and automatic that we do not hear them when we are speaking. The audience hears them, though, and if we regularly and often lace our speech with them, the audience will first begin to notice, then to count, then to tally, and ultimately to tune out.

These audible pauses signal that we are grasping for a word or idea. But because we are speaking at the time, we believe we must con-tinue sounding. So while we wait, we "uhm." It is okay to grasp; it is not okay to serenade an audience with audible pauses until we think of what we want to say.

There is a way you can be sure if you have observed the "pause silently" principle—tape yourself. That way you can hear and notice the audible pauses, locate the spots at which you are prone to use them, and take corrective action when you prepare again. Remember, we commit the audible pause because our tongues operate at a slower speed than our minds. We say "uhm" or "you know" because we have temporarily forgotten what we are going to say next. The *forget* im-pulse lasts but a nanosecond but long enough to produce the "er." The springboard technique really works. When through feedback you spot a word that immediately precedes the pesky "ah," consciously plan to use that word, and it often occurs at the end of a sentence, as a virtual springboard to the next idea, the next sentence. Practice this and poof! there goes the "uhm."

Make Intellectual Like

Arch Lustberg teaches that if an audience likes the speaker, they will listen. The preceding four tips all relate to preparation and delivery. Executing them well will indicate to an audience that the speaker has prepared and knows how to communicate. This will help the audience like the speaker, and the speaker can do some additional things that will encourage the audience to like him or her.

Under most circumstances, if the speaker appears relaxed and in control, and if the speaker can smile, the audience will be disposed toward liking the speaker. Smiling is one of the nearly universal nonverbal cues. It often conveys warmth or friendliness. In some cultures it may only indicate "I am listening." Smiling conveys anger in some circumstances, but it is unlikely that a public speaker who smiles will deliver that message. Smiling most often communicates "pleasant," and pleasant is better than unpleasant or neutral.

The open face complements the smile; often it accompanies the smile. Smiling and raising the eyebrows, and creating horizontal lines in the forehead, achieves an open face. Conversely a closed face is achieved by frowning, which creates vertical lines where the eyebrows nearly converge above the nose. Most of the time, open is good and closed is not good. It is not the easiest of tasks for some speakers to smile appropriately when addressing a group, but learning to do so— and one can practice this—pays dividends in "likeability."

Guard against mastering a phony smile. Speakers who smile at everything, all the time, forfeit believability and likeability. Speakers who attach a smile to everything—Tuesday, downsizing, budgets, or Anglo-American Cataloging Rules—rob the smile of its impact and confuse an audience. Trying too hard to be likeable can backfire. "Appropriate" is a good word to remember in this connection.

There is only one way you can be sure you have observed this principle—videotape yourself before an audience and watch yourself. Do you look happy to be there, or anxious for the speaking event to be over? Do you look confident and relaxed, and do you achieve this by smiling and displaying an open face to your audience? Have you connected with and engaged your audience by making intellectual *like* to them?

Move

We offer you expert advice on movement and presentation. To smoothly orchestrate a presentation, work on balance and stance. Get comfortable without slouching. Face the audience; give them your attention. Consultants at the Frontline Group teach a "see, move, plant, speak" method in which a speaker begins by establishing eye contact with one person. The speaker moves in the direction of the target, stops, finishes a thought or point, identifies another target, establishes eye contact, moves, stations him or herself comfortably, makes the point (a sentence, perhaps), and continues (Frontline Group 2001).

What does this do? Well, it most certainly involves the audience and completely obliterates opportunities for the speaker to commit deer-in-the-headlights gazes or distracting, monotonous, and artificial head-on-neck swivels. It helps the speaker achieve balance and take energy from the floor and from the persons engaged. It introduces purposeful movement and replaces nervous pacing. Because of the intimacy effected by direct contact with individuals, audience members have been observed actually waiting for their turn to be addressed. While it separates the speaker from the notes, their placement at the podium provides a sure location whenever the speaker must consult them. Moreover, notes on the podium free the hands of the presenter who may use them to gesture appropriately or to rest at the sides. Oh, there is only one way you can be sure you have observed this principle—tape yourself in front of a live audience and get some feedback.

Your Turn: Practice the **See, Move, Plant, Speak** technique. Imagine you are addressing a group at a front-center position. You are about to deliver an important three-sentence portion of your talk. *Forest fires destroy thousands of acres and hundreds of homes each year. And do you know what compounds this tragedy?* Stop. **See** an audience member. **Move** toward him or her. Stop. **Plant** your feet. Maintain eye contact. **Speak.** *We cause most of these fires through our own thoughtless, careless behavior.*

We want to tell you something that is absolutely fascinating about this technique. We teach it to managers. We watch as they practice and we coach them to integrate the technique at appropriate spots several times within a talk. That way it occurs as a natural event, totally within the flow of the presentation, and not as a herky-jerky one-time anomaly. Readers, even when we know it is coming, even when we know the very words the speaker will say because we wrote them and have heard them over and over, the See, Move, Plant, Speak tactic creates an electric spark that arcs between speaker and audience member. The movement and eye contact engage the listener. Many await another "visit," hoping their turn with the speaker will come again. That is the kind of attention a speaker longs for; it is available.

Stage Fright

Stage fright is your friend! But usually it goes away and leaves you by yourself.

What Is stage fright? Stage fright is that terrible fear some of us have when we anticipate having to speak before a group. It can be an isolated symptom or part of a full-fledged social phobic syndrome. It can produce mild or serious panic attacks. Its origins or causes may be unknown to us, but it is most probably a learned behavior. Speculation about its causes includes the social phobic one and comprises a wide range of possibilities:

- We fear making mistakes
- We are unfamiliar with the role of public speaker
- We find standing before others humiliating
- We anticipate audience criticism and disapproval
- We think we will be terrible
- We are simply not cut out to be good public speakers
- We don't look good
- We have failed before at speaking in public
  (Bippus and Daly 1999, 63-72)

The manifestations of stage fright are apparent: pounding heart, active bladder, sweaty brow and palms, deer-in-the-headlights stare, quivering lips, blotchy skin, weak knees, rigid posture, and shaky voice. The term "basket case" can describe persons overcome by stage fright.

Our Turn: We can manage stage fright; it need not overcome us!

Drama teachers tell their students that the audience has come for the story, "not to see you." This truism is also a very comforting thought and a wonderful antidote for stage fright. The presentations we make as managers and representatives are not about us; they are about information services, books, budgets, systems, or opportunities. Yes, the audience will notice if we are very bad or very good, and what they take away from the event will be affected by how well or how poorly we present. Fortunately, we have some control over how well or how poorly we present, and knowing the audience has come to inform themselves, not to *see us*, helps us reduce some of the self-focused attention that is a root cause of anxiety and unmanageable stage fright.

As soothing as the *they come for the story* counsel is, it may not relieve everyone's apprehension about public speaking. In her study of self-management techniques for reducing these fears, researcher Karen Dwyer has demonstrated that different methods work for people with differing needs (Dwyer 2000). She puts us on alert that while there are ways to manage apprehension, one size does not fit all. We should be wary, therefore, of lists which purport to cover all possibilities, and we should rely instead on techniques which work for us as individual personality types.

Great actors have observed that they always get stage fright, and most of them are happy that they do. They make it work for them. They draw upon its considerable energy. They claim that the difference between professionals and amateurs is that professionals use and employ stage fright while amateurs are overcome by it.

How can we use stage fright? We can use it to get ourselves up, to respect our topic, and to respect our audience. We can use it to remind us to prepare and practice, the two most important determinants for success, and the two most potent enemies of fear. Some speakers find imaging or positive visualization useful. Proponents of this technique encourage speakers to prepare by picturing themselves looking great, delivering a splendid presentation, and earning visible and audible approval from their audiences. Imagining makes it so, they claim. They are often right. Conversely, negative self-talk is judged by some to have the same effect as negative goal setting. Imagining oneself doing poorly often produces that very outcome.

Interestingly, researchers have discovered that some social phobics, while they may imagine that they perform poorly in public speaking experiences, often score their performances worse that audiences do (Rapee and Lim 1992). This is hardly an endorsement of phobia as a management strategy; rather it is an observation that our worries are seldom warranted. It is also an acknowledgement that some speakers actually frighten themselves into anxiety attacks (Tanne and Rapp 1987).

Fear of being on stage often dissipates once we get there, especially if we have practiced. The Advanced Public Speaking Institute advises that if the fright does not go away, address the problem by moving a bit, laying notes aside so they do not vibrate so, finding the friendliest face you can and establishing contact, and remembering that nervousness "doesn't show one-tenth as much as it feels" (Advanced 2001).

Your Turn: Think about the times when you may have experienced stage fright. Share these experiences with your friends or a discussion group.

Mistakes to Avoid

The following are nearly always serious snafus. Speakers should consider them mistakes:

- "Forgetting that speaking is a form of show business" is an error (Contavespi 1995, 100). Employ some tricks, use pauses to build anticipation and establish eye contact immediately.
- "Being self-deprecating" (Contavespi 1995, 100) can backfire, as can jokes that flop. Control the urge to relax yourself and the audience by telling a joke. If it lays the proverbial egg, you may too. Be careful about making jokes at your own expense, especially about your nervousness or lack of expertise. The last thing you want is for the audience to be embarrassed for you or feel sorry for you. They will not listen to you if they do.
- Cluttering your talk with refuse annoys audiences. There are meaningless words—refuse or throwaway words—and expressions which almost never serve a useful purpose and nearly always distract listeners. Among them are

    1. All the audible pauses like *er, uhm*, and *ah*.
    2. *Basically* and *You know* are usually always lifeless airballs.
    3. *Okay*, as in 2+2=4, okay?
    4. *I know you can't see this screen...* (Then do not show it!)
    5. *So far we have talked about...* (No, we have not: you have!)
    6. *But seriously...* (usually after a seriously failed joke).

7. *I won't bore you with the details.* (How do you plan to bore us?)
8. *Pass these around* (as if we really needed an excuse not to listen to you).
9. *Like* (As in "He was like all angry and said, 'like don't go there.'")
10. *And in conclusion...* (unless you really mean it).

Communication Mythology

At first I thought I did not like Fred at all. But then we had our office retreat, and I got to know Fred, work closely with him, eat with him, and spend some leisure time with him. Now I realize I hate the son of a bitch.

Let us speak carefully about the importance of communication skills, confidently about our ability to improve them, and very cautiously about attributing to those skills more power than they can deliver.

We cannot overestimate the value and importance of communicating well. Exchanging information is an essential skill in personal relationships and in work relationships, and we know of no responsible people who would deny this. The record also clearly demonstrates that people can improve interpersonal and group communication skills by identifying and replacing bad habits with better habits. Unfortunately the record also shows that some people have placed too much responsibility on communication's doorstep. Solid communication cannot solve all problems. We can understand each other very well and still take up the sword.

Part of the problem exists in the hangover-like residue from the 1960s and 1970s. When the human potential movement was in full swing, communication was seen as the key to success. Moreover, disclosure was the centerpiece of a catechism that proclaimed the benefits of full disclosure, of letting it all hang out. "Disclosure begets disclosure," intoned me-generation gurus. These experts did not, as we did, have to sit on the bus next to a convert, a perfect stranger who assaulted us with personal troubles and imperfections, revelations which unburdened and freed the talker but annoyed us. Relationships, even casual ones, cannot exist comfortably where half are free and half are embarrassed. Because "appropriate" was not part of the discloser's vocabulary or communication agenda, that kind of communication did not build a relationship; it discouraged it. Communication can be real and authentic and still be unproductive. Friends who mistrust one another, coworkers who rebel, and nations which war against each other do not do so simply because they misunderstand each other. They may understand each other very well. They disagree with what they understand; that's why they fight.

Similarly, owning and practicing good presentation skills will not guarantee a successful presentation. While communicating well is necessary, it may not be sufficient to win over an audience committed to opposite stands or points of view. Mastering the Lustbergian Principles virtually assures a speaker that he or she will be listened to, but an audience predisposed to opposite positions may not accept what a presenter promotes. Good communication is a key; it does not lock in success.

Therefore, let us not unfairly attribute to communication skills that which they cannot deliver. Without them we flounder and err; with them we have a chance to succeed. Let us hold them accountable for what they can do—exchange information, and let us not burden them with being solely responsible for success.

Is There Any Good News for Managers of Information Places?

Yes there is. Just as poor communication habits have been learned and acquired through practice, managers may learn and acquire good communication habits through a process of identification, elimination or unlearning, replacement, and practice. There are excellent tutorials, workshops, and videocassettes, which managers can access, attend, and use.

That one can improve is rooted in the belief that a behaviorist approach to the issue is both comforting and productive. It is comforting because it holds that we do most of what we do because we learned and practiced it, and that we can "unlearn" or replace bad communication habits by identifying what is unproductive behavior and replacing it with productive behavior. It is good to know that. There is evidence that some shyness, a trait that interferes with communication, is an inherited trait that we did not learn but were given. Nevertheless, some shyness is not programmed. It is learned and can be unlearned. The behaviorist approach is productive because it holds that we can in fact change. The record shows that people who identify and practice the techniques of effective communication improve their skills, their shyness notwithstanding.

One important step that a manager can take to improve the process is to appreciate the value of feedback and get good at giving and getting it. Managers who practice giving and getting feedback learn many things. One of these is, miracle of miracles, that many of us share the same language codes. We are able to apply similar meanings consistently. In part this is due to shared context that complements shared language. Context is created when people share common interests and pursuits like, for example, when they have worked together to construct, understand, and execute a mission statement; when they have studied and explained the same vision statements, policies, and procedures; and when they have committed to similar goals and outcomes.

Good two-way communication helps establish and nurture a context for the corporate culture so it can accommodate and promote the aims of the organization. Managers who give and accept feedback help keep the information place on course.

Information services personnel who paraphrase client questions provide feedback to verify their understanding of inquiries. This can result in more efficient and effective searches. Good managers verify transactions when they ask employees to repeat instructions. Poorer managers ask closed-ended questions like "Do you understand?" or "Have you any questions?" These questions invite Yes or No answers that often mask faulty or incomplete understandings. "Please tell me your interpretation of my directions," is a better way of determining whether a listener has comprehended.

References

Advanced Public Speaking Institute. 2001. Public speaking: Stage fright strategies. Available at www.public-speaking.org/public-speaking-stagefright-article.htm.

Bippus, A., and J. A. Daly. 1999. What do people think causes stage fright? *Communication Education* 48 (January): 63-72.

Chovil, Nicole. 1991/92. Discourse-oriented facial displays in conversation. *Research in Language* 25:163-94.

———. 1999. Communication Articles. Available athttp://persweb.direct.ca/nchovil/articles.html (accessed 29 October 2001).

Contavespi, Vicki. 1995. Unaccustomed as I am . . . *Forbes* 155 (Jan ary 15): 100.

Davidson, Jonathon. 2001. Is shyness a mental disorder? http://webmd. lycos.-com/content/article/1674.50379.

Dwyer, Karen. 2000. The multi-dimensional model: Teaching students to self-manage high communication apprehension by self-selecting treatments. *Communication Education* 49 (January): 72-81.

Fallon, Willam K. 1981. *Effective communication on the job.* 3rd ed. New York: AMACOM.

Filson, Bret. 1991. *Executive speeches.* Williamstown, MA: Williamston.

Frontline Group. 2001. *Executive briefing center presentations.* Capitola, CA: Mandel Communications Division.

Gruhn, Paul. 2001. Terrified of public speaking? Not anymore . . . *Intech* 48 (May): 1.

If you want to lead, first learn to speak. 1992. *Success* 39 (3): 42-43.

King, Don. 2000. Four principles of interpersonal communication. http://2.pstcc.cc.tn.us/-dking/interpr.htm.

King, Paul E., Melissa J. Young, and Ralph E. Behnke. 2000. Public speaking performance improvement as a function of information processing in immediate and delayed feedback interventions. *Communication Evaluation* 49 (October): 365-74.

Lustberg, Arch. 1992. *Perfecting presentations.* Video. Baltimore: Library Video Network.

McNeill, David. 1985. So you think gestures are non-verbal? *Psychological Review* 92 (3): 350-71.

Nelson, Bob, and Peter Economy. 1996. *Managing for dummies.* Chicago: IDG Books Worldwide.

Nichols, Ralph G., and Leonard A. Stevens. 1957. *Are you listening?* New York: McGraw-Hill Book Company.

Nonverbal dictionary. http://members.aol.com/nonverbal2-/adajum.htm (accessed 13 November 2001).

Quotes that transform shyness. 2001. www.shyanfree.com/html/quotes. html.

Rapee, Ronald M, and Lina Lim. 1992. Discrepancy between self- and observer ratings of performance in social phobics. *Journal of Abnormal Psychology* 101 (November): 728-31.

Tanne, Janice Hopkins, and Ellen Rapp. 1987. Tips on conquering paralyzing anxiety: Fearing the worst. *New York* 20 (February 9): 44-49.

ToDo Institute. 1999. Morita therapy. www.anamorph.com/todo/morita. html.

Weaver, Carl H. 1972. *Human listening: Processes and behavior.* Indianapolis: Bobbs-Merrill.

Chapter 3

Leadership and Management

Elsewhere in this discussion we have stated that managers decide and oversee, and that deciding things is a pivotal responsibility. Leaders also decide things. Leaders supply vision and they influence others to behave in certain ways. So do managers. That managers sometimes lead and that leaders sometimes manage need not confuse us if we focus precisely on some of these activities and make whatever distinctions need to be made about functions or job titles. The parlor game of separating leadership from management and management from administration can result in the creation of symmetrical lines and boxes on a sheet of paper; in the trenches the lines blur and the boxes bleed.

Leadership

We point out in the next chapter that management has a long history. It is not just something that developed in the last century. The same holds true for leadership. The *Oxford English Dictionary* dates the first appearance of the word "leader" in the English language to 1300. (*Oxford English Dictionary*, 2nd edition, s.v. "leadership.") However, the word "leadership" did not make an appearance until early in the 19th century. Even so, the concept of leader is easily discernable in numerous texts from the Greeks to Christians to Chinese early writings. In fact history, as most commonly understood, is a chronology of feats of leaders. Only recently has that field focused much attention on the "common soldier" or the "people." What has changed over the centuries is that the concept of leadership has become more broadly conceived in order to meet the needs of more complex social structures. Thus, early leaders were kings, chiefs, military commanders, and the like. Over the centuries, human societies and leadership have evolved together, so that the concept of leadership as viewed at this point in time is much different from that of ten or twenty centuries ago.

Leadership is an essential feature of human activity that takes place in a group. Military successes are directly attributable to several factors, one of which is always leadership. Religious, political, and business group actions nearly always take place with a leader. The leader may not always be formally recognized. Particularly as leadership has evolved, it is less necessary that the king always be appointed. Human groups respond to leadership whether formal or informal. Leadership may shift from person to person within the group. The king is not always king.

The *Economist* in a somewhat tongue in cheek manner suggested that "in America, leadership has become something of a cult concept" (*The Leadership Thing* 1995, 23). It notes that most countries are not as obsessed with the idea of leadership, but that in America it starts early. "Children in elementary school take turns to be class leader for the day"(*The Leadership Thing* 1995, 23). This preoccupation results in numerous leadership councils, university programs, and institutes. Leadership training is ingrained in the fabric of corporate America. Practically every library conference has at least one program on leadership. There are also several library leadership institutes conducted each year such as the Frye Leadership Institute and the ACRL/Harvard Leadership Institute.

Brian Quinn says that a few researchers are now questioning the assumption "that leadership is a critical factor in the successful operation of any organization" (Quinn 1999, 147). These researchers are studying other variables that may influence organizational effectiveness. Gemmill, in particular, considers leadership a social myth "that functions to reinforce existing social beliefs and structures about the necessity of hierarchy and leaders in organizations" (Gemmill 1992, 113). A more balanced view is that of Gibbons who posits "a contingency theory of leadership" (1992, 15). In this view, "Different environmental conditions, particularly resource positions, impact the nature of the leadership challenge" (Gibbons 1992, 15). Thus leadership does not occur in a vacuum, but influences and is influenced by numerous and changing elements. This approach appears to have particular value for libraries. For several decades, libraries have operated in an increasingly complex environment with consistently scarcer resources. We believe that leadership is an important ingredient, but certainly not the only factor in organizational success. Leadership is no more or no less important now than in the past. But, the nature of that leadership has changed, in large part due to the changed environment in which libraries operate. The quality of leadership in a library is important to the success of the library. Because leadership and management are so deeply intertwined, this is an appropriate topic for discussion in a book on management.

What Is Leadership

Will I recognize it if I see it? Most likely, one experiences leadership rather than sees it. Most of us have ideas about what constitutes leadership, but a precise definition often eludes us. Leadership exhibits itself in so many differing combinations of traits, situations, conditions, and styles that it continues to lack a commonly agreed upon definition. For example, while charisma is one of the identifiable traits of leadership, it is not generally considered an essential element of leading. There are many leaders who are simply lacking in this trait. In fact, Kirkpatrick found that "charismatic communication style had few direct or indirect effects on performance" (Kirkpatrick 1996, 44). Thus attempting to define a leader by a precise set of skills and traits may not be the most helpful approach.

Describing as a way of defining leadership does offer possibilities of reaching a common understanding. Barnes describes a leader as "a person to whom others turn for direction, inspiration, moral authority, or support" and "someone whom we trust to guide us toward a shared future" (Barnes 2002, 5). Implicit in that description is the idea that leadership is the act of seeing what others may not and of influencing others to behave in ways they might not solely on their own, pursue. It is important to recognize that this definition requires two things. In order to lead, one must first have vision, and second, one must act upon that vision by convincing others to follow. While other traits and skills may or may not be present, without these two, there is no leadership.

The mid-1990s provide an example of these points. At that time, some librarians perceived the importance of the Web and began convincing their libraries to use the Web to push information out to the campus instead of requiring that everyone come into the library building to satisfy his or her information needs. They licensed and accessed information remotely, developed electronic reserve systems, and used Web pages to deliver a variety of library tools and information to customers' homes, offices, dorms, and other locations. In the meantime, other libraries continued to invest heavily in CD-ROM technology, which as a rule continued to require customers to come into the physical library. Others continued to rely almost exclusively on print, further limiting customer options. Library leaders who invested early in the Web confronted an unknown future and made choices to provide services and collections in a far different manner than had been done in the past. They weighed the risks, created their visions, and convinced their followers to follow as well as those libraries that followed later.

Why Is Leadership Important to Libraries?

Leaders challenge the process. They lead change within an organization. This change may be macro in responding to external forces, such as the continuous impact of technology on libraries, or it may be micro in responding to a staff member's observation that a particular acquisitions process is not serving any purpose.

In order for change to occur, leaders must inspire a shared vision. Often change involves stepping into the unknown. What impact will a unified interface have on the user at a public workstation? Will it be positive or negative? Will it in some way limit the scholar in her search for vital information? Stepping into unknowns such as this requires another trait of leadership—flexibility. The successful leaders allow for other possibilities. Stepping into the unknown sets up the possibility for failure. This is another trait found in many leaders—the willingness to risk failure.

In a general societal view, libraries are rarely considered to be change agents or high-risk operations. The reality is that many libraries have been at the forefront of change in the information age. Library leaders as change agents and risk takers could do much in positioning information places for the information age.

What Do Leaders Do?

What are some of the things that library leaders do? Kim Barnes makes a key observation when she says, "No title confers qualities of leadership on anyone. Leadership is earned through behavior" (Barnes 2002, 5). A library leader may not do everything in this listing which follows, but they do many of them in some combination and with varying degrees of success.

Library Leaders Have Vision

Vision is considered to be the most essential trait of a leader. People are inspired to act and to achieve, taking an organization to higher levels of service by visionary leadership.

Library leaders develop and promote the vision of the information place. They build support for the library's mission and priorities. Without a compelling vision, staff will not reach their potential to be as effective as possible in serving the library's constituencies. Typically, the library director articulates the vision. It is not realistic to believe that a library staff can develop and pursue a vision without the personal commitment of the library director. However, in order to achieve the vision, the library director must involve others in the process of fully defining and establishing the goals to achieve it. As a general principle, public library boards or academic faculty library committees and library staff—particularly professional staff—are all key players in this process. Unless these groups develop genuine ownership of the vision, it will not inspire anyone to commitment and action.

Library leaders move the library toward achieving success in its goals in a changing, seemingly technologically driven world. Not all leaders are ultimately successful, but they do move the organization. Interlinked with vision are values. Library leaders articulate shared beliefs and values. It is difficult to imagine a vision for a library that is not built upon values that are commonly held.

It may appear at first blush that a vision for a particular library is easy. After all, haven't we been about service and collections from the beginning? But vision must be continually articulated within an ever-changing external environment. Technological advances must be incorporated and articulated in new ways. For many people, the card catalog was a value of libraries. Thus when CD-ROM and online catalogs replaced the card catalog, there was a terrific wrenching of values. Unwittingly, we had attached value to a tool rather than to what the tool could do for us. Online catalogs do the same thing as card catalogs, but do it much better and are easier for our customers to use. Thus as the environment changes, leaders must be careful to restate the vision and values in such a way as to ease the transition. While the core values and vision may change little if any over time, the environment in which they operate does change greatly and library leaders must be prepared to articulate them in new ways.

Library Leaders Are Creative

Leaders bring about change. They ask the questions that often have no answer other than "That's the way we have always done it." Library leaders look at things with a fresh eye. They do not accept the status quo, but do recognize those instances when the status quo is the best answer. And there are many cases when the status quo is the best answer. Library leaders draw from a broad range of knowledge, skills, and intuition to find creative solutions to vexing issues and problems.

Library leaders encourage and promote creativity within the staff. By creating an environment where creativity is rewarded and can flourish, a leader is enhancing the likelihood of success for the organization.

Library Leaders Are Planners

Planning is a continuous process. The library leader uses planning to keep the library moving forward through working on strategy. It is essential that the leader work with her staff annually to review the strategic plan and to update the strategies to reflect current realities. It is also a time for reflection and evaluation. What worked and what did not work this past year? What can we do better? Are we missing anything? What is stopping or delaying us from accomplishing our goals and objectives? Budget, external factors, individuals within the organization, time, or any number of things may be identified in this process.

Library Leaders Care for Their Employees

Although there are library leaders who seem to care little for their employees, most successful library leaders are caring and attempt to create a work environment for all employees (staff, students, volunteers) that is conducive to their well-being. They work to help their employees be successful. The leader often sets the tone for this to happen. A leader who is angry, berates employees, is arbitrary in decision making and commands, shows favoritism, and is just not a pleasant person to be around models behaviors that staff will likely emulate. Without a compassionate human touch and recognition of the humanity of relationships, little motivation or inspiration will be found among staff.

Library Leaders Are Risk Takers

Library leaders are risk takers and they accept responsibility. They have the ability to say, "I was wrong" and "The buck stops here." Taking the safe path often proves not to be safe and can lead a library to mediocrity. While risk taking creates the possibility and in fact even the likelihood of failure on occasion, it also is one of the most important factors in energizing an information place. Risk taking is not done "on the fly" or simply for the sake of risk taking. A leader will gather and analyze information, reflect upon it, and in most cases, take a calculated risk. Sometimes, even after all of these steps, the risk must be taken based upon intuition. Although the leader should not ignore the warning flags found in the information gathered, intuition is often what guides a final decision.

Library Leaders Inspire

Charisma is almost indefinable. But it is a very real ability to inspire others. It often is listed as a trait one finds in leaders. However, many library leaders are able to inspire without necessarily being charismatic. Charisma is typically associated with public appeal and public speaking. While library leaders should aspire to be effective public speakers, they may not necessarily achieve charisma. Inspiration through public charisma is only one way and often not the best way in and of itself to inspire. Library leaders can certainly inspire when they provide task cues to implement the vision. In other words, they make certain that staffs know how to perform tasks appropriate to achieving the vision. Library leaders inspire best when they concentrate on what is best in their people. When they can bring out the best in people, by example or by praise or some form of acknowledgement of an accomplishment, they are then inspiring. Staffs want and need someone who recognizes their contributions and accepts their worth. At times, praise is most appropriately given to the whole staff in perhaps a staff meeting. At other times, it is most appropriate with a single individual. At times, it is best in writing and at other times in verbal praise. One excellent opportunity occurs when salary increases are given. While many leaders may be inclined to do a form letter, it is an excellent idea to individualize each letter and to acknowledge some particular aspect of an individual's performance.

Leaders also inspire when they can articulate clearly the vision and values of the library.

The Differences between Leadership and Management

Don Riggs provided a good set of distinctions when he noted recently that

> Library managers tend to work within defined bounds of
> known quantities, using well-established techniques to ac-
> complish pre-determined ends; the manager tends to stress
> means and neglect ends. On the other hand, the library
> leader's task is to hold, before all persons connected with
> the library, some vision of what its mission is and how it
> can be reached effectively. (Riggs 2001, 6)

How important are these distinctions? As we emphasize several times throughout this chapter, leaders must both lead and manage. For the greatest success, they must pay attention to details and to follow-through as well as to vision and strategy. The important point here is not so much that information place managers or midlevel managers identify when they are doing one or the other. The important thing is for individuals to recognize and accept the importance of both and to make time in their busy schedule to do both. Expanding Riggs's distinction to encompass a number of the other traits and activities identified in this chapter will help ensure that the manager is fulfilling her role in making the information place in which she works a successful organization.

Management

This discussion of management shall target the things managers of information places *do*. If we were speaking *POSDCORB-RC*, we would here refer primarily to the "D" for directing. The function of directing is composed chiefly of training, supervising, and evaluating. There are myriad other important functions, and we will get to some of them, but directing is a biggie.

Training

Personally showing others how to perform and seeing to their training by providing on-the-job or in-service training opportunities are major managerial responsibilities. Often the manager functions as teacher. Such managers are educators in a very real sense. Must the manager of a technical service operation be the most skilled at data entry? Not necessarily, but that manager is responsible for seeing to it that the people responsible for data entry receive adequate training, and the manager needs to know enough about processes and product to be able to evaluate employees' data entry performance.

Coaching

This term has been borrowed from the sports world to apply to a manager who teaches, encourages, pulls for, praises, and rewards members of a work team who produce. The team concept applies here. In this connection a team is a group of workers who understand organizational goals and objectives, see their individual roles in helping to achieve those aims, and work cooperatively to make them happen. These understandings do not just happen. Cooperation does not serendipitously materialize. A manager/coach may produce these effects by skillfully preparing employees to work together for the common good—usually customer satisfaction, and by acknowledging their good efforts. Sophisticated observers may find the image of a cheerleader with the proverbial carrot and stick a bit saccharine, but the idea of a manager who trains and encourages, and in the process helps prepare employees for future responsibilities, has considerable appeal. Coaching and employee development go hand in hand.

Mentoring

Mentoring is a term that applies to a special relationship forged between a seasoned employee and a new hire. This relationship can be assigned, as is the case where a boss says, "Doris, you mentor Philip." The arrangement may be informal. Doris may seek out Philip, or the novice Philip may go looking for a veteran to assist him in learning the ropes. The mentor can become a teacher, helper, and confessor in this one-to-one relationship. Because this mentor has been around the block, he or she may have valuable insights to share with a person new to the corporate culture and to the corporate routines. The mentor may tutor, guide, and nurture. Under the watchful eye of a skillful mentor, a new employee may develop quickly. People who have been successfully mentored sing the praises of the process; they believe they truly benefit from the personal attention.

Apparently, the mentor/mentee relationship can benefit the mentor as well. Mentors report that they have learned from new hires with fresh perspectives, more recent formal training, and no corporate baggage. This produces a win-win situation for the organization and the employees.

If a mentor turns out to be a curmudgeon or a poor teacher, opposite results can occur. So leadership should appoint mentors with experience, good communication skills, and a willingness to serve. A mentor should want to be a mentor. Also, if the new hire is shopping for a mentor, the novice should look carefully for personality fit, competence, and a willingness to tutor.

Supervising

Manager, now that the employees are trained, supervise them—make sure they do what they are supposed to do. This can be a scary responsibility. Just how do managers go about doing supervision? How do they learn to supervise?

Chances are, new managers will learn to manage from having had the experience of being managed. Others will model themselves after other managers whose skills they have observed. Modeling managerial behaviors seems to be the learning method of choice.

We believe that getting in touch with the feelings one has while being supervised is an excellent strategy for a beginner. *What supervisory methods worked with me and made me feel good about what I was doing?* When supervising others, a manager might aim, therefore, to help the employee feel okay about being supervised. That is a giant accomplishment.

What does a subordinate need in order to accomplish his or her mission? Close supervision? Left alone? Answers to these questions lie in understanding the complexity of the tasks to be performed, the personalities of the players, tensions between personal and organizational goals, and the supervisory style of the managers. This is not a simple situation for which readily available formulas just wait to be applied. Good supervision requires an artful approach, one that might actually involve asking employees how they like to be supervised. This is not without risk. No managerial decision is.

Evaluating

How well is an employee doing with respect to what is expected of him or her? How can an employee improve performance? Some writers and thinkers agree that these two questions identify the primary reasons for performance evaluation. In some trenches, however, managers use the evaluation instrument to determine who gets salary raises and who gets promoted. Only indirectly does the process have anything to do with "performance improvement."

In management training programs, managers-to-be learn about evaluation checklists, traits methods, traits with explanations methods, and objectives-based performance interviews. They learn the advantages and disadvantages of each. They learn that traits methods are quick and easy but yield little in the way of performance improvement information. How does one move from satisfactory to good in loyalty, for example? They learn tidbits such as "Get the employee to sign the evaluation sheet. If she balks, tell her signing does not mean she agrees with the '3' she got in competence, only that she has seen that she got the 3." In the entire recorded history of management, there is no evidence that a single employee has ever bought that explanation. Students learn that performance-based interviews between manager and supervisee yield the highest results because they are face to face, focus upon preset performance objectives (not traits), and provide greater opportunities for discussing and learning how to improve. They also eventually discover that this method is costly in terms of time required to schedule and conduct objectives-setting and performance-reviewing interviews. Many observers claim that these communication opportunities are priceless.

Out of the training program and on the job, new managers often find that

- There is an imposed evaluation system that may not be tweaked.
- Only the official instrument and no other evaluation conversation or counseling may impact personnel decisions.
- All promotion and salary decisions rest solely on the official instrument.
- A manager may award only a specified number of *superior* ratings.
- A manager may be ordered by a boss, therefore, to change (downgrade) an employee rating if too many *superiors* have been awarded.
- The requirement to document personnel incidents is a major one, mostly as a buffer against grievance procedures, but also as support for instrument marking.
- They and their supervisees may grow to detest and mistrust the evaluation procedure.

- Some managers simply avoid doing evaluations.

Most managers agree that if properly conducted, evaluation sessions offer supervisor and supervisee a great chance to discuss things that matter, such as how an employee achieves a fit with organizational purposes and objectives, how the employee can improve performance, and what role the supervisor may play in supporting employee improvement and personal development. Many employees crave timely feedback from their supervisors; wise supervisors supply this feedback as regularly as necessary.

More on That "Myriad of Other Functions"

Managers deal with interpersonal conflicts all the time. Wherever there are two or more people in one place, actually or virtually, conflict can erupt. A major cause of such conflict is miscommunication. Managers play an essential role in issuing clear instructions, helpful and timely feedback, verification that messages have been understood, and solid remediation when necessary.

Please Like Me
Some managers spend time and effort on getting people to like them, or on getting people to like each other. Far more important than liking is understanding. Employees who understand the aims of the organization and theirs and their fellow workers' particular roles in helping to achieve those aims, do not have to like each other to be successful. Liking is nice; understanding is essential, and it can neutralize even serious personality conflicts.

Dealing with the Difficult
A manager may inherit a staff, some of whom are entrenched and some of whom have earned the label difficult. A manager may simply have to learn to live with this problem. As long as a difficult person poses no threat to organizational objectives, the manager may find that it is easier and more productive to alter his or her own belief system than it is to produce change in the difficult one. Loosening up a bit helps some managers, as does developing a sense of humor, especially about things they cannot change. Nevertheless, there are some recommended techniques for dealing with difficult employees.
There is a rich literature on dealing with the difficult employee and customer/client. One quickly discovers two common threads when he

or she examines this print or virtual literature. One, writers like to give names to the offenders; and two, the act of listening is the most frequently listed coping technique. Among the titles affixed to the troublemakers are the Hostile Aggressive, the Complainer, the Silent Unresponsive, the Negativist, the Know-It-All, and the Indecisive (Bramson 1981). Though over two decades old, Bramson's classic little handbook reminds new managers that interpersonal issues will loom and they will annoy. They need not destroy a manager who learns to listen, demonstrate respect, and model in-charge behaviors for the non-difficult to observe. The author has also addressed the problem of dealing with difficult bosses (Bramson 1994).

In addition to listening and demonstrating respect, managers should remain calm when challenged, and they should do their best to understand why difficult people are engaging in their difficult behavior. Many simply want to vent, to feel that their opinions matter. Jim Ligotti of Sikorsky Aircraft chooses to coach aggressive employees, believing that the personal approach helps him help them to achieve their goals without so much disruption (Thornton 2002).

Angry clients can also cause difficulty for a manager. Drunken customers, smelly customers, and even violent customers pose a real problem, one which usually requires intervention by police or security personnel. By far, however, angry clients cause the most frequent disruptions. They are

> people who are angry at the library: mad because of an overdue notice they think was an error, mad because an item requested two days ago still isn't in, mad because they had trouble finding a parking place. . . . You name it, a patron has gotten mad about it. (Turner 1993, 45)

Dealing with a difficult client also requires a manager to remain calm and listen. Turner adds three other techniques to the list of coping tactics: "Speak slowly, clearly, and in a moderate tone of voice; Take immediate action if you can; [and] If you can't achieve a resolution to the problem, pass the patron on to your supervisor" (Turner 1993, 149).

Motivating the Motivated and the Unmotivated

From what mysterious source comes the urge to want to perform well? How can the manager influence workers to do their jobs well. Can they? Let us just suppose that workers possess clean slates with respect to motivation. What can a manager do to etch some positive inclinations onto those slates? Several things, we think. Treat workers with respect. Acknowledge them. Find ways to let them know they are appreciated. Notice when they do well. Tell them. Demonstrate some trust in them. Keep them informed about things that will help them do their jobs. Consult them once in a while. Listen to them. Invite their comments. Reward them.

Managers may be restricted from offering promotions and monetary rewards as frequently as they would like. They are not restricted from noticing, acknowledging, and trusting, all of which can produce psychic rewards that positively influence motivation. To be sure, people work for money, and those struggling at near minimum wage jobs may be a tough audience for routine pep talks. Yet people work for other reasons too. They want to feel good about themselves, to feel important, to understand that they make a contribution, and to gain encouragement from those who notice them. A manager who provides these kinds of recognitions does so at very little cost, and a sincere "Way to go!" can be a powerful motivational instrument.

Listen to this perceptive comment by Barbara Ehrenreich, author of *Nickel and Dimed in America*, and consider its stirring appeal for recognition and trust:

> Management always seemed to operate on the assumption that the worker is a drug addict, a thief, or, at the very least, a slacker who needs constant surveillance. And yet, I saw people being very self-motivated and self-organized. They pulled together when they were rushed. They supported each other when someone had a personal problem. I often wondered why management didn't make use of this vast potential resource, *which is the desire of people to achieve satisfaction in their jobs* [emphasis ours]. Instead managers fear the people at the bottom whom they perceive as an underclass that will mug them in the parking lot if they get the chance. (Fremon 2001, 26)

Asking for What You Want

Asking for what one wants is an important skill. Most managers have the opportunity to ask their employees what is on their minds, what they want from their manager, and what they would like to have that would help them serve clients better. Many employees will answer these questions, and skillful managers may be able to respond. On the other hand, some employees feel that management does not care, and worse, does not listen. A manager who talks to her employees risks having to hear some negative feedback, but the advantage of establishing communication outweighs this possible disadvantage. Knowing what one's employees think can help a manager respond in ways that communicate respect and care. Employees can feel empowered when managers ask them for help. "Will you help me do this thing?" is a request that invites participation and cooperation. Managers should avoid intoning, "My door is always open" unless managerial ears are also open. Likewise, a manager who requests, "Tell me what you think" may create an expectation in the one who accepts the request, an expectation that the manager is going to listen, perhaps act, but most importantly, respond.

When You Have to Reprimand

Reprimand in private. Spare the feelings of all concerned. Focus on behavior, not the person. Give the person a clear explanation of the problem as viewed by management. Verify the person's understanding of the problem. Provide equally clear instructions on how to remedy the problem. Every serious treatment of this issue, How To Give a Reprimand, includes these kinds of recommendations. Few people like to be scolded or corrected, but most would like to know how they are doing, and if they are not performing up to par, how to do so.

Delegating

Busy managers must let go of some things once in a while. Delegating is a necessity. There is just too much to do, and the attempt to do it all oneself usually leads to disaster and frustration.

Delegation is the act of assigning authority and responsibility to a second party. The wise manager delegates for two major reasons: one, there is not enough time in the day to do everything oneself; and two, spreading authority and responsibility helps develop a staff.

Managers must understand the essential difference between delegating and merely parceling out jobs one would rather not do oneself. Delegating is sharing important tasks, ones which provide opportunities for learning and growth. On the other hand, passing on the responsibility for constructing a department's work schedule because one "really hates that job" and cannot wait to be free of it is hardly delegating. The *delegatee* will see that for what it is: Getting rid of a disagreeable chore.

If every management teacher intones, "Delegating is essential," and if every management textbook admonishes, "Managers must delegate," why is it that some managers find delegating so difficult to do? There are several reasons. One is the belief that if one wants a job done correctly, one must do it oneself. When arrogance and mistrust converge, they operate against delegating. Fear is another reason. Giving up means surrendering control. Delegating is risky. What if those to whom a manager passes responsibility for an important task fail to accomplish it? This will make the manager look bad; it is his failure because it happened on his watch. Reluctance to share the enriching experiences is a third reason. Some managers hog the opportunities so that they can look good. Yet the price a nondelegator pays is an expensive one. Failure to delegate leads to inundation, stress, conflict, and sometimes failure. The information society is too complex a phenomenon and the information agency is too complex an organism for a "do it all myself" manager. The severest penalty a nondelegator pays is the stunted professional growth of the staff and the resultant disservice to clients.

Some Sound Bites from the Trenches

Over time we have conducted numerous workshops and training sessions on interpersonal communication and supervision. On several occasions we have assembled some veteran managers to offer their wisdom and to respond to questions from eager participants. What follow are some of the more notable contributions from the experts and the learners. We present them as discussion points, not as truisms or pronouncements, although we agree with many, such as the first one, for example.

- Clearly explain expectations in relation to service standards.
- Being understaffed, overcrowded and underfunded is never an excuse; it is a situation to address.
- Adopt sound management principles as guides, not as commandments.
- Do not presume every employee acts in good faith. (Whoops! What about trust?)
- Understand that some employees will remain unmotivated.
- Do not hire a problem. (Check references. Make a phone call or two.)
- Carry private tort insurance.
- Document! Write up every infraction.
- Tell people to their face when they are wrong—in private, and without tearing them down.
- Adjust and adapt to change. If supervisees see that you do not buy in, neither will they.

- Prioritize. Some things can wait; others cannot.
- Provide supervisees with a challenge.
- Instill a sense of mission. Work towards integrating personal agendas with that mission.
- Admit mistakes. You *will* make them.
- Acknowledge that one never stops learning about supervision. We still get surprises after years of experience.
- Explain!
- Maintain confidences.
- Teach. Help. Observe.
- Control the tendency to overmanage.
- Do you get angry? Wait. Let some of the strong feelings pass. Then deal with the issue.
- Decide.
- Some things you may have to live with.
- A supervisor does not have to be a best friend.
- Every once in a while, you will have to go toe to toe and eye to eye with supervisees. Prepare for this.
- Busy supervisees have less time to quibble. Unoccupied supervisees have time to contribute to chaos.

Your Turn: You are quite impressed with the applicant's record. You liked the portfolio he brought for you to inspect. His letters were not glowing, but all three testified to the candidate's competency, promptness, and reliability. You get a tip from one of the applicant's coworkers. The "friend of a friend" claims the applicant is poison—a very disruptive person, a carrier of tales, and a subversive. What will you do?

Your Turn: The way I look at it, this organization has bought my mind and talent, not my wristwatch. The people who work for me, on the other hand, are hourly workers. They have specific jobs to do related to production and service. I am responsible for their performance. Yet they grumble when I am at conferences and meetings or when I take my lunch at irregular times. I owe them no explanations. If they do not like how I do my important job, that's their problem. If they think I am "out for myself," let them. My business is not their business. They wouldn't understand, anyhow. Counsel this manager.

Your Turn: One of your employees is a very nice person. But her work is not up to par. On several occasions you have pointed out Adrian's mistakes, even referred Adrian to the procedures manual, but the mistakes mount up. You have placed three notes about poor performance in the file. Adrian has not learned the job, and the probationary period is half over. Adrian seems bright, and many clients enjoy dealing with her; but the poor performance continues. What will you do?

References

Barnes, Kim. 2002. Leading in style. *Executive excellence* 19:5.

Bramson, Robert M. 1981. *Coping with difficult people.* New York: Dell.

———. 1994. *Coping with difficult bosses.* New York: Simon & Schuster.

Ehrenreich, Barbara. 2001. *Nickel and dimed in America: On (not) getting by in America.* New York: Henry Holt and Company.

Fremon, Celeste. 2001. Labor's pain. *LA Weekly*, July 13-19.

Gemmill, Gary, and Judith Oakley. 1992. Leadership: An alienating social myth? *Human Relations* 45:113-29.

Gibbons, Patrick T. 1992. Impacts of organizational evolution on leadership roles and behaviors. *Human Relations* 45:1-18.

Kirkpatrick, Shelly A., and Edwin A. Locke. 1996. Direct and indirect effects of three core charismatic leadership components on performance and attitudes. *Journal of Applied Psychology* 81:36-51.

The leadership thing. 1995. *Economist*, 337, Issue 7944: 23-24.

Oxford English dictionary. 1989. New York: Oxford University Press.

Quinn, Brian. 1999. Librarians' and psychologists' view of leadership: Converging and diverging perspectives. *Library Administration & Management* 13 (3): 147-57.

Riggs, Donald E. 2001. The crisis and opportunities in library leadership. In *Leadership in the library and information science professions: Theory and practice*, edited by Mark D. Winston. New York: Haworth Press.

Thornton, Paul B. 2002. Managing difficult people. www.refreasher.com!difficultpeople.html (accessed 2 May 2003).

Turner, Anne M. 1993. *It comes with the territory: Handling problem situations in libraries.* Jefferson, NC: McFarland.

Chapter 4

A Brief History of Organizational Thought from the Garden of Eden to the Fish Market

"But I have never, ever told another adult what to do on the job."

People reading this chapter are surely asking themselves: What good will it do for me to read a brief history of management? I have to manage today, or tomorrow at the latest. Would that they were asking! Many people discount the importance of management history, and many find the issues of today's management only remotely connected to what they associate with the work world they are about to enter. They have been drawn to the information professions because they enjoy technology, like to search and package information for clients, excel at teaching people to become information literate, or thrive when they tell stories to little ones. These information professionals-to-be may not yet see themselves as deciders and deployers, hirers and firers, trainers and supervisors, handlers of disturbances, negotiators, representatives, and father/mother confessors. The reality of spending half their workdays in meetings has not yet visited them. They are as yet unaware that extinguishing interpersonal brushfires may be an everyday responsibility. They may, like the management student who uttered the lament which begins this chapter, have never supervised another adult on the job. Newly hired managers very quickly discover that managing people can be scary. We think that the more managers know

73

about how management thought has evolved, the more armed they will be for the management encounter.

How One Manages

How one manages may depend in large measure upon how one views the people to be managed. What makes them tick? Will they cooperate? How do I motivate them? Can I motivate them? Why do they work here? What do they want? Is what I want from them at all like what they want to give? What tools are at my disposal?

Through the ages, but mostly during the last half century, these questions have been asked and responded to. There has been a pronounced shift of focus in the last century. Managers used to focus primarily, even exclusively, on task and production. They now focus substantially on the worker and on the psychology and sociology of the workplace. Which of the newer views are valid? Which work? In ancient times managers tied heavy stones around the necks of uncooperative workers and cast them into the river. Clerics who were landowners could keep the peasants in line with the threat of excommunication and damnation. At the turn of the nineteenth century, supervisors could fire workers once they fell short of production standards because there were twenty people in line waiting for a job. These measures are substantially absent from today's managers' procedure manuals, and it is comforting to know that drowning, damning, and firing are probably not the methods or motivators employed by most contemporary managers. Other orthodoxies prevail today: participatory methods, hands-off supervision, feedback, coaching, flattened organizational schemes, quality circles, and "fun" approaches to work and production. Like the more extreme approaches they replaced, they share the same assumption: *Here's how you get people to do their work.* How has this thinking evolved?

The *New* Science

Anyone who has ever read a management textbook has encountered the claim that management science or scientific management is a very young science. The authors of these texts assert that the new discipline has its origins in the work of Henri Fayol and Frederick Winslow Taylor in the late nineteenth and early twentieth centuries, making it barely over a century old. They are correct, of course, but in the process of giving credit to the pioneers, could they possibly create the impression that nobody knew anything about managing organizations until 1890? Well, we have some questions, the answers to which should dispel the impression that nobody ever finished a job until F. W. Taylor fired up his stopwatch. The Holy Roman Empire wasn't managed? Nobody ran the monasteries? Brother Antonio never really knew what to do with his time? Should he pray now or plow now, how bald should his bald spot be, and could he have seconds on the mashed turnips? There was no order in the guilds? The early factories had no bosses? No one ever planned anything until Lyndall Urwick and Luther Gulick said, "Plan" to President Franklin Delano Roosevelt in 1937 (Stueart and Moran 1993, 11)?

The Really Important Question

As fascinating as the history of organizational thought may be to people who are fascinated by history, the most useful purpose in observing how we got to where we are today, management thought-wise, is to discover how people behave in organizations and how managers think about those people and their supervision. We have come from somewhere to get where we are today. Just knowing that history may not protect us always from repeating some errors of the past, but it may help us discover reasonable managerial practice for the present. *Look backward to go forward*, a typical Chinese paradox, provides an interesting exercise in preparation for management (Witzel 2002, 5).

Knowing why people behave the way they do in organizations is a useful intelligence item for a manager. Knowing that people behave that way because of conditions in their personal makeup, personal environment, and the occupational opportunities and constraints they perceive in the work place is a powerful insight spawned in the 1930s. Knowing that workers have free will and that they cannot be programmed need not discourage the manager who artfully can convince the work force that doing things the company way is as advantageous to them as it is to the company. Douglas McGregor's Theory Y managers take this view; his Theory X managers cannot, and they must hover as a consequence.

The Garden of Eden

What if we had only one boss? What if the span of control were two? That is a rather manageable number, no? What if unity of command were clearly and firmly in place, all instructions were direct and simple, and the dress code was about as casual as a dress code can be? What could go wrong, managerially speaking?

Well, according to one widely told story, despite an uncluttered chain of command and a rather reasonable number of work rules—*one!*—history's two very first company workers decided to disobey that rule and order the forbidden fruit cup at the Tree of Knowledge Management Café.

Bad move for them and us, but what is the lesson here? Well, even when things are perfect, something can go wrong, and even a Supreme Being can have trouble with the work force. Nevertheless, everyone reading this has managed to survive banishment, the flood, the plague, and the Ice Capades. So there is hope for managers, even new ones.

How They Used to Do It

We present this quick historical snapshot in the following schema: Holy Roman Empire, guilds, pre-industrial enlightenment, industrial revolution, and the modern era.

The Holy Roman Empire

For centuries the Roman Empire endured, suffered some ups and downs, was really not all that "Holy," and provided some examples of how to manage. While they did not call it "corporate culture" back then, a managerial culture is what those players created. It was based on four pillars: organizational legitimacy, anti-corruption, organizational stability, and effective leadership (Daley 1998, 127). One who searches the managerial dictums in today's texts will find these same themes emphasized in the new millennium. Words like "vision," "mission," and "purpose," key terms in modern management argot, have their managerial antecedents in the empire begun in 57 A.D. Augustus, who ruled until A.D. 14, may not have invented command and control, but he employed it expertly. Not all the Roman administrators and managers were able to check the overly and sometimes criminally ambitious citizens, however, and neither could they check the *it's not what you know, it's who you know* adage that was popular then, even as it is today. Yet long before Max Weber (1864-1920), Diocletian (A.D. 285-305) "created a hierarchical system of prefectures, dioceses and provinces" (Daley 1998, 133). This hardly challenges Weber's primacy as chief bureaucracy guru, but it should put management observers on notice that notions of hierarchy and of ascending levels of power, and of the downward flow of authority, predate modern bureaucratic models by more than fifteen centuries. We know of no management authorities who credit Diocletian with being the father of participatory management, probably because he was not. He did, however, institute governance models in which decision making was a shared responsibility and he practiced "shared leadership" (Daley 1998, 134). Another emperor, Justinian I (A.D. 527-565) dealt with what Daley calls a 'bloated bureaucracy' long before bureaucracy was in fashion (Daley 1998, 138).

We need to remind ourselves that this great empire fell largely because of management failure and destabilizing corruption issues, chiefly the quest for and abuse of personal power. Those emperors struggled to do what managers today strive for: selecting and training the right people for the right jobs—hiring good people and letting them do their thing, and hoping that their thing is the organization's thing, too.

Guilds

Guild management established standards and punished artisans who produced inferior products. The Guilds, which flourished during the Middle Ages from about 400 to about 1400 and which are the antecedents of today's labor unions, made provisions for needy members and their families and enforced strict apprenticeship rules (History n.d., 1). The management was tight, often one-to-one between master craftsman and apprentice, and focused primarily on workmanship and the enforcement of strict admission procedures.

Long before "mentoring" or "coaching," craftsmen and apprentices developed the special relationship of teacher and pupil in the work place. The personal touch was a primary ingredient in the process, as was an intense focus upon quality of product that predates TQM by over six centuries. Artifacts and buildings constructed by these Medieval artisans have endured to this day.

Pre-Industrial Enlightenment Times

A long, long time ago Aristotle (384-322 B.C.) believed that mankind's highest calling was to seek the common good through participation in politics and government, and that the leader's job was to manage this good outcome. He believed people would invest in this for-the-good-of-everyone idea because they were naturally inclined to seek that common good. Much later political philosophers and thinkers about things administrative still believed in natural inclinations, but they observed that the "good" most people sought was their good, not the common good. Eighteen centuries later Niccolo Machiavelli (1469-1527) injected Aristotelian idealism with heavy doses of pragmatism because he believed more in people's bad sides than their good ones. So he invented instruments of control to keep them focused upon maintaining the safety of the state. Enlightenment thinkers in the 1700s believed people would freely pursue those aims which coincided with their own self-interest and that it was government's job to keep enough order to allow the pursuit to proceed (Bagby and Franke 2001, 623-33).

What kind of manager will I become? Good question. We believe the answer to that question is in part contained in the response one has to a pronouncement by Bagby and Frank. Managers form their views of people in the workplace on the basis of

> whether we agree with the ancients that man is a political
> animal, whose highest development lies in the perfection
> of his civic and intellectual virtues. Or, as argued by mod-
> ern political philosophers such as Machiavelli, Hobbes and
> Locke, do we feel that man is a passionate animal whose
> development is essentially self-defined and inescapably
> selfish? (Bagby and Franke 2001, 633)

The most important aspect of this issue is not the answer; it is the question. The question is about the phenomenon of man in the organization, a phenomenon that produced a ferment of incipient ideas that reached full bloom and the status of a science—management—in the 1900s.

The Industrial Revolution (1750-1900)

This movement is important to our view of history, not because of the management developments and wisdom it yields, but because it sets the stage for the future study of ways to accomplish objectives in organizations. Most of the gurus of the scientific management era, which immediately followed the Industrial Revolution, were born in the late nineteenth century and many of the observations they made of Industrial Revolution conditions prompted them to seek better ways to manage people and processes.

The industrial age produced a number of consequential conditions and phenomena. First, it changed the way most workers made their living. Mass production and assembly line methods yielded products and gadgets at speeds unheard of previously. Not only did machinery produce more things quickly, it enabled factories to supplant the work of the guilds. The Industrial Revolution did not completely abolish the apprentice system, but it made the factory the locus of production activity that employed legions of workers who might otherwise have sought to learn trades from the master craftsmen or to work on farms.

Second, the Industrial Revolution changed where people lived. Factories located in larger towns and transportation centers like port cities, so the people who worked in them were drawn to the cities from rural areas. This began a mighty urbanization. Urbanization brought with it giant assortments of new developments and problems: the dramatic rise of a new middle class, crowding, crime, demand for public services like police protection, the need for skilled labor, and child labor abuses.

Large groups of assembly line workers had to be trained and supervised, and the immediate need to develop midlevel supervisors presented itself. Companies sought constantly to produce more and more and to improve the methods of production. Philanthropic titans of industry paid off their social debts by building schools and orphanages, and by supporting causes in which they believed. Two of those causes were education and libraries. The libraries were touted as "people's universities" where workers might educate themselves, or where, as Michael Harris believes, the work force could be held in check through exposure to ideas which the elites held were good for them and which would enable the rich to continue to control the poor (Harris 1973). It is from these kinds of developments that the modern managerial era emerges.

The Modern Managerial Era and What It Teaches Us

People who study managerial practice divide the post-industrial era
into three periods: classical, neoclassical, and modern. The classical
period began about 1890 and was ushered in by pioneers like Henri
Fayol and Frederick Winslow Taylor, who focused primarily on the
job to be done and the best ways to do it. In the United States of America during the 1920s and 1930s, social scientists contributed findings
about human behavior to the managerial equation. Forward thinkers
like Mary Parker Follett helped launch the neoclassical period, which
was basic classical thought laced with the findings of the human relations movement. In the 1940s, World War II involved the United
States of America in producing, moving, and storing mass quantities of
materiel. In addition, the nation trained hundreds of thousands of
troops, stationed them, deployed them, and managed them. All these
efforts presented requirements and opportunities to study both the
movement of equipment and human behavior, as the conduct of the
war required the country to assemble vast quantities of people and the
tools of warfare—tanks, planes, weapons, foodstuffs, and structures.
Mathematicians and statisticians flourished as they applied their skills
to the problems of moving and governing vast numbers of people and
things. Empirical and analytical studies bolstered the human relations
discoveries of the 1930s and helped define a third period of managerial
thought—the modern period. The post-industrial age, the computer
age, and the information age continue the modern period, a time during
which service and information have nudged manufacturing, the essence of the Industrial Age, from its position as the focus of the
American economy and of management.

For our purposes here, the question becomes "What can we learn
from some of the pioneers and visionaries who oversaw the movement
from industrial age thinking to information age thinking?" We believe
that the most useful suggestion we can make is to examine how thinking has evolved and to select from those thoughts and discoveries the
ingredients for assembling a workable, flexible, personal managerial
philosophy. To assist us with this look at the recent past we have
drawn heavily upon two excellent sources: Stuart Cranier's outstanding
book, *The Management Century* (Cranier, 2000), and Stephen Hartman's Internet contribution, "Questions on Organizational Behavior"
(Hartman, n.d.).

Luminaries of the Classical Period: A Few Observations

Fayol and Taylor were instrumental in establishing management as a science. The following sections present some of the contributions of these two pioneers.

Fayol

Frenchman Henri Fayol (1841-1925) is considered by many to be the father of modern scientific management. Fayol was a thinker and a doer who spent his working life with one French mining company and was one of the first of the pioneers to elevate management to a status as a serious subject for study.

Before there was the Harvard MBA, the artifact created by those who believe that management can be taught and learned, Fayol developed and published principles which he derived from his own managerial practice. What follows is a digest of those principles:

1. Division of work into specialties
2. Authority, the right and power to demand obedience
3. Discipline based upon fairness and the application of sanctions
4. Unity of command, the "one boss principle"
5. Unity of direction based upon central authority
6. Primacy of organizational interests; subordination of individual interests
7. Fair value compensation of employees
8. Centralization, specialization, best use of workers
9. Order, the matching of skills and equipment with jobs
10. Equity; application of kindness and justice
11. Stability of work force
12. Initiative; planning as a motivator
13. Teamwork

(Hartman, n.d.)

So, in terms of the development of a personal managerial philosophy, what can Fayol teach us? He teaches us that managerial technique can be learned by those of us who as yet may not grasp it. Scanning the principles listed above provides one with a mighty managerial homily: The chief concerns of the manager are people concerns. How one treats other people defines the quality of his or her managerial practice. What a useful piece of intelligence for the new manager!

Taylor

Historians argue that Frederick Winslow Taylor (1856-1915) is also a cofounder of scientific management. He may have been the very first efficiency expert. He gained fame, and a certain amount of resentment, for brandishing his stopwatch. Modern management owes him a great debt, however, for he made significant contributions to managerial decision making, to establishing reasonable times for the completion of tasks, to the study of motion, to standardization, and to the development of practices which increased production. He was certainly more that just the stopwatch guy.

Taylor's affinity for piecework, a practice which rewarded a worker for achieving production targets, was an example of his interest in goal setting and in motivating the worker to produce, a motivation he thought was based primarily on monetary reward. Subsequent study has added to our knowledge of why people work by identifying powerful motivators like the desire to belong, the desire to make a contribution, and the desire to feel fulfilled. Certainly his thinking about the task at hand and about establishing an organizational structure to best accomplish that task influences modern thinkers who insist, along with Peter Drucker (Drucker 1974, 74), that the most important question an organization can ask itself is "What is our business?"

What can we learn from Taylor that will contribute to developing a personal philosophy of management? We can learn that it is desirable to provide workers with reasonable targets, and it is essential to communicate clearly with workers so that they can understand what is expected of them. This is another essential interpersonal skill.

YOUR TURN: You are the new manager of a department whose job it is to order, purchase, describe, and classify products and ship them to customers. The section is in total disarray. Inefficiency prevails. Look at the digest of Fayol's principles and consider Taylor's contributions. How might they guide your approach?

Neo-Classical Period, 1930-1940: A Few Observations

More than any other phenomenon, the Hawthorne Studies demonstrate the impact of established social science upon management science. More than other individual, Mary Parker Follett demonstrated the validity of humanistic social science upon management science.

The Hawthorne Studies and the Hawthorne Effect

The Hawthorne Studies, so-called because they took place in the 1920s and 1930s at the Western Electric Hawthorne plant in Cicero, Illinois, are still the subject of research today. The Hawthorne Effect is this: There is an effect of the observer upon the observed. You will perform differently, and probably better, if you think you are being observed.

There is more to the effect than the conclusion that being observed, or believing that one is being observed, affects how one behaves on the job. The Hawthorne Studies, especially those portions spearheaded by human relations professor Elton Mayo, signal the impact that the social sciences are to have in influencing attempts to study and understand behavior in the workplace. The Hawthorne experiments had been conceived and conducted in an effort to discover ways to increase production. Many variables were introduced: work breaks, free lunches, music, illumination, increased supervisory attention, and pay benefits. All of these variables had similar effects; they all were associated with increased production. Mayo and his team concluded that the workers were responding primarily to the attention they believed they were getting and not specifically to the changes themselves. It was not the music per se. Each time a change was introduced, the workers interpreted the new wrinkle as an indication that they were being watched. So they worked harder. What is so meaningful about this discovery is not the rather obvious notion that if the boss is watching, a worker will respond to being observed. What truly matters is the discovery that managers may choose from among multiple ways to achieve the *being watched* effect without hovering over or smothering the worker with heavy-handed supervision. Subtler methods work. Music is more than just soothing, lighting is more than just illuminating, work breaks are more than just relaxing, and an encouraging word is more than just a verbal pat on the back. The message received can be "Management cares; they are looking out for us." The result can be better production.

Another finding from the Hawthorne Studies that matters is this: Groups of workers establish their own norms for behaviors. There is a sociology of the workplace that strongly influences the behaviors of participants. Workers who depart from the norms, either by producing too much or by producing too little, earn the disapproval of their peers. This too has an impact on production, an impact that is influenced not by management but by the workers themselves. So corporate culture, that system of beliefs and attitudes which govern behavior in the organization, is as much a creation of workers as it is of organizational management. Thank the influences of the social sciences for this key finding about group influences in the workplace.

Another key conclusion that has resulted from study of the Hawthorne experiments is that feedback matters. Workers respond well to timely feedback—feedback delivered in time to correct a problem. Conversely, feedback delivered after the fact is worse than useless. Untimely feedback which reaches a worker as a "gotcha" frustrates and disillusions the worker. "Now you tell me" feedback only documents that the horse has escaped; it does little to solve the problem of the missing transportation.

A manager wishing to develop a personal philosophy may consider the following Hawthorne-related items for inclusion:

- Supervision requires some observation on the part of the manager, but there are ways to conduct observations in addition to overt watching.
- Workers establish ways of behaving and communicating that influence how they work and relate to each other. Managers may use the grape vine as an instrument for spreading messages they want to send.
- Timely feedback is precious; managers should issue pats on the back or reprimands in ways that have most immediate impact on performance.

Follett

Another social scientist who strongly influenced the neo-classical period was Mary Parker Follett (1868-1933). Unlike the classical mechanical view of the worker, hers was a more humanitarian view, a view that drove her major concern—infusing human elements when dealing with conflict on the job. She saw a more prominent role for participants in the resolution of conflict, a role that departed from the traditional power move on the part of supervisory management. The power move had been a staple of classical thought, as had been confrontation and domination. She believed in integration, "the only positive way forward. This can be achieved by first 'uncovering' the real conflict and then taking 'the demands of both sides and breaking them into their constituent parts'" (Cranier 2000, 71).

Long before "empowerment" became the buzzword it is today, Mary Parker Follett was a champion of involving participants in the resolution of problems and in the creative pursuit of opportunities. Her views on leadership emphasized having an eye for the future and developing a more holistic understanding of the organization and its purposes. She saw leadership as having more to do with vision than with traditional concepts of power, confrontation, and dominance. She saw the humanistic approach as having the best chance for getting an organization focused and moving toward defined purposes. Like many visionaries, she was ignored by some of her contemporaries. Now, however, her contributions are seen as forward looking and important. Even more than Mayo and Hawthorne, Follett enfranchised the worker and supplied the supervisor with fresh approaches. She epitomizes neoclassical thinking.

So how can an appreciation of Mary Parker Follett help one develop a personal philosophy of management? One can consider these principles:

- Compromise involving the input of the several persons in conflict is a technique often preferable to power or dominance.
- Work groups may share power and responsibility; all authority need not come only from the top.
- Team approaches work.
- People issues are paramount.
- Following is as important as leading.

Your Turn: What does it feel like to get negative feedback after you purchased the new car or after you had the article of clothing unalterably altered? How might these feelings help you develop a philosophy of management?

The Modern Period, 1941: A Few Observations

As stated previously, World War II presented the United States with both the necessity and the opportunity to invent, mass produce, and quickly distribute thousands of products. Hundreds of thousands of people had to be trained and deployed. Casualties had to be counted. Morale had to be studied and often improved. Troops had to be clothed, fed, and sheltered. Service men and women had to be separated from the military and readmitted to the work force. New interest in why people act the way they do drove some important research and inspired serious thinkers to more closely examine organizational structure and organizational behavior.

A useful purpose may be achieved by mining the thoughts, teachings, and discoveries of some of the more prominent movers and shakers of this period and then listing some principles which managers might consider adding to their arsenal of management guidelines. Accordingly, we choose to consider some of the contributions of the following modern era stars: Herbert A. Simon, Abraham Maslow, Douglas McGregor, Frederick Herzberg, Peter Drucker, and W. Edwards Deming.

Simon

If deciding things is the most important thing managers do, and we believe it is, and if acting indecisively is the cardinal management sin, and we believe it is, then we must examine and appreciate, and use, the contributions of Herbert A. Simon. Simon won a Nobel Prize for his work on decision making, but unlike the findings and publications of many international prizewinners, Simon's work is immediately understandable and usable in the trenches of our organizations.

Simon has presented us with a three-celled decision model, to which we have added a fourth cell, but for which we claim no share of his prize. The three-celled Simon model consists of *intelligence, design*, and *choice* (Simon 1960). We add *evaluation*.

Intelligence

This is the initial information component. It is an active process, not a passive one. According to Simon, an organization must develop the capacity to look for opportunities to make decisions. Seeking out such opportunities is the proactive opposite of its passive counterpart— waiting for something to happen before deciding to do anything. Intelligence gathering is a chief responsibility for management, but it should also be a shared one. Good managers involve staff in the identifying and gathering of issues that must be addressed, problems that must be solved, and opportunities that should be pursued. The more pertinent information a decider can gather, the more likely he or she is to make a good decision. Simon sez! We agree.

Design

Design consists of two parts: alternatives and consequences. After managers identify opportunities to make decisions, the next step is to list as many alternative solutions as they can. If intelligence provides information that the roof is weak, or that it is indeed leaking, the design phase kicks in when the search for solutions begins. Some possible solutions include

- Replace the roof
- Patch the roof
- Build or move to a new building
- Place a plastic tarp over the books about to be leaked upon
- Discontinue use of the space likely to be inundated
- Do nothing

Each of these proposed solutions has consequences, or advantages and disadvantages. An advantage to replacing the roof may be a more secure environment for the whole building; disadvantages may include cost and the length of time it may take to convince funders, issue bids, employ contractors, and wait for completion. Factor in the inconvenience to the whole operation if an entire roof must be constructed.

Patching the roof may be an easier solution to obtain, quicker, and cheaper. But it may only temporarily address a problem. Next week another section may spring a leak.

Getting a new building may be the best answer, but the cost may be prohibitive.

Placing a tarp over the soggy books or drowned company server is cheap, but certainly temporary and for aesthetic reasons alone is an unlikely remedy.

Discontinuing the use of the affected space may also be cheap, but it does nothing about the problem and only provides temporary relief.

Doing nothing is inexpensive, for now, but deciding not to address the issue is likely to lead to further problems, even catastrophic ones, down the road.

During this design phase deciders try to pick the solution which is most doable, considering time, technical, and financial constraints, and the likely advantages and disadvantages attached to each possibility.

Choice
Choice involves the manager in selection of the best solution available.

Evaluation
This is our addition. A manager observes to see whether the decision is implemented, what results it produces, and whether study of those results suggests an alteration in the decision or indicates that it should

continue unchanged. Evaluation feeds the intelligence stage and may trigger more design activity or just reinforce the original decision.

Simon claims that there are two basic kinds of decisions. Programmed decisions respond to routine conditions in the environment. nonprogrammed decisions respond to novel circumstances in the environment. A programmed decision can guide one's route to work, a decision to have lunch, when to add toner to the copier, or when and how many book pockets to order. A nonprogrammed decision is one involving the selection of a mate, choosing an elective surgical procedure, switching from Dewey to Library of Congress Classification System, or designing a new for-fee service for one's information agency.

One uses the Simon model when constructing a nonprogrammed response, the kind of response which addresses rare opportunities, which may be quite expensive, and which may commit a person or organization to travel a very important path. If one were to employ the Simon model when deciding which kinds of mustard—spicy, hot, horseradish, or Dijon—to apply to a lunchtime pastrami sandwich, one would probably annoy luncheon companions and surely return late for the afternoon work period. Employing the Simon model is useful practice when deciding matters of great consequence; it is wasteful when deciding routine matters. The eight o'clock hour can signal the start of a set of established routines for closing the building at 8:30. So the chime of eight bells triggers preplanned activities; it does not invite use of the Simon model. (What do we do now? What are the advantages of alerting customers that we are about to close? Which lights do we extinguish and who extinguishes them? Who locks the front door?) Determining which decisions should be constructed to respond to routine circumstances and which require Simon's prize-winning directives is an important managerial function. Managers at all levels deal with this issue.

Here's another useful observation about the Simon model. It has prescriptive and descriptive properties. It can "prescribe" a way to make a decision by guiding the manager through a process. Managers may also use the model to critique and/or repair decisions that have already been made, by them or others. That is its descriptive property; like its prescriptive cousin, it can help a manager "doctor" a decision.

Simon is not without his critics. They have assailed his model for assuming too much—that a decider can array all possible alternatives, and that one can know all possible outcomes. The process appears to be logical but it is predicated upon a fictitious notion about rationality, they argue. The decider's capabilities are finite; one cannot "see" into the future and unerringly anticipate events.

Simon's response is as equally reasoned as his model. In effect he says, "Look, no one is promising the best decision. What may be in store for the logical decider is a good decision, not necessarily a perfect one." We agree. We think his idea of "satisficing," which is finding *a* needle in the haystack but not necessarily the sharpest one, may be all that is required. Simon is telling us that a rational decision process is preferable to one which is irrational, helter-skelter, or in no way scientific (Simon 1976). Should one jettison a rational model for other devices—proverbs, for example? He ably dismisses that strategy in his excellent "Proverbs of Administration" article (Simon 1946) in which he points out that proverbs usually have opposites. He is right. *Look before you leap*? Well maybe so, but *He who hesitates is lost.* Wise sayings are shorthand for rational thought, and they abandon the decider when even slight changes occur in the environment. We think the proverbs provide inconsistent models for managerial behavior, but we also agree with serious observers who point out that the proverbs ought to be studied, not abandoned in favor of a search for always correct, always applicable, scientific formulas (Hood and Jackson 1991). The main problem is not that proverbs have opposites; the main problem is that some managers use them, regardless of the circumstances, to rule their decisions. Sometimes the laws of the situation demand that we do put all our eggs in one basket!

So, what principles might a manager draw from Herbert A. Simon?

- Deciding is an active, aggressive, even entrepreneurial process.
- The Simon model provides a path for the decision maker.

Your Turn: You open your refrigerator and are greeted by unidentifiable food objects, fuzzy textures, and odors that bring you to your knees. The electricity is on, the motor is dead, and the plug is plugged in. You have just gathered intelligence; now design, choose, and evaluate (apply the Simon model).

Maslow

Abraham Maslow was interested in motivation. Why do we behave the way we do in organizations? His Hierarchy of Needs consists of five levels, each of which is pursued in sequence, and none of which can be achieved until all the levels below it are achieved. Taken as a whole, according to him, the hierarchy model helps explain a significant part of personal behavior in the organization, and it also provides clues that may help a manager provide motivational cues.

The hierarchical levels of need are, from top to bottom,

- Self-actualization—being the best one can be
- Esteem—feeling good about being good at what one does
- Belonging—seeking and getting the love and appreciation of others, especially significant others
- Safety—feeling secure and protected
- Psychological—feeling okay about basic needs like food, drink, and shelter

If Maslow is correct, then people have to be earning a living wage and feel confident about their security in the workplace before managers can expect them to be motivated to invest themselves in the goals of the organization. Maslow teaches that people will not be motivated to pursue higher needs, that they will not have higher needs until they have met the basic ones.

Here is the way this works. A manager may not expect workers who are hungry or who fear that they cannot provide for their children to be invested in the "team." Until they are secure, they will not be motivated to surrender personal goals to those of the organization. Managers should not be surprised that minimum wage workers neither will be moved to be as polite as they can be to clients nor likely to believe managers who exhort them with platitudes such as "You are the backbone of this organization; we could not open our doors without you."

In addition, a manager who supervises those who have achieved satisfactory levels of psychological and safety needs will discover that these workers are now motivated more by the desire to contribute, to be recognized, and to achieve than they are by wage concerns. Therefore, wise managers provide ample opportunities for motivated employees to participate in self-development. Fed, clothed, sheltered, and safe employees desire to learn, to excel, to participate, and to feel important. Those motivations now drive them.

There are minimum wage workers who know how to treat clients with courtesy, and they take pride in doing so. Some of them will seek to self-develop and advance themselves. Some wage earners who are in comfortable circumstances will not "graduate." They may settle in after having achieved level four. These exceptions do not render Maslovian theory irrelevant, but they teach us that there are exceptions which probe the rule. To those who would argue that motivation comes from within and that managers can do little to motivate an unmotivated worker, we would respond that understanding the "why" and "what" of motivation helps the manager to provide those things which contribute to a worker's desire to achieve, to move upward, to seek rewards for the psyche as well as for the pocketbook.

What does Maslow contribute to our collection of managerial principles?

- Needs motivate people and they pursue them in sequence from the very basic to the very sublime.
- Managers may, in the staffing and directing of organizations, help workers pursue needs and accomplish personal and organizational purposes.
- Insecure workers are less likely to have or participate in a "vision" for the organization, and managers should not be surprised by this.

Your Turn: Despite your warnings, counsel, and imposed penalties, Chris is continually tardy. Chris is an excellent performer, but the tardiness is disruptive of work flow and injurious to staff morale. How might you employ Maslovian principles to address this problem? What deployment (scheduling) options might work?

McGregor

Douglas McGregor authored the influential book, *The Human Side of Enterprise* (McGregor 1960), in which he laid out his thoughts and discoveries about things managerial and gave us Theory X and Theory Y to consider. From his observations of how managers manage, he concluded that some managers managed as though they believed workers hate to work, must be closely supervised, and will not surrender personal goals to those of the organization. He labeled this Theory X. On the other hand, he observed that some managers managed as though they believed workers like to work, perform best when supervised less intensely, and will surrender personal goals if managers can explain to them how their aims and company aims can complement each other. He labeled this Theory Y.

Theory X and Theory Y earn frequent mention in contemporary conversation about management. People often refer to "Theory X managers" as though managers so named are locked into X-type practice. Theory X also has been infused with negative connotations. Theory X is "bad," in other words. Conversely, Theory Y has been infused with "niceness" and goodness. A Theory Y manager is people oriented, kindly, and supportive. A Theory Y manager lets people do their things and is beloved.

McGregor never intended for his theories to be perceived in so simplistic and confining a way. He saw X and Y as styles occupying positions on either ends of a continuum, to be sure, but he never meant to posit goodness or badness. Neither did he believe that managers were forever consigned to a given style. Most managers operate some-where in the middle of the continuum, and most good ones know when to shift styles depending upon the work to be done and the characteris-tics of the people to be supervised.

Theory Y gives great comfort to the proponents of the "work is as natural as play" school of thought. People are often at their best when at play. They are focused, motivated, and engaged. Managers who try to blur the lines between work and play, and employees who are able to cross the line, often find that workers like work more and are more productive as a direct result.

A Theory X view may enable some managers to do what needs to be done. There are some times when circumstances demand that they supervise more closely. There are some workers who, under some cir-cumstances, respond positively to close supervision. They react posi-tively to a kick in the pants—to negative reinforcement.

Managers owe McGregor a great debt. He has supplied them with options, an array of possible ways to train and supervise that accom-modates given circumstances. Wise managers artfully appraise those circumstances, which include the task and the characteristics of the workers. Contingencies matter. They require a deft touch, not a heavy-handed formula approach. McGregor demonstrated this both in his published work and in his managerial practice. He thought it, and he did it!

McGregor did not stop with X and Y. He also laid the ground-work for Theory Z (Cranier 2000, 115). Theory Z, sometimes loosely referred to as Japanese management style, was popularized by William Ouchi in his book Theory Z (Ouchi 1981). Centerpiece provisions of Theory Z, such as guaranteed lifetime employment, consensual deci-sion making, collective responsibility, and the holistic view of the worker (his health, happiness, personal life, children's welfare), demonstrate McGregor's influence and signal another explicit departure from the classical mode of "organization/task first."

From what McGregor supplies, what can we add to the growing list of principles considered for inclusion in an arsenal of managerial practices?

- How one views the worker may determine how one manages. Trust plays a major role. Even X managers can display trust.
- The Y view, the one that holds that workers desire responsibility, deserves a chance.
- Much can be learned from contemplating the meaning of the expression, *The human side of enterprise.*

Herzberg

Frederick Herzberg in a very real way partners with Maslow in providing insights into motivation and worker behavior. Herzberg studied the question of why people work and the phenomenon of job satisfaction. He discovered that "True motivation . . . comes from achievement, personal development, job satisfaction, and recognition (Cranier 2000, 111). He also coined KITA (kick in the ass) to describe a technique designed to alter motivation, so he was also a "carrot and stick" man when he determined the situation called for positive and/or negative reinforcement (Cranier 2000, 111).

Managers in training should notice two important lessons/developments contained in Herzberg's contributions. One is the sharp departure of his findings from classical thought. Classical thinking focused on the job to be done and the organizational directives and structure required for its completion. Classical notions ruled all the way through the mid stages of the Industrial Revolution. Workers were replaceable, even expendable. Along come Maslow and Herzberg (and others, of course) who show that production is affected by influences other than economic. People work for a variety of different reasons. Motivation matters. Managers can do things to improve worker attitude and performance. How a worker is "getting along" may determine how he or she views the job.

This new scientific management has provided us with different, and probably more accurate, ways to think about the nature of work and the training and supervision of employees. There is a powerful little equation, $B = f(IE)$, that encapsulates an essential complex observation. We cannot attribute this equation to Herzberg or Maslow, but we see how it captures vital organizational truisms contained in their work.

> *B* stands for behavior in an organization.
> f stands for "function of. "
> *I* stands for "individual" and includes everything the worker brings to the job: attitudes, intelligence, motivation, feelings, disposition, and skill.
> *E* stands for "environment" and includes ingredients like work conditions, equipment, support, supervision, and other workers.

What a practical insight the originator of this equation provides for the modern manager! If a manager wants to understand what is going on, he or she will have to understand that workers behave, perform, and produce the way they do on the basis of how they are feeling, whether or not they had a good breakfast or a fight with their significant others, whether or not they have been properly trained and coached, whether they like their jobs, whether they get along with coworkers, and whether they think management "cares." Classical managers cared about establishing standard times for transferring so many bricks from the pile to the railroad car. Today's managers know they must take a more holistic view of the worker, and they owe pioneers like Maslow, McGregor, and Herzberg a giant debt.

What can we extract from Herzberg for inclusion in our arsenal?

- Because it matters whether people like their jobs, managers should help them do so.
- Job satisfaction and motivation are closely related.
- Recognize achievement; doing so positively affects motivation.

Your Turn: Theories X and Y do not lock a manager into performing in certain kinds of ways; what they do is provide an array of options to be applied in different situations. The labels do not enslave. They suggest. What do you think about this? How might you employ X and Y notions?

Drucker

More than once Austrian-born Peter F. Drucker has been referred to reverently as *Saint Peter Drucker.* There is a reason for this. More than any other contemporary thinker about things managerial, he challenges and influences managers. He does so because he sees, understands, and is consistently insightful. People are drawn to his wisdom and profoundly affected by it.

Managers of information agencies will do well to observe his teachings, which focus upon

- Figuring out what it is the organization is supposed to be doing
- Understanding how what one does furthers this cause; knowing what one is doing
- Knowing why one does whatever it is one does
- Knowing what to expect
- Clarifying instructions and expectations
- Recognizing that business is substantially a human and intellectual process

Managers of information places are squeezed by shrinking revenues, challenged by competing technologies for the time of clients, often incapable of inventing novel approaches, sometimes inimical of and resistant to change, frequently suspicious of entrepreneurship, and often unsure of their future. They may fail to explain to potential clients what it is they can do for them, opting instead for pious promises they cannot keep, like "promoting lifelong learning." They would do well to consider Drucker's message.

Drucker may be best known as the father of management by objectives, a method for establishing targets and taking specific steps to reach them. It is a process that requires management to

- Establish objectives
- Analyze tasks
- Establish performance standards
- Make long-range decisions and plans
- Build teams
- Communicate
- See the business as a whole, as a system; integrate management
- Understand how the business (especially the information business) fits in with other enterprises

- Monitor achievement

(Heller 1985, 174; Cranier 2000, 121)

There is an unmistakable linear expectation to MBO that invites scrutiny. Does it rest upon an expectation that times are rather stable and the environment is placid? Can we "know" the future? Does a five-year strategic plan make sense in uncertain times? To critics of a process they term unrealistic in the face of rapid change, we offer these questions: Is *not* having a plan an invitation to fail? Is *not* establishing objectives or targeting outcomes a very smart idea? Can plans *not* be flexible? May we *not* preestablish a maneuver to employ should we encounter blockage? Isn't that why God invented Plan B? If you do not like MBO, can you come up with something better?

Drucker-inspired principles for consideration as additions to our arsenal include

- Let people know what is expected of them and hold them to that standard
- Management is a job for educators and developers of people

Deming

Well, someone has come up with something he thought was better than MBO. Enter W. Edwards Deming, a physicist and statistician who believed that quality control was the best way to ensure production economies. He was a great advocate of good organizational communication. He believed his fourteen management points, which evolved into total quality management, provided the best hope for organizations who wanted to flourish in times of great change and competition. His followers who traveled the USA and gave TQM workshops to multitudes of eager managers claimed that TQM trumped MBO.

Basic to Demings's teachings and fourteen points are a number of tenets and exhortations:

- Embrace and accommodate change.
- Do not expect overnight results.
- Do not think that by inspecting you are improving quality, or as trainer Arch Lustberg has repeated, "You don't fatten a hog by weighing it."
- Do it right the first time.
- Plan for the future.
- Consider the next customer; make what is required of/available to the next customer easy to deal with and use-

ful. The next customer may be the purchaser of a product
or the next department to receive what you issue or send.
- Invest in worker education.
- Involve the whole organization in these efforts
               (Hartman n.d., 11-12; Cranier 2000, 161, 167-69).

Deming may have eschewed aiming at production targets, or objectives, but it is fair to say that he substituted the relentless pursuit of
quality for the preoccupation with objectives. He may not have counted
things, but he certainly noticed and counted steps in the process of creating things of quality. His emphasis on purpose and planning dovetails
with MBO; his emphasis on in-service training, eliminating targets and
numerical goals, promoting worker pride, and providing educational
opportunities adds to the MBO orthodoxy.

Speaking of orthodoxies, they emerge and will continue to emerge
from the whispers of their predecessors. TQM extracted what is
"good" from MBO. Quality circles, task forces, empowerment teams,
and learning organizations are cloned from the ribs of their ancestors.
Gurus will insist that their potions are superior to, not just different
from, the "older" and dated acronymed approaches. Experts will write
more books like *Zen and Creative Management* (Low 1976), *Murphy's
Law, the 26th Anniversary Edition* (Bloch 2003), *The One-Minute
Manager* (Blanchard 1982), *The Seven Habits of Highly Effective People* (Covey 1990), and *Fourth Generation Management* (Joiner 1994).
They will announce principles like Lawrence Peter's: *In a bureaucracy
people tend to rise to a position of incompetence where they languish*
(Heller 1985, 206-07). They will continue to invent things like the
Joiner triangle, a new management philosophy that defines customer
quality and provides the groundwork for future corporate culture"
(*Fourth* n.d., 2).

Deliverers of hopeful messages will continue to find receptive
audiences hungry for methods that work. Consultants and academics
will continue to translate into the idioms of current practice the meth-
odologies they discover in foreign lands. Critics will continue to assail
the new teachings. For example, they once claimed that Japanese management style, an orthodoxy credited with helping to revive an industry
that was reduced to ashes to a position that rivaled the United States of
America's, was more derivative of industrial age mill towns (paternal-
istic, holistic, involved in the workers' minds and pocketbooks) than it
was "new." It was only applicable in a tight island culture, they in-
sisted, while flourishing corporations were *using* it in the Americas and

elsewhere. And so it goes. Meanwhile, here are some Deming- and TQM-inspired additions to our assortment of managerial principles:

- Tweak the bureaucratic model so it can respond to the demands of a changing environment. The bureaucracy can accommodate task forces, quality circles, and empowerment groups.
- Plan.
- Train the workforce.
- Go ahead and count things, but be sure what you count gives an accurate depiction of your dedication to quality.

What Is Next?

If modern management principles like MBO and TQM were third generation stuff, one could have forecast with certainty a fourth generation. It has surfaced (Joiner 1994) as an extension of TQM. Fourth generation tools put theory to work, are ferociously customer and quality focused, and offer up training opportunities for employees.

On to the Fish Market

Critics will have a field day with the book, *Fish!* The fish market thing is unlikely to achieve the status of MBO, TQM, or any of the famous managerial regimens, but it presents the interested manager with a very intriguing assortment of ideas about the workplace. The major contribution it makes to managerial thought is its attention to the topic of attitude on the job.

There is a fish market in downtown Seattle. Customers descend upon it in droves. Citizens who work in and near town purchase and bring their lunches (yuppies, their yogurt) just to watch and be entertained by what goes on there. The employees are involved. They arrange displays, they banter with customers and crowd, they throw and catch fish, and sometimes they throw fish *to* the customers. Most often the customers drop the flying tuna or other airborne seafood; perhaps they are distracted by the shouted commentary that announces the flight ("Lobsters at twelve o'clock!"). Occasionally they make an error-free reception and the crowd goes wild. The employees enjoy themselves so thoroughly and so demonstrably that the customers and audience share in their delight—and they return.

The fish market people are convinced by strong associative relationships between their methods before and after adopting the show business model, and increased sales and profits, that their collective decision to enjoy their work and involve their clients is the reason for their remarkable success. Even those of us who do not hurl halibut for a living can learn from them.

Here are the principles that guide the fish market staff:

- I can choose my attitude; I may not always get to choose my work, but I can always choose how I approach it.
- Play; enjoy what can be very tedious; join with fellow players to form a winning team.
- Make their day; respectfully include clients; welcome them to join in; let them know we are not just in this for ourselves; we are here for them.
- Be present; make the discovery that this can work.

In the book, *Fish! A Remarkable Way to Boost Morale and Improve Results* (Lundin, Paul, and Christensen 2000), Mary Jane, a manager concerned about motivating a department within a financial institution, a department occupied by "zombies" that has earned the nickname *toxic energy dump*, happens by the market and observes the remarkable exhibition of joy on the job. Fish market employee Lonnie relates the market story over a period of several visits with Mary Jane. In the process of explaining things, Lonnie makes it clear to the reader that this is not about throwing fish. It is about attitude. It is about choice. It asserts that we can choose how we approach our jobs. It argues that happiness at work is possible and infectious, and that it leads to better feelings and better production and better rewards.

This homily, this parable, is replete with pithy sayings and insightful revelations such as, "I have created a prison and the walls are my own lack of faith in myself" (Lundin, Paul, and Christensen 2002, 38) but readers should not be deceived by the simple clarity with which a very useful message is delivered. Nor should serials catalogers, systems managers, knowledge architects, or information service providers dismiss what *Fish!* teaches simply because they do not sell or catapult fish for a living. The essential message of *Fish!* is that attitude matters, one can choose an attitude to adopt, a good attitude is more fun to have than a bad one, and a good attitude helps produce good results.

After having viewed *Fish!* "the film that started it all" (Fish! 1998), or having read the book, an information agency staff or department might productively ask itself some questions. We invite you to take your turn with these:

- How would I describe my attitude on the job?
- How could I improve my attitude?
- How does my personal happiness about my job affect the quality of my work?
- How comfortable am I with play on the job? Does my scolding parent stifle my natural child?
- What if I thought work were fun?
- Does my being creative matter? Would I be more creative if work were fun for me?
- I may not always get to choose my work, or my work partners, but can I choose what attitudes I bring to my work environment?
- Do we please our clients; do they seem happy to be dealing with us?

Applying Our New Wisdom

Every time we attend a stress management workshop, a conflict management workshop, an assertiveness workshop, a humor workshop, or a time management workshop, we often wonder things like

- Will reciting my new mantra or breathing deeply really work to relieve the stress I feel every time I select the wrong line at the bank, and more importantly, will I attract a curious crowd?
- Will an antagonist, the person with whom I am in conflict, invest as much in compromise as the workbook suggests?
- Will my boss understand when I stand up to her?
- Will Clotilda appreciate the new, more jocular me?
- If I make a list, check it twice, and strike the things I have accomplished, will the staff think I am too anal?

In order for a play to succeed, the prop people have to do their thing, the cast has to know their lines and perform them well, and somebody has to provide an audience. When we have offered conflict management sessions for health care practitioners like nurses, social workers, and infection control practitioners, we have always noted a most alarming fact about that drama: The persons with whom these people are in daily conflict—clients, supervisors, and medical doctors—are never in attendance. The absentees may not perceive the seriousness of the conflicts, or they may consider themselves too busy to attend. But they are not present and they do not participate with their colleagues in the acquisition of conflict management techniques. They are not in the same movie as their colleagues. They may not understand, and they may even resent it when workshop participants all of a sudden try out their newly learned skills on them.

When we attended week-long sessions in interpersonal communication and human relations at the National Training Labs in Bethel, Maine, a facilitator presented us with some very sage advice: *Don't hug the bus driver.*

The bus driver was not at our seminars and training groups. He did not participate in our intense experiments in self-disclosure, authentic communication, and other touchy-feely topics. He will not understand, not having been with us for all the exploration of our human potential, if we board the buss and haul off and hug him just the way we did with our T-Group buddies.

Similarly, managers must understand that a group with no track record of working cooperatively or joyously, or even just in the same space, is unlikely to respond positively to changes in behavior they observe in recent workshop graduates. They had no part in observing their colleague's metamorphosis. They may not appreciate "the new Fred" or welcome any activities that get dumped on them without warning or preparation. Resistance to change is a mighty inclination. Preference for the status quo is prevalent, and some people will oppose innovation on principle, the principle being that change is threatening.

Therefore we advise managers to pay special attention to how they introduce needed change to their staffs. Solid communication is a key. Giving people ample opportunity to comment and question is essential, as is winning the support of upper level administration. Bring people along slowly, if that is what it takes. This is not an argument for the preservation of what is. It is a caution that managers must deftly employ good people skills or run the risk that their excellent new ideas will be rejected, not because they are bad, but because they are new and poorly championed.

Most people need a rock to hang onto when the waves of change come crashing in. One such rock is a system of values. Before introducing change, wise managers reaffirm organizational values with their employees; they engineer a process in which everyone participates in the reaffirmation. Managers reassure staffs that the plan is to retain values held dear, and that a contemplated change is designed to enhance core values, not erase them.

Your Turn: Review the "principles" listed in this chapter. Are there any you think are useful? Do you disagree with any? What is your opinion about examining the thoughts of managers from years, even centuries, ago?

References

Bagby, Lauri M. Johnson, and James L. Franke. 2001. Escape from politics: Philosophic foundations of public administration. *Management Decision* 39 (Issue 8): 623-33.

Blanchard, Kenneth H. 1982. *The one-minute manager*. New York: William Morrow and Company.

Bloch, Arthur. 2003. *Murphy's Law, the 26th anniversary edition*. New York: Putnam-Penguin Group.

Covey, Stephen R. 1990. *The seven habits of highly effective people: Restoring the character ethic*. New York: Simon & Schuster.

Cranier, Stuart. 2000. *The management century: A critical review of 20th Century thought and practice*. San Francisco: Jossey-Bass Publishers.

Daley, Dennis M. 1998. The decline and fall of the Roman Empire: Lessons in management. *International Journal of Public Administration* 21 (1): 127-43.

Drucker, Peter. 1974. *Management: Tasks, responsibilities, practices*. New York: Harper & Row.

Fish! Catch the energy, release the potential! 1998. Burnsville, MN: ChartHouse International Learning Corporation.

Fourth generation management. Reviews. http://hallinvesing.com/management_leadership/1460.shtml (accessed 4 January 2003).

Harris, Michael. 1973. The purpose of the American public library: A revisionist interpretation of history. *Library Journal* 98 (September 15): 2509-14.

Hartman, Stephen. Questions on organizational behavior.http://iris.nylt.edu/-shartman/mbat0299/120_0299.htm (accessed 10 August 2002).

Heller, Robert. 1985. *The pocket manager: An alphabetical reference guide to management*. New York: Dutton.

History of Guilds. Available at http://renaissancefaire.com?Renfaires/Entertainment/History-of-Guilds . . . (accessed 9 September 2002).

Hood, Christopher, and Michael Jackson. 1991. *Administrative argument*. Brookfield, VT: Dartmouth Publishing Company.

Joiner, Brian L. 1994. *Fourth generation management: The new business consciousness*. New York: McGraw-Hill.

Low, Robert. 1976. *Zen and creative management*. Garden City, NY: Doubleday.

Lundin, Stephen C., Harry Paul, and John Christensen. 2000. *Fish! A remarkable way to boost morale and improve results*. New York: Hyperion.

McGregor, Douglas. 1960. *The human side of enterprise*. New York: McGraw-Hill.

Ouchi, William. 1981. *Theory Z: How American business can meet the Japanese challenge*. Reading, MA: Addison-Wesley.

Simon, Herbert A. 1946. The proverbs of administration. *Public Administration Review* 6 (Winter): 53-67.

———. 1960. *The new science of management decision*. New York: Harper.

———. 1976. *Administrative behavior: A study of decision-making processes in administrative organization*. 3rd ed. New York: Free Press.

Stueart, Robert D., and Barbara B. Moran. 1993. *Library and information center management*. 4th ed. Englewood, CO: Libraries Unlimited.

Witzel, Morgen. 2002. The history of ideas: The economic principles of Confucius and his school. http://thoemmes.com/economics/confucious_intro.htm (accessed 9 September 2002).

Chapter 5

Human Resources

Innumerable people have credited the little butterfly wings of helpfulness and kindness by librarians and staff the world over with making a difference in their lives. There is no doubt that the greatest resource of any library is its staff. No matter how great the quality or quantity of books, journals, and electronic databases, they mean little without the expert management of library staff. A top quality staff can work wonders, even with a limited collection. But a poorly trained or managed staff will be ineffective no matter the size of the collection. To reach its potential and achieve its mission, the staff of a library must be carefully selected, properly trained, appropriately supported, and well led.

Relationship with Staff

Most managers inherit a staff hired by their predecessors. Fortunately, there are very few library managers who feel it is appropriate or necessary to fire all professional staff in order to name librarians of their own choosing to the various positions in the library. It may well be that one of the defining characteristics of a good manager is the ability to work with staffs not of her choosing. It is important not only to be able to work with that staff, but to help it to excel. One of the most important tasks of a manager is to create a work environment that actively promotes the success of every employee. This is not an easy task and it requires continuous effort on the part of the manager. An excellent start in creating this environment is to have in place or to develop a mission statement, goals, and a strategic plan. Managers should see to it that all employees become familiar with these documents and find them relevant to their particular work situations. Without these documents, it would be difficult for anyone to know what the desirable work environment would look like.

Following up on these documents with sets of standards or expectations for employee performance is a necessary and challenging next step. This is not done in isolation, but through consultation and negotiation with the employees. The expectations should be meaningful and achievable. However, the employees should also feel that they are stretching to reach the expectations. Most people appreciate meaningful work and expectations that match their abilities. One rarely hears petty complaints from staff that find their work fulfilling. Setting clear expectations which are challenging and that satisfy the employees' desire to find meaning in their work is often the difference between high morale and excellent performance and poor performance with low morale.

Another managerial attribute necessary in developing a high quality work environment is attentive and empathetic listening. When an employee discovers a problem and takes it to the manager/supervisor, she does not necessarily need to have the problem solved by someone else. She can probably resolve or solve it herself. What she often needs is someone who will listen and at most offer other perspectives or options to consider. If the manager attempts to solve all problems rather than letting the staff solve the ones most appropriate for them to solve, then a situation of unhealthy dependency develops. The ability to know when to solve a problem and when to listen empathetically and perhaps point the employee in the direction of solving it herself is not an easy skill to master. It probably only comes for most of us as a result of many years of learning and experience as a manager.

The complexities of staff relationships and the manager's role may be well described in the following quote. "Nor is it Homer Nods, but We that Dream. . . ." (Pope, *An Essay on Criticism 1961*, 180). One explication of this statement is that although what Homer wrote has remained the same, our interpretations of his writings have changed over the centuries. It depends on where one is standing as to what interpretation one may give to an event. Managers often work from a different perspective from that of staff. Coming around to view things from other perspectives may be one means of ensuring that manager/staff relationships remain viable.

Effective managers usually have a very visible role in supporting and encouraging their staffs. It will always take a lot of time and energy on the part of the manager, perhaps time she would prefer to spend working on spreadsheets. But the priority should always be with staff issues. The results from a staff that feels supported by their manager will always justify the effort and time. Although it may take a number of meetings between the employee and the manager, and may involve some mentoring, the results can be rather amazing. Low performing employees can be motivated to much higher levels of performance with the proper encouragement and support.

Continuing Education and Training

Although the lines between continuing education and training can at times blur, the two are usually distinct activities with differing goals. Continuing education is usually long-term focused and is less specific in nature. Training often refers to a specific skill that is to be learned in relation to the requirements of the job.

Many small public and academic libraries provide quite limited budget support for either training or continuing education. Support for attendance at professional conferences, a good venue for continuing education, is often meager as well. While there appears to be increased expectations that librarians keep up to date with their skills and knowledge, the support for doing so is often not adequate. Based on a survey reported in a recent publication in the CLIP Note series, the authors concluded that "library funds to support increased travel seem to have, at the very least, remained static" (Gaskell, 2001, 3).

For a small investment in staff, managers have an opportunity to greatly improve the information place return on investment through continuing education. It seems only logical that managers should do all they can to ensure that all staff have sufficient financial support for continuing education and training. They also need to ensure that every staff member is encouraged to take advantage of these opportunities. This is done partly through including these activities in evaluations, but also through setting an example on the part of the manager. If the manager does not stay up to date and participate in professional associations, there is little incentive for staff to do so.

Mentoring

Mentor was the name of the Ithacan noble whose disguise the goddess Athene assumed in order to act as the guide and adviser of the young Telemachus. The *Oxford English Dictionary* also states that from this first usage, the meaning has come to signify "an experienced and trusted counselor" (2nd edition, s.v. "mentor."). Mentoring is a highly regarded practice in all types of businesses and organizations as one of the best ways to help new managers or to prepare an employee for management.

In its statement entitled "Ethical Guidelines for Library Managers," the Library Administration and Management Association (LAMA) exhorts managers to "take responsibility for developing professional excellence and for mentoring others" (1994, 183). Thus, mentoring is specifically noted as not only an essential element of a manager's job, but an ethical responsibility as well. Managers who do not have an ability to mentor others are probably managers we would not want to work for—at least not for very long.

Many businesses and organizations have developed formal programs for mentoring. Within the information environment, professional associations such as the College Libraries Section of the Association of College and Research Libraries (ACRL) have developed mentoring programs which pair newly appointed college library directors with more experienced directors (Hardesty, 1994, 7). There are also many libraries that have formal mentoring programs, but there is the likelihood that there are many more informal mentoring efforts occurring than formal. While many formal programs pair the protégé with someone who is not his supervisor, informal mentoring is more likely to occur between a manager and her employees. Whether formal or informal, mentoring is most effective when linked to the mission and goals of the library.

Mentoring has a long history within the world of information place management. Perhaps one of the best-known mentoring environments was that at Emory University, when Guy Lyle was director. Many a young library school graduate benefited from the experience of beginning a career at Emory under Lyle (Lyle, Farber, and Walling, 1974, vii). Of course, Lyle also authored the classic text on college library administration that continues to bear his name. It is interesting to note that mentoring is not mentioned in this text.

Critical knowledge and insights about the library in which one works as well as of the profession at large is passed on through mentoring relationships. Much of this information is simply not available through books or journal literature. This type of knowledge is best passed on through such activities as advice, feedback, focus, reflection, and support. The sharing of experiences and perspectives by mentors is one of the most effective methods of transferring knowledge from one generation to the next.

In a career field predominantly female, mentoring appears to have particular value. Whether male or female, rarely does one simply take on a management role. One must prepare for the responsibilities it entails. For males, society provides many cultural supports for growth into this role. For females and minorities, these supports are less abundant. Thus the profession must assume some responsibility for developing these supports. Mentoring is one of the most effective means of creating this type of support network. Recent efforts, particularly by ARL and other large libraries, to recruit women into management positions have resulted in a greater number of directorships currently being held by women. Mentoring advances this process.

What Mentors Do

The range of activities included under the rubric of mentoring is practically limitless. At times, the mentoring relationship may be more in the realm of coaching or even counseling. Coaching and counseling are more specifically goal directed than mentoring and often are more short term. But if the primary focus remains on the aspects of mentoring that transcend coaching and counseling, the relationship will not suffer.

Listening

One of the most important activities of mentoring is that of listening, particularly a type of listening that is both attentive and accepting. The protégé should feel safe at all times to ask questions and express feelings. Attentive listening by the mentor will help keep the process from deteriorating into simply a telling of war stories. While the sharing of experiences is an important part of mentoring, there is a danger that it will become focused strictly on the mentor doing all of the talking. Thus mentors must be aware of their listening skills and provide a context in which the protégé can talk and share concerns.

Advising

Mentoring consists of conversations in which the manager shares not only decisions, but also a careful analysis of the thought processes involved in reaching the decisions. A discussion of the events leading up to the decision often forces the manager to reflect more deeply on the decision. The protégé obviously gains from this deeper reflection.

Assigning

Mentoring may include the assigning of special projects to the person being mentored. The mentor should ensure that the individual is prepared to take on the project and should feel reasonably certain that she can successfully complete the project. These special projects should never be busy work, but should provide the person with an opportunity to learn more about the many facets of management.

Shadowing

Mentoring may mean asking the protégé to sit in on particular meetings so as to gain insight into other aspects of the manager's job. Understanding the dynamics of group interactions is an important skill for managers and debriefing the protégé is a helpful way for her to practice and gain skills in this area.

The range of learning experiences that may be tapped into for the growth of the protégé is practically limitless. Being a mentor requires creativity and awareness of opportunities on the part of the manager. The richness of the experience is greatly enhanced by these two qualities.

Evaluation

Formal evaluation of employees is for many managers a major time-consuming annual event. Yet evaluation is one of the most effective means of communicating with employees. Evaluation takes many forms, but to a large degree is determined by the parent organization. Typically evaluation takes place annually and follows a set pattern. Frequently the format will vary between that done with professional librarians and paraprofessional staff. Because the expectations differ, the way in which performance is evaluated also differs. For paraprofessional staff, a standard rating system is often used. This rating system most likely will be one used by the parent organization for all agencies within the organization. For librarians, other professionals, and managers, there may not be a standard form. It may well be that librarians will submit a dossier or a portfolio of their accomplishments during the rating period. Whatever instrument is used should be consistent for all librarians, while allowing for individual differences in developing a career path through job performance.

Fortunate is the supervisor who has good employees and for whom the evaluation process can be a tool of positive reinforcement. In cases such as this, the evaluation may even take place in an informal setting. There are many instances of the supervisor and employee taking a walk in the park or around the campus as they discuss the employee's performance. However, when there are critical issues to be discussed or serious performance shortcomings, the evaluation discussion is more appropriately conducted in a formal setting.

Some supervisors spend inordinate amounts of time preparing the evaluation form. While it is necessary to spend enough time to produce a thoughtful and precise evaluation, it is not necessary to turn it into a masterpiece. Often for long-term employees who consistently perform well year after year, there is little new that the supervisor can say in the evaluation. This does not mean that the manager should not point out noteworthy accomplishments. But if the employee consistently provides excellent customer service and that is one of the areas being evaluated, there is little more that needs to be said. Thus it may be that taking the employee out to lunch and formally thanking him for his contributions to the overall mission of the information place is the most appropriate action for the manager.

Managers may also use the formal evaluation as a time to provide support and encouragement for particular career growth, particularly for the professional librarians. Managers may be able to point out areas in which librarians can develop strengths that will enhance their careers. Often this may be simply to encourage the librarian to undertake a new responsibility or task related to their primary job responsibilities—to take the ball and run with it. In fact, it is not unusual for librarians to tentatively propose an idea to see if the manager will support them in pursuing it. At other times, the encouragement needs to be in areas such as research, publications, and other professional contributions. For most academic and many public librarians, these activities enhance their careers.

Your Turn: It is time to do the yearly evaluation for the untenured manager of the circulation department of your college library. This unit consistently draws praise from clients who appreciate the services of an obviously well-run department. However, the manager is not active professionally and does not appear inclined to become so. How will you prepare for and conduct this performance review?

Salary Administration

Salary administration is one of the most important responsibilities of a library manager. Library employment does not often place one in the ranks of the highly paid. Limited financial resources for salaries means that the manager must try to manage these funds in the most fair and equitable manner possible. Wise salary administration speaks tangibly of a manager's commitment to her employees.

Beyond wise management of salaries, it is imperative that the manager be an effective spokesperson to the parent organization on the value of the library staff and work closely with that organization to ensure that library salary issues are addressed. Thus the manager must both administer the current funds available and be an advocate for increased funding as the situation warrants. Much of the data used for administration of funds is also helpful in advocating for additional salary funding.

Salary administration often involves working with a fixed and rather complex set of data, only some of which will be quantifiable. While organizations can set up a variety of schema for equitable salary scales, factors come into play that only human judgment can decipher. For example, a scale based on seniority may appear on paper to offer the most straightforward means of achieving fairness. But it will not help in hiring or retaining a technologically proficient librarian. The marketplace factors into this equation and adjustments must be made if one is to compete for the best automation librarian. But is it fair to pay a reference librarian $5,000 less annual salary than an automation librarian, assuming both have the MLS? What about the senior librarian who has consistently performed well, but has chosen to continue to do the job she does best. By doing so, she has turned down opportunities to be a middle or upper level manager. Should she be in the same salary range as a much less experienced librarian who has moved into middle management? Are there inequities between male and female employees? What do historical trends reveal?

One of the most serious problems a library manager may face is salary compression. New hires are usually able to negotiate their starting salary and continually push the starting salary scale higher. Long-term employees without this negotiation advantage are left to fend for themselves on annual seniority or cost of living increases. Only occasionally are they in a position to negotiate salary increases based upon other factors. Annual increases often do not keep pace with starting salary increases. Thus starting salaries usually rise faster than those of long-term employees.

Another factor that must constantly be assessed is the competitiveness of salaries in relation to other information places locally, regionally, or nationally. How does one obtain this type of information and how can it be analyzed appropriately for the manager's local situation? Additionally, how competitive are salaries in relation to comparable positions in other industries?

The manager should develop qualitative and quantitative data for studying salaries. Many salary scales are fixed by governmental or other authorities and appear to be out of the manager's hands. Even with fixed scales, the manager may have some options. She may discover that some library employees are classed at a lower level than they should be. She may discover that the scale unintentionally, or perhaps intentionally discriminates against a particular class of employees.

Qualitative data such as comparative job descriptions or job market analysis often are quite useful in spotting inequities in salary administration. Quantitative data that compare actual salaries of comparable jobs also are helpful in documenting problems. Usually, quantitative data are most effective when presented in charts and graphs. The manager will find a number of quantitative ways to view information. A good starting point is to create a chart that graphically lays out the actual salaries being paid to her employees. In reality, there may be several charts beginning with one comprehensive chart that includes all staff. Other charts may focus on salaried and hourly employees, male and female, special experience or education, job market factors, and seniority in relation to pay. As these charts are developed, the manager should be able to spot numerous features not before apparent. So an analysis begins with the gathering of basic information and preparing it so as to be able to view it from a variety of perspectives.

Gathering data from the local, regional, and national marketplaces provides critical documentation. ALA publishes salary data annually that can be purchased. *Library Journal* publishes an article each year on placement of library school graduates and the starting salaries. Some peer libraries conduct annual salary surveys. Often libraries within a local region share data upon request from a manager, or in some instances share survey results if they have done a salary survey recently.

Upon obtaining data from these sources, the manager will usually receive much good assistance and advice from the parent organization's human resources department. Often there is an individual within this department who has expertise on compensation and thus can help the manager review and analyze the data. The expert can also be very helpful in pointing out the types of data that need to be reviewed and/or gathered. He can also suggest ways of formatting and presenting data. Ultimately, though, it will be up to the manager to make some decisions regarding the data, how it is documented, written up, and presented to the appropriate officers of the parent organization. While in many cases city managers, school boards, or the corporate parent may establish boundaries, there is much the manager can do within those boundaries to ensure a fair hearing for her staff.

Typically it is necessary to document the employee's performance as well as the market or internal conditions that warrant the salary increase. While each situation is unique and the manager will have to be sensitive to her local environment, there is no substitute for being well prepared when requesting additional salary funds. To the parent organization, salary is a long-term commitment. Although other operating budget lines may in fact be long term, there is not the level of commitment to them that exists for salaries.

Managers will never be wrong for being zealous advocates for fair salaries for their employees. They can gain respect from the parent organization as well as from their employees, and everyone benefits.

Your Turn: A female paraprofessional in your cataloging department has discovered that a male counterpart earns $500 a year more than she does. She has been employed in your library ten months longer than he has. He has a bachelor's degree while she has a high school diploma. They both perform similar jobs equally well. She is upset and has asked for a salary adjustment. What would you do?

Selecting Staff

In filling position vacancies, it is important for the library to establish procedures that ensure fairness, maintain communication, and project an image of the information place as a desirable location in which to work. Several important steps make this happen. It is essential that a good working relationship be established with the Human Resources department of the parent organization. It is also important to become thoroughly familiar with their procedures and deadlines and work within that framework.

There will always be some type of paperwork establishing a paper trail of the actions taken in the filling of a vacant position. If the position to be filled is a permanent funded position and the manager is simply replacing the incumbent, this paperwork is likely to be routine and easily handled by the manager's administrative assistant. If the position is a newly approved position, additional documentation will usually be required.

This is an excellent time for a review of the job description. Usually the parent organization will require that a job description be submitted along with a request to fill the position. Often the parent organization will have a boilerplate format for the job description, but it is up to the library to fill in the details. Regardless of the local procedure, the manager and supervisor should review and update a job description at any time there is a vacancy. In all likelihood, the parent organization has a preferred format for the elements to be included in a job description. There is usually enough flexibility in the parent organization's job description format to permit the inclusion of library specific elements. The manager will usually find it beneficial to seek assistance in American Library Association publications as well as other professional publications that offer excellent library-specific boilerplates and suggestions for the writing of a job description.

Written Criteria

There are many libraries that hire staff without a clear idea of what criteria they are following in their selection. While the position description frequently lists desirable characteristics (e.g., attention to detail, interpersonal skills, collegiality, and intellectual curiosity) these are usually general in nature. It is helpful for the individuals involved in the hiring decision to meet and discuss criteria in greater detail. This fleshing out helps ensure that everyone is working from similar assumptions.

The criteria should consist of a list of what characteristics are important for a potential employee to possess. While there are some characteristics that are common for all positions in the library, others are specific to the given position. Some of these criteria can be identified through a review of the job requirements. Additional characteristics may be identified through a review of the mission statement. If the mission statement identifies teaching as an important part of the mission, obviously that should be considered an important characteristic, whether the position is directly involved in teaching or supports teaching in some way.

Supervisors and coworkers also can offer much good guidance on the characteristics desired for a particular job. Obviously any list will have limitations, but by going through the process of developing a list, all individuals who may have input into the hiring decision will have an opportunity to gain a sense of the type of candidate most likely to succeed in that particular environment.

Unwritten Criteria

There are also unwritten criteria for candidate selection. Even with writing out a list of selection criteria, there are usually some unwritten criteria that are just understood. It is not unusual for the interviewer(s) to be unaware that they are operating from a set of unwritten criteria. One way to get at these unwritten criteria is to set up a briefing session for all individuals involved in the interview prior to selecting which candidates to interview. It is also advisable to set up a debriefing session after the interviews have taken place.

Some of the unwritten criteria may include such things as the need for an individual to actively contribute to the intellectual health of the organization, the ability to be a team player and the perceived fit between the organization and the applicant. More evident, although often still unwritten, is the public service attitude of the individual and the chemistry between the applicant and the interviewers. The more that one can identify all of the factors important in the selection process, the more likely one is to be successful in identifying and hiring the best candidate for the position. However, there are times when something else must be added to the mix. One supervisor with whom we are acquainted, after trying logical and analytical approaches to hiring, finally decided that she would make all future selection decisions on "gut instinct." This approach may be used very effectively as a complement to the other strategies identified earlier.

Advertising the Vacancy

Upon approval of the request to fill a position, the next step is advertising the vacancy. Sometimes the human resources department of the parent organization will handle the advertising, although many libraries handle the advertising on their own. If human resources handle the ad, they will usually review the ad with the library manager before placing. Advertisements must be written with care taken to ensure that all legal requirements are met. The manager also must ensure that the ad correctly emphasizes the essential elements of the position and its requirements.

The manager usually has a role in determining which advertising channels should be used. For a variety of good reasons, it is desirable to advertise professional positions as broadly as possible. This may include advertising in national professional journals, the local newspapers, a state library job line, and postings at schools of library and information science either within the region or across the country. Particularly in the current employment climate when there are so few applicants, it is even more necessary to advertise widely. Other reasons to advertise widely include diversity goals and improving the quality of the applicant pool. For paraprofessional positions, placing the ad with the state library job line and local newspapers is usually sufficient. More recently, information agencies have been posting position vacancies on their Web pages. While this may not gain the wide distribution of other forms of advertising, it does often result in additional candidates applying for positions.

Who writes the job advertisement? Who makes the decisions about which publications should be contracted to carry the ad? Often these decisions are based on past practice, but leadership should certainly review these decisions regularly to ensure that they are achieving the desired results. Frequently, someone within human resources will write the ad based upon information gleaned from the job description. This can be a good check on the clarity of the job description, although it also reflects the ability of the person writing the ad. Depending on the local situation and the relationship with human resources, the library manager may write the ad. In some instances, the library manager may also serve as the primary contact with one or more of the library publications.

There continues to be debate over whether an ad should or should not state a closing date for receipt of applications. It seems to be a personal preference with good arguments for either position. In any case, the manager will need to follow the guidelines of the parent organization. If the guideline is such that a deadline is not permitted, the library manager may get approval to state something to the effect of, "To receive full consideration, application must be postmarked by. . . (a specified date)." Another option would be to state that the position is "open until filled. Review of applications will begin by . . . (a specified date)."

After a position has been advertised, either the library or the human resources department of the parent organization will receive resumes and applications. While the human resources department will usually send the applicants a form for identifying whether or not the applicant belongs to a protected status group, it is important for the library manager to send a brief letter to applicants thanking them for their applications and stating whether all information needed for review has been received. Particularly for the academic library, that may mean that it takes longer to complete the hiring process. Still, it is important for the library to promptly send a letter of acknowledgement to all applicants for a position. This creates an important positive impression with the applicants. Too often libraries only acknowledge an applicant with a brief letter stating that someone has been hired for the position. Actually, many times libraries never communicate anything to applicants. They go through the process and hire someone, but never inform the remaining applicants that anything has occurred. While perhaps unintentional, it is also quite rude. Communication between the library and applicants for a position with the library is one of the most critical and yet one of the most neglected aspects of the hiring process. The effort to communicate at critical points in the process pays excellent dividends in terms of the image of the library. Numerous applicants have received insufficient or even no communication from libraries to which they have applied. Thus, when they experience good communication, the positive impression created is very evident.

Review of Applications

At an agreed-upon date, the manager should begin a review of applications. The nature of this review will depend on several factors. One is the size of the applicant pool. In the not-far-removed past, a library could expect to receive forty or fifty applications for a single reference librarian position. Currently many libraries are happy to receive even half that number. With a larger applicant pool, it is more likely that the applications making the first round cut will exceed the number the manager wishes to interview. One way to do a second round cut is to set up brief telephone interviews with each of the candidates who made the first round. Typically questions and discussions in this setting should be very focused. The manager must be careful to not allow this to replace the full interview. But telephone interviews are quite effective in reducing the size of the applicant pool and certainly provide the interviewers with information not available in a written resume.

Many corporate and academic agencies now use the search committee to review applications, select candidates to be interviewed, interview candidates, and make a recommendation to the manager. While the director, particularly in smaller libraries, may be involved in the process, much of the responsibility rests with the search committee. In small agencies with only two or three professionals on staff, it is likely that all will be involved with the hiring process. This has had the effect of reinforcing the collegial environment and it allows the search committee members to be much more invested in the success of their decisions. It has the disadvantage of being much more time consuming. In some instances, an organization will lose out on its best applicants because of the time delays of this process. It also is desirable that paraprofessional, clerical, and other support staff have a role in the hiring of professional librarians. Particularly in smaller libraries, this may be a role within the search committee itself. In a situation where the librarian to be hired will be supervising members of the support staff, those staff should have an opportunity to interview and provide feedback to the search committee. In many public libraries, the process is usually much less involved and typically only the manager and the direct supervisor are involved in the process.

Screening and Narrowing the List

For professional positions, it is expected that at least some of the candidates will be from outside the local area. Many libraries or their parent organizations have budgets that pay the expenses of applicants who are coming from outside the local area to interview. Because of the expense incurred by the library, it is useful for the manager to obtain as much information as possible about the candidate before scheduling an interview. A telephone interview can be important in helping the manager make the decision on whom to invite for interviews. Another useful strategy is to use the placement service provided at conferences of the professional organizations such as the American Library Association, the Medical Library Association, Special Libraries Association, and the American Society for Information Science. There is a great economy achieved when managers can interview multiple applicants who appear at conference interview sessions.

There is no magic number for the number of applicants who should be invited to interview for a position. Often this depends on a number of factors. Budget to pay applicant expenses may play a role in the decision, although it is assumed that one would not advertise nationally unless the budget is adequate to pay for someone to come in from the other side of the country. The actual number of applicants who make the final cut may also be a factor. Sometimes only one applicant rises to the final round. At other times a half dozen applicants may rise to the final round. Most information places attempt to interview at least three applicants in person.

Sometimes there is difficulty in narrowing the number of applicants to a manageable number to be interviewed. For many libraries, interviewing three candidates is ideal and five candidates is a maximum. But if there is a strong applicant pool and a library can only narrow the list to seven or ten or twelve applicants, the telephone screen can be very effective. The search committee chair or the manager calls candidates to inform them that they have passed the first screen or cut and asks them to participate in a brief telephone screening interview. An appointment is then made for this interview. Typically, no more than fifteen to twenty minutes are needed for this interview. While it is customary to use the same set of questions with each candidate, occasionally there is something in an application that needs resolution before a decision can be made on furthering the candidacy of a particular applicant. Telephone screening interviews rarely fail to narrow the field significantly.

Scheduling Interviews

After the initial set of applicants has been selected for in-person interviews, managers usually contact them by telephone and a date and time for the interview is agreed upon. In public libraries, interviews typically last no more than a couple of hours. In academic libraries, interviews may be scheduled to last one to two days. This is because in many academic libraries, librarians are organized as faculty. Thus, the collegial model calls for extensive contact between all of the librarians and the candidate in an effort to ensure that there will be a good fit. In some instances, it is appropriate to extend the interview contact to teaching faculty and other college administrators as well.

Properly preparing for the actual interviews is a critical element in determining the success of the search. Upon selection of candidates for face-to-face interviews, the manager or the chair of the search committee calls candidates to schedule the interviews. For academic positions, the interview may be a day or a day and a half in length. For candidates traveling from outside the local area, the manager or committee chair should discuss with the candidate how their expenses related to the interview will be covered. In some instances, the candidate incurs the expenses, then submits a voucher to the library for reimbursement. In other cases, the library will make the transportation and housing arrangements and be billed directly for these expenses.

After the date and time have been agreed upon, the manager should immediately send the candidate a package of information about the library. Typically this would consist of such things as the most recent annual report of the library, an organization chart, a copy of the library's mission statement, general statistics about the library, information about the parent organization such as the college or university bulletin, and an itinerary for the interview. The itinerary is particularly important for the academic library interview. The manager might also include any recent newsletters or articles about the library, organizational chart, and any other information she feels may be useful to the applicant in preparing for the interview. There should also be a cover letter that states in writing the terms of the interview (e.g. how expenses are handled, date and time, etc.)

Every candidate interviewed for a professional position should
receive a copy of the library's mission statement in advance. It is also
advisable for individuals interviewing for staff positions to be made
aware of the library's mission statement and its importance to the
workplace. This accomplishes two important goals. First, the candidate
has the opportunity to decide if she or he is in agreement with and can
support the agency's mission. Sometimes when the agency is part of a
religious or political institution, the candidate may feel uncomfortable
with a particular mission. Or it may be that a key element of the mission is teaching and the candidate may not be comfortable with performing in that facet of the mission.

The second goal accomplished is that the agency can explore in
detail the candidate's commitment to its mission. Particularly for professional applicants who will have the greatest opportunities to interpret
and carry out that mission, the interview process should be designed to
help the interviewer(s) determine the ability of the applicant to contribute to that mission. This can be done in a number of ways. The direct
approach is sometimes necessary. One might ask the candidate if she or
he received a copy of the mission statement in his interview packet. If
so, the interviewer might ask for comments on it or, better yet, ask a
specific question related to it. For example, if classroom instruction
were a part of our mission, we might ask, "Would you comment on
your abilities and experiences in teaching?" A rather weak approach
would be to ask him what he thought of the mission statement!

Your Turn: You are on a search committee interviewing candidates
for a professional library position. You have been assigned to ask the
candidates questions about the mission statement. What are some questions you would ask? You may refer to chapter 1 for a sample mission
statement.

Conducting the Interview(s)

In many situations, the candidate may go through two or more interviews with different groups or individuals. While the primary interview may be with the search committee, there often are interviews of
varying depths with other individuals or groups, such as the agency
manager, an academic vice president, or library board members. In this

section we shall speak primarily of the interview with the search committee, although many points are relevant for any of the interviews.

Since the interview with the search committee is typically the most critical, many information agencies arrange for it to take place during the morning when the candidate is likely to be at peak performance. Other activities and interviews are then scheduled around this time.

A good manager will orchestrate arrangements and schedule the interview in a comfortable room away from distractions. Someone should introduce the candidate to the search committee. Someone on the search committee should make some introductory remarks and start the interview questions. That individual or others on the committee should prepare to keep the interview moving forward and on track. Awkward moments often occur during interviews. The search committee members should work to move out of awkward moments quickly.

It is advisable that the members of the search committee have in hand a set of questions that they will ask during the interview. A good manager will assemble and distribute a set of questions to cover important points. Frequently these questions are distributed among the committee so that each person asks at least one question. They are certainly not limited to just those questions. In fact, if the candidate and committee develop a good rapport, the dialogue may proceed in unexpected and fruitful directions.

Many personal questions are neither appropriate nor legally permissible. Since some of these questions may be open to interpretation, it is best to obtain a list from the parent agency human resources department or, even better, to invite one of their staff in to conduct training with library staff involved in interviewing.

There are a number of activities that can serve to help the agency and the candidate get to know one another better. Some activities to consider including are

- tour of the library,
- tour of campus or city hall or other appropriate civic buildings,
- interview with search committee,
- open time allowing the candidates to explore the library on their own,
- interview with information agency director,

- introduction or interview with mayor or city manager, academic vice president, library board member, or other appropriate individuals,
- lunch with selected professionals,
- presentation to all staff with question and answer period,
- perhaps concluding with dinner at a nice restaurant with the director and one or two of the librarians.

Interestingly, it is at the dinner where the most critical information is sometimes exchanged. Both the information place manager and the candidate have an opportunity to display their best social skills in conversation and etiquette. They typically demonstrate diplomacy. Either may be quite entertaining in this social setting. This may be a desirable trait of the candidate that was not revealed fully during the formal parts of the interview. Of course, candidates have been known to drink alcohol excessively during dinner and exhibit unacceptable behavior. Other times, a candidate may relax, but in doing so, may become indiscreet.

It is important to remember that this is a two-way street. The library must make a strong positive impression with the candidate as well. Developing a well-thought-out itinerary and following it are good first steps in this process. On the date for the interview, the candidate should at no point be left to wonder what is going on. Library staff that has particular responsibilities with the candidate should be well qualified to work positively with the candidate. After all, it is just as important for the library to make a good impression as it is for the candidate. A poor attitude on the part of the person conducting a tour of the facilities for the applicant or a poorly organized interview will have a negative impact on the candidate's response to a job offer from the library. Good communication and a well-organized interview are important perceptions which assist in getting acceptance of the offer of the job.

Contacting References

When should references be contacted? Advice varies on this point with some preferring to do so before investing in the costs of an interview. Other managers contact references after the interview. The director or the search committee should always contact references at some point before making an offer of employment. Reference calls are usually brief and focus upon two things. One is for the purpose of verifying that the individual is who he says he is and has done the things attested to on his application. The other covers specific attributes of the candidate that relate directly to the job for which he is being considered.

How should the manager handle references? Some managers believe that it is counterproductive to ask for letters of reference as a part of the application package. This is because reference letters at this stage are often canned and are not specific to the position advertised. References requested when the candidate is under serious consideration typically speak more directly to the candidate's abilities in relation to the particular position. It also is an added and frequently unnecessary expense for hiring managers in terms of time and effort, particularly when so many advertised positions receive numerous applications. Yet occasionally one still sees advertisements which ask that letters of reference be included in the application package. It often appears that these are the same advertisements that ask for five reference letters rather than the standard three!

It is more typical for a manager to include a statement in the advertisement asking that names and contact information of references be included with the application package. References are typically contacted by the hiring manager after a candidate has made the cut to the point of being invited for an in-person interview. The reference may be asked to provide a reference for the candidate either by phone or by letter. At that time, before investing in the costs of the interview, it is important that the manager verify that the individual is who she says she is and that she has attained the education and experience stated in the resume. Additional information, which the manager may wish to solicit, may be useful as well. Either phone or letter works well in helping the manager obtain additional information about the candidate as well as verifying the information on the application. When conducting a reference interview by phone, the manager should plan the conversation in advance, with questions written out. The manager should plan to take notes of the reference's responses. While the questions should be written out in advance, it is good to leave openings for the reference to provide additional information. While it is generally assumed that a candidate lists references that will have positive things to say, it is surprising how many applicants fail to notify someone that he or she is being used as a reference. This can lead to interesting exchanges!

Your Turn: You are seeking a person to fill a high-stress position with lots of interaction with clients and considerable supervisory responsibilities. Compose three questions you will ask an applicant's references.

Many human resource departments now advise supervisors to state that they are not permitted to serve as references for their employees and to refer the caller to the human resources department. This has occurred because of the number of lawsuits regarding references. Many human resource departments will only verify that the candidate worked for an organization and the dates of that employment. A manager should not view this as a negative comment about the candidate. Since this is a standard procedure within the organization, it says nothing about the applicant's performance during employment with that organization.

Making the Offer

After all candidates have been interviewed, the manager and the staff should make a decision on offering the position as soon as possible. Typically, with perhaps three candidates, a public library can conduct all interviews within three or four days. In an academic library the process may take up to two weeks. The decision may be easy as one candidate stands out from the rest. It may be difficult as there may be two or three candidates offering differing strengths to the organization. Or there may be no candidates who are satisfactory. If that is the situation, most organizations select more candidates for interviews from the already identified pool. If this becomes necessary, it sometimes creates an awkward situation with the candidates previously interviewed, since they would typically expect a decision within a short period of time.

Making the offer to a candidate is often one of the most pleasant tasks of a manager. Before making an offer, the manager should review the process with the human resources department. There are sometimes restrictions that this office places on the manner or the terms of an offer. For example, relocation assistance and certain other fringe benefits may be available for one class of employees but not another. If a manager includes a term not usually available to the class of employee under consideration, the library is usually obligated to provide that benefit. This is particularly troublesome whenever there is a significant cost associated. In other instances, managers have been known to miscalculate salary and make an offer higher than what had been budgeted. Because an employment agreement may constitute a legal contract, the library must find a way to cover the cost of the error.

The manager should follow up a verbal offer with written confirmation. Again the manager should be aware of the personnel office policies on the offer. In many organizations, the offer is in the form of a contract. In other instances, it is simply an offer of employment, but is not a contract. The candidate may give a verbal acceptance, or may ask for the written offer before accepting. Typically, many candidates will ask for time to consider the offer. Usually there is no reason not to give the candidate a reasonable time in which to consider an offer.

After a candidate has accepted a position with the library, the manager should notify all of the other applicants that the agency has filled the position. For those who also interviewed, the director may call to inform them of the decision. The manager should send a letter of notification to those candidates not interviewed, if they have not previously been notified that they are no longer being considered for the position.

A final important step in the hiring of a new employee is to conduct a new employee orientation. There are numerous items of information to share with the new employee. Instead of doing it from memory, which can result in gaps in the orientation, managers should create and employ an orientation checklist to be used with each new employee. This helps to ensure that new employees receive information necessary for their successful transition into the organization

How to Fire an Employee

Despite the best efforts of the manager, she sometimes finds it necessary, for the well-being of the organization, to fire an employee. Quite properly, this is one of the most difficult decisions the manager makes. It is not one to be taken lightly and often causes days and weeks of agonizing for her. However, when it becomes the most prudent course of action, she should take it without apology.

When considering termination of an employee, the manager should consult with someone within her human resources department as soon as possible. Personnel from this department can advise and assist the manager throughout the process. It is also very helpful to have a neutral and professional third party reviewing reasons and actions. Personnel in this department are trained to provide professional perspective on employee/employer relations.

The manager should carefully document the reasons for considering this course of action. Documentation should take place whether there is any indication of possible cause for termination or not. Normal performance reviews, usually annually, provide the foundation for documentation. However, the manager should follow up much more frequently if a serious problem is identified in the annual review. The documentation process may continue for months or even years before a decision is made regarding the employee. At a minimum, the documentation should include specific information regarding the employee's performance and the ways in which it does not measure up to the job description expectations. The documentation should include notes detailing meetings between the employee and the supervisor in which the employee's performance shortcomings were discussed. It also should include steps or suggestions made by the supervisor to the employee for how they might improve performance. Finally, it should include some idea of a timeline by which performance should meet the minimum expectation.

When the manager makes a decision to terminate an employee, she has a number of options to choose from in terms of specifically how the termination will be carried out. First is to decide the location for the conversation. It may take place in the manager's office, a conference room, in an office provided by human resources, or in some other room deemed appropriate. The primary consideration is that the location should be one that provides privacy. If the employee has had several conversations with the supervisor regarding his performance, he may be at least somewhat prepared emotionally for the termination. However, often even with specific warnings, employees are quite surprised to discover that they are being fired.

Second, the manager must decide whom to include in the termination discussion with the employee. There should be at least one additional individual besides the manager and the employee. This helps to reduce the tension somewhat between the manager and employee. It also assures that any recollections of what was or was not said during the conversation are reasonably accurate. Oftentimes a good choice for the person to be included is someone from the human resources department. Another choice is the immediate supervisor of the person being terminated.

Third, the manager needs to decide whether the employee is to be terminated or will be permitted to resign. Particularly for personnel in professional positions, the option of allowing a person to resign is frequently offered. This often depends on the situation. If the individual is simply not able to meet performance expectations, this is an acceptable option. However, if the individual has committed an egregious act (falsifying time sheets or other forms of dishonesty), termination is the most appropriate course of action..

Fourth, the manager must set the effective date of the termination. Will it be immediate or at some future date? Particularly in situations in which the professional librarian appointments are faculty appointments, American Association of University Professor guidelines should be followed. In many instances, these guidelines call for up to twelve months notice of termination. If an employee will remain in a position for some period of time after notice of termination, it is important that the termination conversation set up guidelines for employee behavior during that time. An angry employee being terminated can wreak havoc on the morale of a staff in a very short period of time.

Your Turn: Managers, when should you do all of the required documentation for termination of an employee? Do you do it at the time of termination? Discuss your answer.

Termination Meeting

After all decisions of this type, it is time to call the termination meeting. Opinions on the best time for a termination meeting vary. Assuming the termination is not the result of an action requiring immediate termination, we recommend that the termination meeting take place early in the week. The employee is more likely to avail himself of positive networks of support if it occurs early in the week. If the termination occurs on Friday, or even late Thursday, there is a stronger likelihood that the employee cannot find networks of support over the weekend. He faces two consecutive nonbusiness days of "idle time" during which he cannot job hunt. This could allow a lot of negative emotions to build within the employee and slow his recovery from the firing.

The meeting itself should be short and to the point. The manager should clearly state the purpose of the meeting. The manager should then outline the reasons for the termination. The manager should make it clear that the decision is final. This is not a negotiation meeting and there is no wiggle room. The employee may then be given an opportunity to ask questions or to make a statement. However, at this time the manager should avoid getting personal or responding to any hostility or inappropriate questions. Do not let the employee sidetrack the discussion or try to place blame. By keeping the focus on the primary reason for the meeting, the manager can reduce the likelihood of miscommunication. There is no avoiding the fact that meetings of this type are extremely unpleasant for both the manager and the employee. The manager must expect that the employee will react with more emotion than normal—whether that emotion be anger, remorse or tears, Mr. Cool, or whatever. Any or all of these responses by the employee are natural and should be allowed, but not played up to. At the point where questions regarding the termination appear to be over (usually in less than fifteen minutes) and the employee is trying to cope with the information, it is usually appropriate for the manager to leave. Depending on the nature of the role of the other person in the meeting, it is often appropriate for that person to remain with the employee for a somewhat longer period of time. Because the manager has up to this point taken the lead role in the termination, any employee anger or other negative feelings are directed toward the manager. The third person can be comforting to the employee, who may not perceive him or her to be a threat in the way that the manager is perceived.

Your Turn: You have a well-documented case of consistent poor performance. You schedule a termination interview at which the employee to be fired pleads financial hardship, begs for another chance, and promises to do better. Respond.

In the process of termination, the manager should respect the dignity and self-respect of the terminated employee as much as possible. One of the chief ways to allow dignity and self-respect to remain intact, albeit damaged, is to allow the employee the option to resign. Resignation should be considered as an option except in cases of grievous offense or when the employee indicates an unwillingness to exercise that option. No one can go through the process of being terminated without feelings of doubt and fear of the future. The manager can do her part to respect these elements by the way in which she handles the termination.

She and others can reassure the employee that in a different work environment, he is likely to achieve more success.

It is important at this time to communicate to the rest of the staff regarding this action. Rumors start very quickly in situations such as this. Thus communication is important for staff morale. If the employee has been terminated, the manager can word the communication in such a manner as to indicate such. If the employee is being allowed to resign, the manager may permit the resigning employee to communicate to the rest of the staff that he is resigning. However, the meeting should set the parameters of this in that the employee must submit a written resignation within a certain period of time and that he will communicate his decision to the staff after he has given the manager his written resignation.

Being Fired

One of the facts of the information place is that managers are sometimes fired. Despite their best efforts, managers are just as vulnerable to termination as any other employee. However, because a manager has been in a position of some power, her termination often has greater impact. The bigger they are, the harder they fall. The hazards of termination of a manager are oftentimes greater than that for line employees. Although termination is often the result of incompetence, it can also occur for other reasons. New college presidents, provosts, city managers, CEOs, division managers, or library board members who want to hire their own people in critical positions may terminate incumbents and replace them. Thus the manager is always taking the political temperature of the environment in which he works. He is always looking for the warning signs of trouble ahead. While he should not spend a lot of time worrying about this type of thing, he should certainly be assessing the situation and carefully reviewing information regarding his relationship in the environment.

If the circumstances of termination are not substantive, (e.g., performance related) the manager is on much more firm ground for negotiating the terms of departure. In many cases, even performance related departures might be negotiated to the manager's advantage. Few if any organizations want a messy termination on their hands. Thus most will consider a reasonable request that avoids the likelihood of a messy termination.

The information place manager should not count on his supervisor's being skilled in personnel matters. Do not expect the supervisor to be particularly skilled in documenting and handling terminations. They may well be skilled, but that is often not the case. Thus the manner in which the termination of a manager is handled may not follow the rules—or the procedures—suggested in this chapter!

Managers are sometimes fired, but they are often given the option to resign. Thus they are often faced with the decision of whether to stay and fight the termination or to resign as requested. If the proposed termination is nonperformance based or performance criteria weakly supported are the ruse for termination, the manager may well be able to remain on the job and prevail in the termination proceedings. While a risk, it is in some cases the correct course of action for the manager. There are two primary risks with this course of action. First is that the information place will likely suffer during the course of the proceedings. Morale can suffer, long-range planning may be postponed, and even funding can be negatively impacted. Second is the fact that should the manager lose, the ability to negotiate terms of departure may be seriously impaired. Most organizations are more willing to negotiate generous terms to avoid a messy fight, but are less willing to do so after a messy fight has already occurred.

Forced to resign under pressure, usually the manager may negotiate a number of benefits. One benefit would be favorable letters of recommendation. While the letters would not likely be enthusiastic, they would at least not say anything that would damage his professional reputation or harm his chance of a management job in another organization. Another benefit is severance pay. Depending on the circumstances, it is not unusual for this to amount to one month's salary for each year of service. Continuation of health care benefits for a specified time is usually a part of any termination package. Provision of outplacement services is becoming a more common practice. Often this amounts to paying the costs of placing the manager with an executive recruitment firm. Portability of retirement benefits may also need to be negotiated in this process. Personal counseling may also be a negotiable item, particularly if the manager feels she may have difficulty in coping personally with the termination.

Regardless of the fairness or the lack of fairness in the termination, the manager should handle himself professionally in public situations at all times. On the other hand, the manager should seek a support system. There is simply no way to avoid some loss of self-esteem in this type of process. Whether it is with trusted family or friends, it is healthy for the manager to turn to those in times such as this for support. Often the manager feels a sense of failure and self-esteem suffers greatly. Many managers are self-reliant individuals who willingly accept responsibility for their actions. Thus they accept responsibility for their termination. Managers typically exhibit an internal rather than an external locus of control. Thus they believe that they, and not fate or luck, control their destiny. Therefore, a termination is something they feel they could have avoided had they acted differently and controlled the situation in some manner. Frequently this results in the manager's taking on too large a share of guilt and blame. To be able to discuss the situation with a trusted friend is the start of a difficult healing process.

The good news out of all of this is that many managers do move on to better positions and become even better managers. In some circles, there is a belief that being fired is an important lesson many managers need to learn. Whether true or not, a manager who has been fired for whatever reason often becomes much more sensitive to the devastating effects of firing and is much more judicious in the use of this power.

References

Gaskell, Carolyn, and Allen S. Morrill. 2001. *Travel, sabbatical, and study leave policies in college libraries*. Chicago: College Libraries Section, Association of College and Research Libraries.

Hardesty, Larry. 1994. College library mentor program. *College & Research Libraries News* 55 (January): 7.

Library Administration and Management Association. 1994. Ethical guidelines for library managers. *Library Administration & Management* 8 (Summer): 183.

Lyle, Guy Redvers, Evan Ira Farber, and Ruth Walling, eds. 1974. *The academic library: Essays in honor of Guy R. Lyle*. Metuchen, NJ: Scarecrow Press.

Oxford English dictionary. 1989. New York: Oxford University Press.

Pope, Alexander. 1961. *Pastoral poetry and an essay on criticism*. Ed. E. Audra and Aubrey Williams. New Haven: Yale University Press.

Chapter 6

Political Behavior

Library and information place managers are frequently heard half-jokingly making the statement that "the job would be fine if I didn't have to deal with people." This is usually in reference to political behavior by individuals within the library or the political behavior of people in other organization units with which the library must interact. A manager who finds herself in a highly politicized organization will experience some of the most trying difficulties of her career. While the topic receives some attention in organizational behavior literature, it appears to have received almost no attention in the library literature. This lack of attention should not be viewed as indicative of any lack of political behavior in libraries. It may be indicative of the limited amount of study devoted to the subject, even in the field of organizational behavior. This is particularly unusual in view of the fact that political behavior is one of the most common topics of discussion in most organizations.

Several studies of organizational politics have discovered a high degree of agreement among managers on a core set of actions that are considered to be political behavior. Most people feel that they know it when they see it. One often hears organizational politics called "office politics," or "the political game." These terms usually connote a negative view of political behavior. A value neutral definition states, "Organizational politics involve intentional acts of influence to enhance or protect the self-interest of individuals or groups" (Allen et al 1979,

77). Political behavior is a vital part of organizational structure and may be either positive or negative for the organization.

No library with a staff size greater than two would be complete without its internal organizational politics. In fact, no work organization is complete without this salient human trait. "Self-interest and limited resources guarantee that political behavior will be evident in all organizations" (Gray and Starke 1988, 504). Libraries are organizations that almost daily reach the limit of their resources. Library managers are constantly making choices on which materials to buy or which programs to pursue. Every choice made has the potential to eliminate or reduce the level of support for some other choice. While librarians and library staff generally consider themselves to be altruistic, self-interest is in place, even in altruism. Status, ego, financial incentives, power, personal interests are all areas of self-interest that may motivate particular political behavior. Altruism does not make a library immune to political behavior.

The mission of a library is too critical to allow it to be caught up in abusive political behavior. This type of behavior consumes valuable time, reduces the efficiency of the information place and often leads to resentment on the part of staff whose time it consumes. This may then result in the loss of some valued employees. Persons engaging in negative political behavior rarely seem to leave the organization. Negative political behavior subverts library goals and prevents it from achieving its mission. This behavior also diverts human energy that otherwise might be devoted to tasks that support the library mission in positive ways.

A library with a highly politicized environment is in a no-win situation. Such an environment will consume the manager's time and destroy the library's effectiveness. It might be said that a library's effectiveness suffers in proportion to the amount of inappropriate political behavior occurring. Thus it is important for the manager to understand the nature of political behavior and to anticipate and recognize it. The manager must then be willing and able to take appropriate actions to reduce negative political behavior to an acceptable level as well as to increase the appropriate political behavior that enhances the library's mission. It is important to note, given the nature of human beings, that negative political behavior is never entirely eliminated. The goal is to minimize political behavior that is unacceptable so that it becomes nothing more than simply a minor annoyance within the library.

This chapter will outline, discuss, and provide some examples of political behavior, both inappropriate and appropriate. It also will discuss ways to keep a library from becoming highly politicized and what to do if a manager finds herself in a situation that is already politicized.

Finally, it will explore the impact of technology, such as e-mail, which has potential as a powerful new tool for executing political behavior.

Political Behavior

Political behavior is an important operational part of every organization. Limited resources are a fact of life in all organizations. Because limits on resources place constraints on organizations, political behavior is an important process for determining how those resources are allocated. Political behavior is necessary in order for the library to receive its share of resources from the parent organization. Political behavior is involved as well in how the library manages those limited resources that it receives from the parent organization.

Another important aspect of organizations is that all individuals within organizations possess the human trait of personal goal orientation or self-interest. When self-interest and limited resources combine, political behavior inserts and asserts itself in the organization.

Political behavior is comprised of both intent and an action or actions. Intent usually arises from personal goals of an individual. If those goals are in conflict with library goals, inappropriate political behavior is likely to occur. This person may then act on that intent by engaging in a variety of political tactics.

Appropriate political behavior requires that the personal intent be congruent with the goals of the library or subordinated for the good of the organization. The tactics employed with appropriate political behavior must be congruent with the purposes of the library as well. It is unlikely that the tactic of attacking or blaming others would be an appropriate political behavior no matter how aligned the intent is with the goals of the library. Appropriate political behavior has less latitude in the tactics employed than inappropriate behavior in that those tactics must be congruent with library goals. As a result, there is a smaller range of tactics available for use by individuals engaged in appropriate political behavior.

Political behavior of either type occurs both within and among the library staff and externally. It is often incumbent upon the director to have sharp political skills in order to negotiate budget increases, a new building, or an automation system. This type of appropriate political behavior takes place in a larger arena. While it is assumed that a director will act with political appropriateness, that is not always the case.

Intent is individualized to the specific person acting and usually is based on personal goals. It is not particularly amenable to generalization. Intent changes from person to person and commonality of intent does not appear to exist. However, *means* are succinctly outlined in the typology developed by Robert W. Allen, et al. This is not a comprehensive list, but does include the more common types of political actions. While any of these behaviors may be used positively, they are often used inappropriately or for inappropriate purposes. They are

1. Attacking or Blaming Others
2. Using Information
3. Building an Image
4. Building Support for Ideas
5. Praising Others, Ingratiation
6. Building Power Coalitions
7. Associating with the Influential
8. Creating Obligations/Reciprocity

(Allen, et al 1979, 79)

Inappropriate Political Behavior

Which of the eight behaviors listed above might a manager encounter in a library environment? All of them and more! Political behavior is probably one of the favorite topics of discussion by library staff. We are aware of or have worked in libraries where some or all of the above behaviors have occurred. In fact, we suspect that most of you work in or know of a library where some of the listed behaviors are taking place. This discussion may help you correctly identify the nature of the behavior and choose an appropriate course of action to deal with it.

Attacking or Blaming Others

This behavior frequently flourishes in situations where technical and public services departments do not have a good working relationship. No matter what the nature of the problem or issue, each blames the other. The attacking and blaming frequently takes on a personal tone in addition to the anonymity of the departmental voice. There are often individuals within each area who attempt to rise above these behaviors, but unless the managers of the two departments are willing to create a different environment, there is little that can be done to change the situation.

Interestingly, this type of behavior even shows up in annual reports. Sometimes managers write into annual reports statements that blame the faculty because "their students" are not using the library or do not know how to use the resources of the library. Annual reports of public libraries or other information agencies may in carefully measured statements attack segments of the local political structure or their local funding agency for lack of resources to accomplish the library's mission, particularly if goals for that year were not met.

Using Information as a Political Tool

Information is something librarians know a lot about. Therefore, when they choose to manipulate information for political purposes, they are often quite effective in doing so. This behavior can be seen in department heads that share very little information with their peers or the administration about activities within their department. Often when they do share information, it is useless information simply put out to fill up space or even at times to mislead. When another department commits to a course of action or change in procedures that could have benefited from the sharing of information, these department heads quickly blame them for proceeding without proper consultation. They demand cooperation on their terms, but other managers never know what those terms are until they violate them. These individuals are quite skilled manipulators who often carry an air of aggrieved innocence.

Certainly using information as a political tool is easily found in a library setting. Many librarians are in key positions to obtain particular information and to use it to gain political advantage. The fact that many of them do not do so is a testament to the professionalism of most librarians.

Creating and Maintaining a Favorable Image

It is usually a good thing to create and maintain a favorable image. In fact librarians typically prefer that other people think favorably about them. But when the intent is incongruent with the goals of the library, it is inappropriate. When the image itself is false or if the image is being created in order to achieve a political purpose harmful to someone else in the organization or to the organization itself, it becomes an inappropriate political behavior.

Taking credit for the accomplishments or good ideas of someone else is a common form of image building. Directors or managers who insist on being listed as co-authors of grant proposals or articles to which they made no direct contribution are not uncommon.

Rarely does this behavior get acted out in isolation. It is usually used along with other political behavior and particularly bears a close relationship with using information as a political tool.

Developing a Base of Support

The inclination is often great for a librarian to build a base of support and the opportunities are certainly out there. Consider the possibility of a children's librarian who builds a base of support among parents and manipulates that support for purposes that may be inimical to the organization. This might be done through bringing in professional storytellers for a cost greater than what the library can afford. Thus the budget for some other areas of the library may have to be cut in order to support this program cost. Academic librarians have numerous opportunities to build strong bases of personal support among key faculty. This support may then be used to try to avoid cutting journal subscriptions in particular disciplines in which the courted faculty work—even though the library is being forced to do a general reduction in total number of journal subscriptions.

In and of itself, building a base of personal support is good and could also result in a strong base of support for the library. While most librarians develop bases of personal support for positive reasons, there are those who do otherwise with usually negative effects on the library. A librarian may use that base of support to bring excessive or inappropriate pressure to bear on budget decisions or even a promotion or pay raise. We know of one instance where a librarian threatened to quit his job and manipulated several members of his power base to call and e-mail the director over the pay dispute.

Ingratiating: Praising Others

This is probably not as common in libraries as in other types of organizations. The relationship between the information place and its clients is not typically such that this type of behavior is useful. Even so, it is likely that most individuals working in information places have met someone, usually a supervisor, who has used this tactic. While the person giving the praise may sound sincere at the time, the overabundance of praise, particularly for work or actions by someone else, soon illustrates the insincerity of the praise giver. Usually the praise giver is careful to only praise those whom he views as being in some way useful. This is closely related to developing power coalitions.

Developing Power Coalitions

Developing a power coalition is a popular tactic within information places. Power coalitions within a library are often dangerous and destructive, particularly when used to promote the purposes of an individual or department at the expense of the rest of the library. Maybe because there is so little power to go around, many people who work in libraries are attracted to developing power coalitions. This tactic is often used in conjunction with associating with influential persons and developing a power base.

Examples abound in personal experiences of many library managers and in news reporting. It is not unusual to read of an outreach librarian in a public library whose program is being cut in a general library budget reduction. In response, this librarian utilizes her power coalition to restore her budget at the expense of other library departments. In academic libraries, power coalitions are frequently developed with faculty or with key administrators to be used to maintain or change a particular policy, procedure, or program.

Associating with Influential Persons

There are those people who will only take coffee breaks or lunch with influential persons. They do not deign to associate freely with those who are not perceived to be influential. This is closely associated with developing power coalitions, praising others, and developing a base of support. A number of library directors have been confronted and defeated by this type of situation. This can happen when there is a middle manager who decides to use these behaviors for his individual purposes. Sometimes a library will go through four or five new directors in a very short period of time because this individual has built up such a powerful array of political tactics that he uses to subvert leadership. New directors often never have a chance to survive this behavior unless they are experienced and adept in dealing forcefully with it.

Creating Obligations and Reciprocity

Another very common practice is to create obligations and reciprocity. If a librarian is in a position to have particular information and make it difficult for the user to intuitively obtain the same information, the user becomes dependent on the librarian. If we think about it, even our classification systems, which we feel everyone should use, create obligations, because few users ever gain much understanding of them.

In one library we are familiar with, a librarian who was responsible for a particular department physically arranged materials in her area in such a manner that she was the only one who could locate needed items or information. Thus everyone from faculty to other library staff had to depend on her to locate information. This political behavior created obligations for the users of information in her area. Because she was so friendly and helpful, everyone praised her wonderful public service attitude. Of course, no one raised the possibility that had her collection been better organized, she could have used her time more productively than being Miss Fetchit! One wonders if this situation perhaps developed because of some type of insecurity on the part of the librarian. It also reflected a lack of clear guidance by the library administration on expected performance behaviors.

Most individuals engaging in inappropriate political behavior use a combination of the above described behaviors. They also are skilled at disguising such behavior through identifying the behavior as something other than what it actually is. For example, they may attack a supervisor who has made a change in procedure. But they disguise their opposition by expressing concern over the impact the change will have on the quality of service provided by the circulation department. Thus they are using three behaviors. First, they are safely attacking a supervisor. Secondly, they are creating a favorable image of themselves in that they have a concern about quality of service. Third, they are developing a base of support, because everyone is in favor of providing high quality service.

Some years ago in a medium-size library, a midlevel manager was highly effective in his use of seven of the eight behaviors listed. The behaviors were effectively disguised and had created a highly politicized work environment. The library was planning to initiate major building and automation projects that would more than double the size of the staff. Neither of these projects was able to gain any traction because the highly politicized atmosphere was consuming everyone's energy and time. Key staff had left because of the seeming ability of this individual to change the rules of engagement daily. In a dysfunctional situation such as this, it is critical that the administrator take decisive actions to break up the political fiefdom. There is no single formula to guide a manager in how this is to be done. Whatever actions the manager decides to take, it is important to observe due process. This protects the integrity of the process and the library and helps to ensure that the perpetrator will not be able to utilize the process to his advantage. Sometimes termination of an individual's employment is necessary. Typically, that is the action of last resort. The particular situation described above was depoliticized when the director and a new associate director began a deliberate and well-planned set of actions that (1) transferred the offending individual to a set of responsibilities that included no staff supervision, (2) isolated the individual physically and organizationally from other staff, thus eliminating his power base and power coalitions, (3) reduced the individual's access to organizational information, and (4) did it in such a way that the individual found only shifting sand as he attempted to blame others, maintain power coalitions, obtain information, and create favorable images for himself. Several months later, this individual found a job at another library and left.

Your Turn: Describe a specific political behavior or set of political behavior you have witnessed in an organization that you believe to have been inappropriate. What impact did this behavior(s) have on the organization? Classify the behavior using Allen's typography.

Technological Enhancements

With the advent of new technologies that facilitate communication in the workplace, it is not surprising that political behavior accompanies these developments. Some types of behavior are now more easily accomplished and have far-reaching results. The use of e-mail for office communications is now common in the overwhelming majority of American workplaces. Its power, speed, and penetration mean that it has a high potential for abuse. Kuzmits points out that "even though an employee may engage in organizational politics face-to-face, over the phone, or in a written note, e-mail provides the sender with opportunities and channel enhancements not found in the other three channels" (Kuzmits et al 2002, 77).

Some employees will choose e-mail over other communication channels because it allows them to engage in political behavior with less effort, energy, and time. It allows a certain degree of anonymity and avoidance of face-to-face confrontation. For many individuals and for certain forms of political behavior, this is ideal. The technology is easy to use. The sender has powerful choices in making either wide dissemination or selected distribution of a communication. Blind copies and forwarded messages can be sent to people other than the original recipient. These functions are appropriate and useful when used ethically. But they can easily be used to cause damage to another individual and/or the library if the intent is to do so.

Distribution lists are useful in facilitating communication. Used for the wrong reasons, they can do much harm to a library. Senders may purposely exclude individuals from a distribution list for political reasons. By excluding someone from vital information, they may be able to cause the excluded person to appear incompetent to the individuals who received and used the information. Typically, when this happens, someone is using information as a political tool. This tactic was already in use in a number of libraries, but it is greatly enhanced in the electronic environment.

The unreliability (real or imagined) of electronic information is also useful in facilitating inappropriate political behavior. Often individuals will assert that they never received a particular e-mail communication. This, in turn, is supposed to relieve them of responsibility for taking a particular action for the good of the library. This is not a successful excuse, since any sophisticated e-mail user can check and learn from the system that the recipient did in fact receive and open the e-mail and did delete the message in question. Denying receipt of an e-mail is still occurring in libraries, although typically by less sophisticated users. Unfortunately, there is still enough unreliability in electronic communication to make this a plausible excuse.

The lack of social cues inherent with e-mail means that its use for these purposes may be less than desirable for certain types of political behavior. If the content is open to interpretation and serious misinterpretation, and it often is, this can backfire on the sender. Also, because the e-mail creates a visible record, it also can have consequences for the sender. In a telephone or face-to-face communication, it can be difficult to document or sort out who said what. E-mail is often just as ambiguous, but the written record does provide tangible evidence of the communication and some indication of the nature of the communication. The freedom of information, "public record" aspect should make e-mail users circumspect about use. Their communication may become part of the public record.

How an Organization Becomes Politicized

What are some actions that are likely to lead to creating a library environment that is highly politicized? One of the most obvious is to reward those who engage in political behavior. The reward can be in the form of promotion, added resources for that individual's department, or any other actions that take scarce resources and allocate them favorably to the individual engaging most obviously in political behavior. As others in the library see this type of behavior being rewarded, they too will begin to engage in political behavior.

A library that has few rules or policies to guide behavior also creates an ideal breeding ground for political behavior to develop. A similar situation occurs when rules or policies are communicated ambiguously. This allows individuals to define situations to fit their own needs and desires.

When competition for resources is high, political behavior is more likely to occur. Libraries are typically stable organizations that make do with what they have, but there are times when the processes for allocation of resources can create excessive competition. When this happens, a manager will seldom experience a more bitter attack. A prime example occurs when a library must reduce the number of journal and magazine subscriptions. Members of the library staff, as well as library users, particularly faculty at a university or scientists at a corporation, are quick to criticize the manager for whatever process is adopted to make these cuts. They will also blame the director for not making the budget case strong enough so that the library can maintain or even add to the current journal collection. Unless the manager handles the situation carefully, positions are quickly polarized and the negative results can last for years. In one academic library, the faculty of one department maintained and frequently vocalized a grudge against the library for almost ten years after a journal reduction project. Library managers are often able to avoid this situation by scheduling regular reviews of magazine and journal holdings (e.g., every five years) and adjusting the collection to meet changing needs rather than adjusting the collection to meet a budgetary restraint.

Reducing Negative Political Behavior

To reduce the possibility of negative political behavior, managers should try to minimize resource competition among library departments. This can most effectively be accomplished by replacing resource competition with externally oriented goals and objectives. For example, the goal is set to provide information literacy instruction. Instead of focusing on the ideal array of resources, a number of options should be considered with various costs and benefits projected. Eventually this can be narrowed down to those options whose costs are within the parameters of resources available. Nothing tells us there is only one way to achieve the goal of an effective information literacy program. The benefits might not be as great as if one had unlimited resources, but creative and realistic assessment of how to use the resources available will result in a viable program. Focus on the library mission and encourage each department to be creative in developing ways to enhance that mission with whatever resources they have available.

The other key action in reducing negative political behavior is to put in place a clear process for evaluation of both individuals and departments. Insofar as possible, managers should make the rewards as immediate and directly related to performance as possible. Libraries typically are not able to offer much in the way of financial rewards, but even intrinsic rewards are highly valued by employees (praise, employee awards, and recognition). Managers should not be reticent about giving out praise wherever and whenever it is deserved. Frequency does not negate praise if it is earned and if the praise is appropriate to the situation.

Appropriate Political Behavior

No library organization would be complete without those who disparage the trait of office politics. Never mind that those who disparage are often the most persistent in the practice. This is perhaps one of the most frequently discussed topics among staff in many libraries. As such, it is an important management issue.

Is political behavior by members of an organization a bad thing? What would it be like to work in an organization in which political behavior was not a part of the organizational fabric? Is there political behavior that is bad for the organization? Likewise, is there any that is positive? What is the manager's role in response to political behavior? Many librarians have made the statement that they would prefer to work in an apolitical environment. Would they really prefer this type of workplace?

We should be prepared to accept the idea that politics are an essential facet of organizational behavior. After all, politics lubricates the wheels; politics gets things done. A search of library literature failed to locate any mention of internal politics. The outcome of political behavior does often show up in library news as library directors are often fired as a result of either staff unrest or conflict with the library board or academic administration. These outcomes are rarely achieved without some degree of politics taking place. But it seems that no one has specifically studied what political behavior is taking place in libraries that leads to these drastic actions or less. This is unfortunate because "politics is one of the most important, yet elusive, concepts in organizational behavior" (Gray and Starke 1988, 498). No library manager has the option to opt out. All must deal with political behavior in their organizations. Even to ignore it is a form of dealing with it.

There are two levels at which political behavior operates. There is the internal behavior among staff as they work to improve their position either personally or for their program. There is the external behavior that usually involves the director, but often involves anyone involved in library outreach.

In fact, there is acceptable political behavior as well as unacceptable. While we do not necessarily advocate situation ethics, there is some behavior that is appropriate in some situations and not in others. Often, it is the intent that helps clarify the distinction. Appropriate political behavior by library staff includes supporting goals of the library and supporting library management, representing the interests of their subordinates and programs, acting as conduits between upper and lower levels of the organization in achieving understanding, and working with their peers. The ability to work with peers is often an important factor in hiring decisions and frequently is listed in job ads as one of the desired traits.

Political behavior can be a positive force in and outside the library. There is a small body of research in organizational behavior that identifies a positive relationship between adroit political behavior and budgetary successes. Several studies done in university and nonprofit settings appear to indicate a relationship between political influence and size of budget and percentage of budget as part of overall budget (Pfeffer and Moore 1980). Studies of this type are particularly relevant to libraries. Anecdotally, one can read library news articles (*Library Journal, American Libraries,* and *C&RL News*) and easily conclude that the most successful libraries, whether academic, public, or special, are those that are well funded. Not surprisingly, there is often evidence in these news notes indicating that the library director has been quite successful in behaviors that can only be termed as political in nature.

Image building is one of the most commonly used means to build positive political alliances. This has to occur at the personal level as well as institutionally. Thus, dressing appropriately, taking the boss or a board member to lunch, and attending appropriate social events at which certain personages of importance to the library are likely to also be in attendance are all possible activities that can be used to improve image. While this may sound very Victorian Age, there is increasing psychological evidence that these things work if carried out without ostentation.

Potential managers must also be enthusiastic and supportive of the larger organization and adhere to group norms for that organization. It is not uncommon for city managers, mayors, provosts, and others to whom a library director reports, to very specifically explore these points with candidates for the position. There may be questions about the view of oneself as a team player and the candidate may be asked to describe the ways in which he or she has demonstrated loyalty to an organization in the past. This is positive in that a person should not work for individuals he or she does not respect nor represent an organization he or she cannot fully support.

Having an air of confidence about work activities is a very powerful political behavior. This confidence should be genuine and sincere. False modesty, on the other hand, is transparent and annoying, and can really lower an individual in the eyes of others. Perceptions of an organization are often created by the perceptions of the director of that organization. Thus it is appropriate to draw attention to one's own successes as well as the successes of the library. There is a fine line between the braggart and the sincere, but one should work to find that line and stay on the sincere side of it.

Networking—enabling the manager to know other people better through informal interaction—is a very important political behavior. Networking is defined as "the developing of contacts or exchange of information with others in an informal network" (*Webster's New World Dictionary*, 3rd edition, s.v. "networking"). Although often used as a device to further a career, it has many uses as a political tool for the library. It also allows other people to get to know a manager better as a person. This often results in improved communication that obviously is important for obtaining desired results. Networking is very much a part of image building, yet goes beyond image building in that it ensures that the library has friends in the right places.

Building a Healthy Political Climate

An information place mission statement is critical in the building of a healthy political climate. Goals, strategic initiatives, policies, and procedures are all developed from the foundation of a good mission statement. A number of experts have noted that "organizations make it easier for employees to engage in political behavior by providing few rules and policies for guidance" (Kcacmar and Ferris 1993, 71). If a manager comes into an information place that does not have a mission statement—or that has a poorly developed and understood mission statement—developing one should take top priority. In the process of developing a mission statement, communication channels are cleared and that also helps in reducing the amount of negative political behavior.

Political behavior is apparent in the ways we choose to communicate. Thus, to build a healthy political climate means that we should start with an examination of communication patterns and issues within the library. Is there good two-way communication between the director and the staff? Do staff members speak up in meetings? Do they feel free to speak openly even if their statements might be critical of some action or policy of the director? Note that the focus of these few paragraphs is on the director. If the director does not engage in good communication practices, the rest of the staff certainly may not be expected to do so.

With the professional staff in particular, managers should cultivate an atmosphere that encourages give and take and open, honest discussion of issues. There will always be honest differences of opinion on many issues facing a library. Do we offer a new service? Do we keep the dust jacket on new books? Do we offer outreach service to particular clientele? A new ethnic minority is rapidly growing in population. How do we best serve them? Do we filter Internet sites? Librarians discussing these types of issues, even heatedly at times, can help the library make the most reasonable decision for that particular time and place. Frank discussions that can take place with little or no personal rancor are healthy for an organization. Fortunate indeed is the library director who can foster this type of communication within the library.

How does one begin to build such an environment, particularly where it has not previously existed? Several key points should be observed. Determine which group or groups of staff should participate in discussing a particular issue. Should it be all staff? Should it be just the paraprofessional staff? Should it be just department heads or perhaps the public services department? A key element is to consider who will feel impacted by the issue. Whichever group will be impacted should be involved in discussing the issue. Will the group actually be making a decision on the issue? Or will they simply be providing input for the director who will make the decision? This is an important distinction and often is key to the form the discussion takes. For some issues, providing input to the director is appropriate. However, insofar as possible, the staff discussion should lead to their making a decision that the director then accepts. As this trust relationship develops, negative political behavior decreases and open discussions become the norm.

As a director works to build this type of environment, it is probably best to begin by sending issues to the group that actually have an answer or that are likely to result in a consensus from the group. Libraries face no end to the issues that must be addressed. If the group begins with issues that drag on for years with no results, they can easily become discouraged. When this happens, the group may lose momentum and purpose.

The director also must be careful in working with a group to not become the 500-pound gorilla in the room. If the director, even subconsciously, begins to give the group the conclusion he wants it to reach, political behavior will rapidly increase. In these situations, even if the director makes a decision to proceed in a particular way, it may not be carried out, either because it is not a good decision or because it does not have the necessary support within the library. An example of this is a situation in which an academic library is attempting to develop a comprehensive program of library instruction to deal with the challenges of electronic access to information. As the professional librarians are developing a multifaceted approach to the problem, the director insists that a one-credit course on information literacy be offered as a part of the approach. The course was approved and offered as a centerpiece for the information literacy program, but enrollment never materialized. The course remained on the books for a few years and then was quietly dropped. This occurred because the librarians never supported the required course and because the external climate was also not supportive of this offering. In this case, not convincing the staff, and not acting with political appropriateness, doomed the project.

An additional key point in developing an open environment is to clearly define an issue and provide background information on it. Whether the director or another staff member is bringing the issue forward, it is always helpful to outline the issue in writing and to have researched the issue in advance. Providing the results of that research (literature review or poll of similar libraries) is efficient and always appreciated by other staff involved in the discussion.

Your Turn: Discuss some other ways in which an administrator might foster a healthy climate of discussion within a library/information place. How might the administrator create a true risk-free environment for voicing viewpoints that may challenge the status quo?

Political behavior is as much a part of library organizational culture as the reference desk, circulation desk, and cataloging. Because it is inherent in any library organization, library managers must be able to recognize, understand, and deal appropriately with political behavior by encouraging appropriate and discouraging inappropriate political behavior. While the library's mission, goals, and strategies may be congruent with the needs of the community it serves, these can be thwarted easily by inappropriate political behavior. Managers must be prepared for the impact of technological communication channels and how these change the power and use of political tactics. A library manager will be more successful if she is adroit at appropriate political behavior and can model it for her staff as well as use it effectively in the external environment.

References

Allen, Robert W., Dan L. Madison, Lyman W. Porter, Patricia A. Renwick, and Bronston T. Mayes. 1979. Organizational politics: Tactics and characteristics of its actors. *California Management Review* 22 (Fall): 77-83.

Gray, Jerry L., and Frederick A. Starke. 1988. *Organizational behavior concepts and applications*. 4th ed. Columbus, OH: Merrill Publishing.

Kcacmar, L. Michele and Gerald R. Ferris. 1993. Politics at work: Sharpening the focus of political behavior in organizations. *Business Horizons* 36 (Jul/Aug): 70-75.

Kuzmits, Frank, Lyle Sussman, Art Adams, and Louis Raho. 2002. Using information and e-mail for political gain. *The Information Management Journal* 36 (Sept/Oct): 76-80.

Pfeffer, Jeffrey, and William M. Moore. 1980. Power in university budgeting: A replication and extension. *Administrative Science Quarterly* 25 (Dec): 637-53.

Webster's new world college dictionary. 1997. New York: Macmillan.

Chapter 7

Budgeting

Good budget management skills are critical for the information place manager. In fact, budget management should rank near human relations skills in importance. Budget management skills may in fact be an indicator of a manager's skills in other areas of information place management. Library staffs are quick to gain an impression of the manager by the way in which she makes budget decisions. It is quite likely that a poor budget manager will experience problems in other areas of management as well. In part, this is because budget decisions often relate very directly to staff or patron concerns and often have immediate and visible outcomes. Thus this chapter reviews some basic principles, discusses several elements of the overall process, and offers a few practical ideas and suggestions regarding budget management.

Image of the Information Place and the Budget

Libraries in general are considered a public good. Few people dare question the value of a library. Libraries are nearly always perceived as the good guys, the white hats. We have all heard the library called "the heart of the campus" or the "most important cultural agency in the community." That does not mean, though, that the decision makers will provide adequate funding for library programs or staffing. In fact, the opposite is often the case. So while the rhetoric is nearly always supportive, the funding to support the rhetoric is much more difficult to obtain. Librarians have been extremely successful in developing the good guy persona for libraries. In the past century and a half, librarians all over the world have fulfilled their mission well and have thus reaped the benefits of grateful communities. But obtaining adequate budget support requires more than goodwill. While we are better off with it than without it, we should not rely upon it exclusively. Managers should utilize goodwill as one part of our budget strategy, but they must do much more in order to be successful in building adequate budget support.

Libraries have been quite successful as well in creating an impression of being underfunded. While there is no doubt that there are many libraries that are underfunded, there are likely just as many that are undermanaged. A poorly managed budget may create the impression that a library is underfunded. The only benefit one usually receives by creating the impression of being underfunded is sympathy. Building successful programs and accomplishing the mission is what leads to successful budget support.

Image Errors

One of the biggest errors in budget management is to blame library woes on poor budget support by the parent organization. While this may be an effective short-term strategy, alienating the budget deciders is not a wise course of action. The library may in fact be underfunded. But it is political suicide to blame the parent organization or particular individuals within that organization. More than one library director has learned this lesson the hard way.

One library director was quite successful in placing the blame for the library's woes on the university administration. Students complained about the lack of current books on topics of interest to them. Faculty complained about the paucity of journal titles in areas in which they were teaching or doing research. This director's response, privately and publicly, was that the low funding provided by the university administration was the culprit. This director ignored the fact that he frequently underspent his budget. Also ignored were the lack of internal library controls for periodicals and continuations and poor acquisitions procedures for firm order books. Although he experienced some success in enlisting students and faculty who were all too ready to blame the university administration, he was eventually forced to resign. In part, his forced resignation came about because in general he did not have a good relationship with the administration and in part because the administration was fed up with being blamed for what they perceived were internal problems within the library.

A manager can develop a much more successful approach when he works in various public forums to create a positive impression of the library, its collections, and its programs. Whether one works at it or not, one creates an impression! A balanced and honest approach is called for in which the manager points out areas of the collections and services which are strong as well as acknowledges those areas that are weak. The strong areas should be emphasized repeatedly and the budget should be utilized to make them even stronger. This can usually be done without neglecting weak areas. Acknowledge weak areas, but do not dwell on them in public forums. In a private forum, such as a budget hearing, discuss honestly and frankly an area of weakness. Then present a proposal, which will lead to a solution. While the financial aspect may be the most important part of strengthening an area, it is usually not the only factor to be considered. Always try to meet the budget decision makers halfway—however one might define halfway. What, other than request increases in the budget, has the library done to correct the weakness? If the weakness is a collection issue, is weeding appropriate? Has an assessment been done? If the weak area is a service issue, have there been opportunities for the staff to participate in continuing education? Does the service have its own mission statement? Does it set up standards for the level of service to be provided and does it publicly acknowledge those standards? In other words, has the manager taken all of the appropriate actions to correct the problem and now simply needs budget support to complete the task?

Psychological Errors

Psychological factors frequently come into play when information place managers sing the chorus of "scarce resources." First, like those nasty germs that have become resistant to various antibiotics, the budget decision makers have heard the song before and they know their part very well. "Well, you know things are just really tight this year. I wish we could do more for you, but . . ." Or they hear the manager's comparisons to other departments or lifestyle expenditures and their eyes glaze over and their minds tune out. Or they hear library managers spout out such things as "meet their needs," "produce lifelong learners," "make self-reliant inquirers," and "broaden horizons," and they have no clue what it is that we are about. How can they fund something they don't understand?

Scarce resources is a catch-all excuse we librarians have used for far too many years. It is somewhat like the hypochondriac who is always sick. What we really mean is (1) I don't want to order that stupid book you are requesting or, (2) if I keep repeating this phrase often enough, maybe the library will get more money. Of course, neither of these thoughts has anything whatsoever to do with the library's mission. The truth of the matter is that many libraries—academic and public—are in fact very well funded! While it is always possible to do comparisons to police or fire departments or athletics or lifestyle expenditures and come up looking like poor country relations, those are usually not appropriate comparisons. In addition, there is no solid evidence that any substantive improvements in budgets occur as a result of this approach.

This is not to deny that some libraries are in fact very poorly funded. It is also the case that some libraries funded by millions of dollars are underfunded while others with far less funding are quite adequately funded. There do not appear to be any known cases of a library being overfunded! A library's funding adequacy depends in large part on its mission—what it is trying to accomplish. When managers create the "poor me" perception of the library, it can become a self-fulfilling prophecy. The truly successful libraries avoid this perception. It is quite likely no library will ever have all the money it feels it deserves. Neither will Bill Gates!

Another psychological barrier managers create with the mantra of scarce resources is hoarding. Staff hoard supplies, faculty hoard book orders, and even budget managers are guilty of hoarding funds until the last minute just in case there is an unexpected expenditure or need. Hoarding places the emphasis in the wrong spot. The emphasis should be on having the tools necessary to do the job—not expending energy hiding supplies. This is a costly and ineffective means of dealing with a common situation. Supplies which are hoarded often do not get used. In fact, many supplies end up being thrown away because they have been hoarded beyond their useful life. A staff member who needs a particular supply item may not be able to obtain it because someone else is hoarding it.

Instead of focusing upon collection development, faculty frequently hoard book orders in an effort to ensure that they have expended whatever funds the library may have allocated for books in their discipline. Of course, this creates havoc with collection development as well as the acquisitions department. In many colleges and small universities, the library typically allocates some portion of its book budget by discipline.

Faculty often and mistakenly have considered these allocations to be a departmental budget, and thus their prerogative to control and manage. The impression is now ingrained by decades of the practice. Thus faculty are frequently more concerned with expending the budget than they are with collection development!

Faculty of course, want and need some guidelines on expenditures. Give them guidelines (based on a formula, if you like), but state clearly that the budget allocation is simply a projection of the amount the library expects to spend on that particular discipline in that particular year. Also be very explicit in stating that the final expenditure may be more or less than the projection. This should not be a major concern of the faculty. Finally, managers should emphasize to faculty that they should submit orders based on their perceptions of need, regardless of the budget projection. The faculty role is much more valuable when they alert the library to needs than it is when they attempt to control a book budget.

The role of the library manager is to obtain an accurate perception of the needs and to assure that the budget meets those needs. If the manager uses some type of artificial formula to allocate the budget at the beginning of the year, how is he going to accurately determine what the real needs are? Tactfully, what he is doing is helping faculty focus upon the real mission of the library in the way that they can be most supportive—which is by giving him information regarding the teaching and research needs, which should be supported by the book collection. Faculty frequently have little understanding of budgets. Budget is the library manager's responsibility. Turn faculty loose in the area where they can be most helpful to the library mission.

Finally, the library manager also may be guilty of hoarding. While it is prudent to maintain a contingency fund to cover unexpected last-minute expenditures, hoarding takes this strategy to excess. Some managers even hoard so as to have funds to return to the parent organization at the end of the budget year. This is not prudent budget management and in fact creates the opposite impression—the belief that the library is overfunded.

The library mission should be reflected in the budget. If technology is important to the mission, it should be reflected in the budget. If children's programming is important, it should be reflected in the budget. The more clearly the manager can relate the mission and the budget, the more likely it is that she will be successful in obtaining adequate budgets each year. Award-winning libraries invariably are libraries that have achieved this congruence. Thus, when it comes time to present and defend the library budget planned for the upcoming year, the manager's task is made easier if she has achieved this congruence.

Definition and Principles of Budget Management

The budget is "a stated program that reflects the goals and objectives of the library and defines the manager's authority to act" (Stueart and Eastlick 1981, 164). Budgetary control and financial management are the keys to efficient utilization of those dollars invested in the organization for the attainment of its ends" (Wasserman and Bundy 1968, 227). The International Management Institute defines it thus: "A budget is not only a financial plan that sets forth cost and goals, but also a device for control, coordination, communication, performance evaluation, and motivation" (Stueart and Moran 1998, 204).

Every manager should bear in mind certain basic principles of budgetary control and financial management. First is the principle of planning. The information place manager will be held responsible for assessing the needs of the community the library serves and for developing a budget adequate to fund programs and resources to meet those needs. A second principle is that the manager should have a primary voice in the planning of how the library activities will be performed. A third principle is that fiscal responsibility should be merged with program responsibility. Finally, there is the principle that the manager should be held accountable overall for proper management of the budget.

The Nature of the Information Place Budget

Library budgets are often quite complex. The way in which books are purchased is very different from the way periodicals are purchased or electronic products are licensed. Often very few people, other than the library manager, have a good understanding of a library budget. Thus it is important for the manager to understand the budget well enough to be able to explain or discuss it with external constituencies (faculty, tax-paying citizens, parent organization administrators, etc.). This understanding begins with a well-written mission statement. The manager always should be able to show the relationship between mission and budget. If the library/information place is in the business of acquiring and classifying information, then its budget should reflect that. A manager or administrator who has a clear understanding of what the organization is supposed to be doing is more likely to be successful in managing the budget and in explaining it to others.

Library budgets produce tangible results in the sense that how they are expended usually results in physical accumulations, provision of services, or physical plant improvements. Library budgets are political in that the manager must maintain excellent working relationships with the accounting office, vendors, supervisors, library boards, and faculty committees. Library budgets are psychological in that the adequacy of funding and how that funding is expended may affect the well-being of customers and patrons as well as the manager and others who work in the library/information place.

Elements of the Budget Process

Planning is the essential first step in the budget process. This planning should begin with the library mission and goals and should reflect both. It should also include a manager's review of needs, a literature review, and consultation with staff. All of this information is *developed* in a document as a proposed budget to be presented to the parent organization. At some point shortly after receipt of the budget proposal, many parent organizations will schedule a hearing. This opportunity for *presentation* should be utilized to make the best case possible for the library and its programs. The presentation may include opportunities for negotiation or those opportunities may occur later in the process. At some point each year, this phase of the process is completed and a new budget is approved for the next budget cycle. The library manager's responsibility then shifts to *expending* the funds in a wise and efficient fashion and in general following the plan developed by the proposal. Finally comes the *accountability* phase of the process, in which the expended budget is reviewed and a final tally made of the expenditures. Increasingly, accountability requires including program impact reviews or outcomes that can be related to budget expenditures.

Budget Planning

An important characteristic of budgets in nonprofit organizations such as libraries is that they cover fixed periods of time. Typically the time frame is twelve months, although in some cases it may be for twenty-four months or even thirty-six months. Thus planning and budget development for a future budget period usually take place during the expenditure phase of the current budget period. It sometimes happens that activities are taking place simultaneously on three different budget periods, e.g., planning for the future, expending the current, and accounting for a past budget period. This is particularly common in twelve-month budget cycles. Since twelve-month budget cycles are the most common, most of this discussion will assume that time frame.

Budget planning is often a continuous activity for the library manager, at least at the informal level. For a twelve-month budget period, the formal phase of planning is likely to occur over a period of two or three months and begin some six to nine months prior to the beginning of a new budget cycle. During this planning period, it is most important that the manager solicit information from all operational areas of the library regarding budget needs. Many a director has been met with cynicism when soliciting budget needs information. The response frequently received is "Why bother? We don't get anything anyway!" One response to this type of attitude is to review the past history to determine if perhaps long ago that individual or department may have submitted a single request that was not funded. However, if the opposite is true and that particular unit has made its needs known repeatedly without results, the complaint could be legitimate! At other times, the type of response received is indicative of other problems such as poor morale or customer service burnout. A wise manager will assess such possibilities in this type of situation and act to ameliorate problems that may show up here, whether or not they are related to budget issues.

An important part of budget planning is the reading of professional literature. Developing trends are often discussed in the literature and helpful information can be gleaned in terms of new programs that may be developed to take advantage of the trends. Libraries are quite generous in sharing the results of their own experiences with new programs. Thus the manager can make more accurate planning assumptions if she has the benefit of someone else's experience to draw on. Yes, those "how we do it good in our library" articles do have a place and a value in the literature of librarianship.

Another element of budget planning is contact with library vendors. A number of library vendors, particularly subscription agents, distribute twelve- to-eighteen-month forecasts of costs that are usually fairly reliable. Many vendors also will provide suggestions or options their company offers for handling financial aspects of a major purchase or commitment of funds. While they obviously have their own self-interest at stake, many are quite sincere in their efforts to work with a manager. For example, it is a common practice to ask vendors (two or three) to provide cost estimates to be used in planning a budget for a capital item or other major expenditure. The manager should probably use the highest figure for budget planning, but would actually make his decision of which vendor to use at a later date, based upon a buy quote. In this scenario, vendors' representatives often provide additional information that the manager will find useful for budget planning purposes. An important caveat is that the manager should always act in an ethical manner when dealing with vendors in this manner. Relationships such as this are easily subverted to unethical conduct on the part of either or both. It is nevertheless important for managers to develop good communications with a variety of library vendors.

An additional factor in budget planning is the general mood within the parent organization. Is it a good budget year or a lean one? There are many code words and sources of information for making this determination. The main thing is that the manager should be careful in her timing. Obviously, if the parent organization is filled with optimism regarding the upcoming budget year, the library budget manager should be more assertive in her proposals. If the organization is in a financial down cycle, prioritizing library expenditures becomes more critical. These financial cycles occur in all types of organizations and the manager should be aware of their impacts on her budget proposals. Few organizations are immune to these up and down budget cycles. Library managers should understand the nature of these cycles and optimize that understanding for the benefit of the library.

Developing a Budget Proposal

Having gathered data from a variety of sources, it is now time for the manager to develop the proposal for review by the parent organization. The format is usually predetermined by the parent organization. The manager should make an effort to adhere to this format unless excellent reasons exist to do otherwise. This proposal document will reflect the results of the manager's planning efforts. Typically it will include narrative information as well as certain types of quantitative information. The narrative information defends current programs whenever necessary, but is usually oriented toward new programs or enhancements to current ones.

A vital requirement of the budget proposal is to document, document, document. It is best to use a mix of quantitative and qualitative data that support the chief elements of the budget. There is no hard and fast guide on this matter. Each local situation provides its own special set of data.

Usage data can be used for the quantitative side, but must be handled carefully. While usage may go up in most years, there is always the possibility that it will be down in a particular year. How does one explain that? Until recently, usage in many libraries varied little from year to year. In the current electronic environment, some libraries are now reporting significant decreases in book circulation. Gate counts and reference desk queries may also be decreasing as well as print journal usage. Lower gate counts may also indicate lower in-house usage.

While usage of print resources and print-based services appear to be declining, libraries are experiencing significant increases in usage of electronic resources and services. These changes do not appear to be a simple quid pro quo. Usage of electronic resources may allow for a much greater range in how the patron uses the information. Even when examined quid pro quo, it is not unusual for the number of electronic usage transactions to far exceed those previously recorded for the same resource in print. Interpreting these changes is especially difficult at this time. Is it simply because this is new, or do people make more use of information available through libraries because it is now easier to access and perhaps manipulate? One of the truisms of information is that the more difficult information is to access, the less likely the user is to make the effort. By making access easier, librarians may finally be able to document support for this truism. Regardless of the difficulties of explaining and interpreting usage data, information place managers often find it appropriate to incorporate this type of information into their budgeting proposals.

Another difficulty encountered in both the print and electronic environments is to understand exactly what is being counted. Standards and definitions for the print environment have been in place for quite some time. But for the electronic resources, standards are still in flux. While some standards have been approved and adopted, many vendors and libraries have not yet put them in place. This difficulty is a caution to managers to use usage counts carefully. Combining outputs-derived data with outcomes helps overcome part of this difficulty as well as build a stronger case for budget requests.

In the past, library managers often have not known why patrons used or did not use certain services and materials. They also have not known, except for the occasional anecdote, what difference may have resulted from the patron's experience with the library or information place. At best, the manager might know which resources were or were not being used, but it was always difficult to define precisely the underlying causes. To get at outcomes-based data, managers need to ask such questions as "How is the user changed because he checked out material from our library" or "How did the parent organization change because someone obtained access to a particular research report through our information place?" Answering these types of questions often means that managers use quantitative and qualitative data in outputs and outcomes. Continuously documenting outputs and outcomes, both qualitatively and quantitatively, is essential for good budget planning.

It should go without saying that this is taboo, but unfortunately many managers still turn in budget proposals which are poorly written and contain numerous spelling, grammatical, and mathematical errors. One way to avoid this problem is to have another member of the library staff read the proposal and mark any obvious errors or vague references.

In submitting the budget proposal, the library manager should abandon meekness. He should be an assertive but not a shrill presenter. He should focus on accomplishments, mission, strategic plan, programs, and needs. He must state needs in terms that will be understood by the people in the budget review process. Budget people usually grasp quantitative documentation quite easily. However, quantitative documentation can be quite dry (but so are budget people!) and may be greeted with some degree of cynicism. Everyone is well aware that statistics can be used to tell whatever story one wishes to tell. Quantitative data often have unexplainable ups and downs, so the manager must present these data carefully. A mix of quantitative and qualitative data is probably most effective. A mix of outcomes and outputs is also effective. He could tell a story of some incident that will illustrate the effectiveness of the library programs. Anecdotal evidence used properly can be very effective. If the manager has been successful in fulfilling the mission, her users also are saying good things about her and that word gets back to the powers that be. Thus, anecdotal evidence is likely supported by information the budget hearing attendees learn from other sources.

New programs or enhancements to current programs frequently require a somewhat different approach from the inflation-adjusted increases for standard items such as supplies, telephone costs, postage, etc. Because they are new, a more thorough explanation is usually necessary. However, one should be careful to avoid information overload as well as the use of too much jargon. These types of funding requests are most likely to meet with success when focused on expected outcomes, how the mission will be enhanced, and the target audience that will benefit because of them.

Budget Proposal Presentation

Library managers are often called upon to attend a hearing regarding the budget proposal they have sent forth. The process varies from location to location, but some general principles apply to all situations. The manager should view this hearing as perhaps his best opportunity to present, discuss, and gain support for the library's mission.   The manager must provide the hearing officers with relevant and clear information. The manager must prepare by documenting all requests and by either implicitly or explicitly tying them to the library mission statement. It is astonishing that many budget managers develop poor or skimpy documentation to support their budget proposals. Even more amazing, however, are the many budget managers who are poorly prepared to defend their proposals in a hearing. It is quite embarrassing to limp through a hearing with poor responses and "don't knows!" A well-written and properly documented budget proposal will make the budget hearing itself much easier. But the manager must prepare to respond appropriately to the unexpected as well as the expected verbal questioning.

The budget hearing is usually attended by the manager's immediate supervisor and perhaps by others on the supervisor's staff. These individuals frequently provide feedback to the supervisor immediately after the hearing. One or more individuals also may attend from the financial manager's office (e.g., vice president for finance or the city budget manager). The hearing typically is brief but full of tension for the budget manager. Questions asked are as varied as the individuals participating, but typically focus on the parts of the budget where the manager has requested either new funding or an increase in funds. Some individuals will examine the previous year's library budget and ask questions about any unexpended funds from that budget period. The manager should be prepared to answer all questions honestly and forthrightly.

In preparing the budget proposal for the hearing, it is probably wise for the manager to avoid giving the impression that the library is either the fat cat or the poor church mouse of the city or campus. Acknowledge current resources and how well those financial resources have supported accomplishing the mission. Assuming that the library mission is well aligned with the parent organization mission, it is well to focus on the library mission and how well it accomplished and supported the parent organization in the current budget cycle. Then point out that to continue to accomplish that mission and to be able to better support it, certain increases are necessary both in order to maintain pace with inflation and to achieve greater programming/resources success. Inflation is probably best documented with national projections. The *Bowker Annual, Library Journal,* and other publications contain much data about inflation factors in library costs. Often it is useful to chart both local data and national data together for presentation at a budget hearing. To the degree possible, the discussion of inflation should be brief, because what you really want to talk about are the new programs or enhancements to current programs and how those support the parent organization's mission. The need for improved programming and resource support beyond inflationary factors will require both documentation of current successes and creating buy-in for future goals.

To the extent that the manager is well prepared, the budget hearing officers will be empathetic to her requests. A poorly prepared proposal and presentation will simply not be successful. To the degree that the budget has been wisely managed in the past, the budget deciders will acknowledge and more positively view the likelihood of future accomplishments. The decision makers want to put money where they know they will get results. Thus if the manager can demonstrate excellent past performance, she is more likely to be approved for future increases. Quantitative and qualitative data as well as outputs and outcomes are vital to success in demonstrating the accomplishment of the mission.

Expending the Budget

After completing and submitting the budget planning documents and surviving the budget hearing, the next step is for funding authorities to provide notification of the approved budget. This usually occurs near the end of the current budget cycle, although there are numerous instances where the budget does not get final approval until a month or more into the new budget cycle. The budget may be approved as presented or it may be modified in any number of frustrating ways. The one thing that will probably not happen is for a budget to be approved for a greater amount than the library manager requested!

One of the essential elements in expending a budget is to develop a good relationship with the personnel in the parent organization business office. A satisfactory relationship with these people develops from a combination of courtesy and common sense as much as from sound business practices. Library staff working with the business office must maintain adequate records for the library as well as adhere to common practices with respect to signatories, authorizations, and deadlines. With the high number of transactions between the library and business office, it is inevitable that some difficulties and misunderstandings will occur. But good personal relationships between the two departments can go a long way toward helping to resolve most differences with a minimum of difficulty.

The approved budget is a guide—a planning and action tool. Many writers view it as a control mechanism, and it is that as well. In essence, though, the budget is a tool for accomplishment of the mission. The budget manager should make every effort to expend the budget wisely and completely.

Wisdom

Expending the budget wisely means making good choices in how and when certain expenditures are to be made. It includes evaluation of products and vendors in order to obtain the best value for the library and its users. It also includes an openness to new ideas and possible immediate action on those ideas.

Wisdom also includes looking ahead to long-term impacts as well as short-term impacts. Sometimes the impact of a particular budgetary decision may not be entirely evident when the decision has to be made. The manager sometimes takes a risk based upon her experience and wisdom. Wisdom is sensing user needs and responding through budget action at the appropriate time. Wisdom is often composed of knowledge and intuition.

Another aspect of wisdom is flexibility. Sometimes programs and needs change rapidly. They don't always stick to a neat twelve-month cycle. Flexible managers are willing work with these changes rather than losing an opportunity to move the organization forward in the accomplishment of its mission. A good working relationship with the business office may mean that the manager will be permitted to exercise greater flexibility.

Completeness

Typically, the manager should expect to expend all funds provided in a budget. Of course, there may be some areas of the budget over which the manager may not have complete control, such as personnel and fringe benefits. But for those areas over which the manager has full control, there is a responsibility to fully expend the funds. Seriously under- or overspending the budget is an indication of either poor budget planning or poor management! Two elements are necessary to ensure proper management of the budget. First, the manager should ensure that appropriate processes are in place for ordering, receiving, and paying for items against which funds are expended. Second, the manager should have in place tools that will allow accurate monitoring and projecting of budget expenditures. Both the processes and the tools should be reviewed frequently to ensure currency and efficiency.

Several kinds of analyses are necessary for accurate monitoring and projecting of budget expenditures. These include a review of past history, awareness of spending patterns, review and reconciliation of library accounting system reports with the parent organization accounting system reports, and the development and use of spreadsheets for specific tracking/projecting activities.

Past History: Books, Scores, Compacts Discs - First, and perhaps for some budget lines most important, is past history. For example, let us say that in the previous budget year, the book budget was $96,000 and the library placed orders for 2,620 titles, but received and paid for 2,250 titles and actually spent $88,400. This is approximately an 85 percent fill rate, which is fairly typical for many small libraries, academic and public. Therefore, we can assume that there are no unusual factors in the acquisitions process and that the average price of $39 a volume is fairly accurate as well. Thus to fully expend the book budget in the current budget year (assuming the budget remains $96,000), this library needs to increase its orders to just under 2,900 titles (2900 X fill rate .85 = 2465 X average price $39 = $96,135).

Inflation is not factored into the above example, in part because its impact on book budgets has been modest for a number of years. However, it is easy enough for a budget manager to factor in whatever inflation rate is current and adjust the purchasing accordingly. The average price can vary somewhat from year to year based on other factors, e.g., acquiring an expensive reference set or purchasing in notoriously expensive areas such as the sciences. However, the variance is typically less than 2 percent. In most instances, inflation and various aberrations can be identified easily and accounted for by using a three-year historical time frame.

Past History: Periodicals and Electronic Materials - Most materials budget lines such as video, compact discs, and scores will track somewhat similarly to the book budget lines. Two major exceptions exist in every library materials budget. Periodicals have experienced phenomenal inflation rates for the past thirty years. Of more recent vintage are electronic or digital materials, many of which are still trying to find their price point. As a result, there is often not sufficient past history for comprehensive budgetary analysis of electronic materials.

Many library materials budgets are dominated by periodicals costs, but electronic materials costs are rising rapidly. Libraries have been successful only partially in obtaining budget increases equal to the inflation rate for periodicals. Most libraries have had to move funds from the book or other budget lines to cover periodical costs. But periodical inflation has turned out to be a long-term problem. Moving funds was a short-term solution that only hurt the other budget lines without solving the periodicals problem. Another action, which has been taken by numerous libraries, has been to reduce the number of periodical subscriptions. While this has had the positive effect of weeding out some low- and no-use titles, it has usually been undertaken in a crisis mode. This has often resulted in hastily devised procedures for determining cuts, has usually had negative public relations consequences, and has not always been of the greatest benefit to collection development efforts.

A more effective approach that is used by some library managers is the "continuous periodical review." In this scenario, a library selects a certain percentage of its periodical titles for review. If a library selects one-third, then it will have reviewed its complete collection every three years. Usually the titles selected for review are in the same or related subject areas. Useful information to include in the review includes such items as cost, usage data (usually a sample), usage/cost (divide the cost by the usage), indexing/abstracting information, and abstract of the recommendation from *Magazines for Libraries* (11th ed., 2001). In academic libraries, faculty are very interested in participating in these types of reviews. The manager must be very careful in setting up the review to ensure that the faculty are clear that they are simply reviewing and recommending to the library—not dictating. Often this is a time when it can be agreed that certain subscriptions should be discontinued and new ones instituted. If the library is under some budget pressure, this can usually be accomplished by canceling a larger dollar amount than new subscriptions require.

There is a psychological factor here that seems to play a big role in acceptance of the changes in the subscription list. Doing the journal review for the purpose of keeping the library collection aligned with the curriculum or community needs is acceptable in a way that doing a journal cancellation project because of a budget mandate is not. At one time, a periodical subscription was a lifelong commitment. Libraries were reluctant to cancel a subscription because of the sanctity of a complete run. To approve the start of a new subscription was frequently a belabored process involving years of consideration. That is much less true today. Academic curriculums are changing rapidly, the journal publishing climate is more unstable than ever, and student use of journals is changing daily. Thus some type of regular journal review is a necessity in most small libraries.

The rise in electronic materials costs has major implications for the library manager. Much of the cost for periodicals is now being shifted to electronic formats. On the positive side, most electronic products are significantly enhanced over their print cousins. The value added often permits the library to improve access and justifies the transferring of funds from one format to the other. A problem with this approach is that some publishers are requiring that a library maintain its print subscription in order to obtain access to the electronic. This places many library budgets in a double bind of trying to pay for both print copies and their electronic equivalents. However, it seems likely that this is a transition period. Many new titles are being published in electronic format only and some of the traditional print titles are discontinuing print as the electronic version catches on with the users.

There are few hard and fast rules for dealing with periodicals and electronic materials budgets. At this time, inflation is decreasing for print periodicals although it continues to hover around 10 percent per year. For electronic materials, consortia purchasing is useful in keeping prices in line. However, there is now greater pressure on even consortia to pay higher prices. This is the area where budget planning is the most critical. Managers must stay current with trends in electronic publishing and developments in consortia licensing issues and plan accordingly.

Established Spending Patterns - Most other library budget lines, such as supplies, memberships, telephone, and postage, track very similarly to themselves from year to year. A manager should watch for unusual expenses in any of these areas and she should develop strategies early in the budget cycle to deal with them.

One can gain from budget history some knowledge of when expenditures occur in the budget cycle. For example, the binding budget may see little activity during the first several months (assuming a July/June beginning of budget year). But as volumes are complete on a calendar year, the binding is heavily spent in the January through June part of the budget cycle. The periodical budget will typically be 90 percent expended sometime in the first or second quarter of the budget year because subscription renewals must be processed in time for the calendar year subscription cycle. Budget expenditures rarely divide themselves out in twelve even amounts. Thus, as one reviews the budget throughout the year and adjusts spending accordingly, it is important to understand where and when certain activities affect the budget.

Budget Reconciliation - Libraries often maintain their own purchasing system. This has happened because of the high number of specialized purchasing transactions which many libraries have each year. The volume and nature of library purchasing means that in many cases it is best handled within the library. However, for some libraries, the parent organization places all purchase orders. The library may be required to follow certain procedures in sending a requisition to the parent organization purchasing department which in turn issues an official purchase order. In other libraries, there is a mix of purchases generated by the library and purchase orders generated by the parent organization. For example, the library may generate purchase orders for all materials purchases, but the parent organization would generate purchase orders for computers and furniture or for purchases over a certain dollar amount. The manager should acquaint herself with the procedures of the parent organization in this area and work within those procedures to ensure an efficient flow of the paperwork connected with expending funds.

Because many libraries do at least some if not all of their own purchasing, it is not unusual for the library to work with two accounting systems—its own and that of its parent organization. While seemingly awkward, this actually offers several advantages. First, many automated library systems offer an accounting module as a part of the acquisitions subsystem. This accounting module usually interfaces very well with library vendors, particularly book and subscription agents. Second, they also can provide quick feedback and excellent management reports. Because it is maintained within the library, it is more current than that of the parent organization. A third advantage is that it interfaces with the other automated system modules so that, for example, as soon as a book is ordered, it can be shown in the public access catalog as being on order.

In most instances the library accounting system will be more current and detailed than that of the parent organization. For example, the parent organization may track book purchases as a single line item whereas the library may track book purchases in numerous lines (children's books, adult books, fiction, nonfiction by discipline, or reference books). This added detail is useful to the manager in planning and decision making as well as budget control.

Managers who operate with two accounting systems will find it useful to reconcile the two systems on a monthly basis—although a quarterly reconciliation may be acceptable for some smaller libraries. The accounting system of the parent organization allows for a good system of cross checks. Errors in one system will frequently be detected by the other. The parent organization system is often not as detailed as the library system, thus it can offer a different view of the budget. Auditors will usually only examine the parent organization's accounting practices. Finally, it allows the manager to communicate with other managers within the parent organization using a common language. The accounting system of the parent organization is the official record of the budget and the one to which the manager will be held accountable. Reconciliation between the two is of great value in helping the manager properly manage the budget.

Additional Tracking/Project Tools - Spreadsheets provide another strategy for managing the budget. Information place managers benefit tremendously when they become power users of spreadsheets. Most libraries have an accounting system as a part of their automation system. However, these systems are designed for the general benefit of all purchasers of that particular system and thus are not easily customizable to the local situation. Spreadsheets fill in this gap, as they are infinitely customizable. They are particularly useful in predicting budget outcomes at various points throughout the year. A case in point is the student labor budget. In a student labor budget, there may be sixty, eighty, one hundred or more students working from five to sixteen hours a week at varying pay rates. Absenteeism and turnover are frequently factors in this budget. Most student labor expenditures occur during the fall and spring semesters of the academic year. However, with a well-designed spreadsheet, one can track this budget and predict expenditures with a high degree of accuracy. It can be used to predict the impact of an across-the-board salary increase for all student employees. It can be used to predict the adding of student labor hours in one department without decreasing them elsewhere. One also can ascertain the impact of a higher average pay rate because of more returning students (assuming that students receive seniority increases in pay). With each payroll period, the tracking becomes more accurate for the remainder of that budget year.

Assuming that the manager has done proper budget planning, made appropriate use of the library's accounting system, and designed useful spreadsheets, there should be few surprises at the end of the budget year. In fact, if the manager sees that there will likely be a problem keeping the library budget in balance for the year, he should inform someone higher up as soon as possible. There have been numerous occasions of library managers who did not realize they had a budget shortfall until the final report came out of the parent organization budget office. This creates an impression one certainly does not want to have conveyed. On the other hand, if the manager identifies a shortfall she is not otherwise able to cover from other budget lines, alerting the provost, academic vice president, or city manager in advance can be a positive step. If the manager is able to explain the shortfall in a reasonable manner, it is likely that because of the advance notice, these people can adjust their much larger budgets in such a way as to use funds from another budget to assist the library in covering the shortfall.

What constitutes a shortfall? Every situation is different. In some small organizations, $100 may be a serious shortfall. In large organizations that are overly focused on budget, any shortfall is a serious matter. There are a few libraries in which the manager devotes most of his time and energies during the last weeks of the budget year to ensuring that the budget will be spent down to within $1.00 of the amount allocated. This has been known to occur even in libraries with budgets greatly exceeding one million dollars. Typically, on a one to three million dollar budget, the manager should expect to bring the budget at a few thousand dollars over or under the allocated amount. It would raise questions about the manager's ability if a budget of this size were over- or underspent by twenty thousand—particularly if the manager were not aware of that type of variance until the final budget report came out. But two, three, four, five thousand dollars over or under may not likely be cause for concern.

The library manager should work to ensure that the library follows the best purchasing and accounting procedures. Working to develop good oversight of the systems pays handsome dividends in terms of the library's efficiency and management as well as its image.

Accountability

Shortly after the conclusion of a budget cycle, the parent organization will issue a final accounting statement of library expenditures against budget allocations. All invoices from the previous budget cycle should have cleared by this time and, if library procedures are adequate, this accounting should show that all funds have been expended fully and in the appropriate manner. If the library has followed through on its procedures and has followed good budget management practices, there should be no surprises at this time.

Unfortunately, some library managers have difficulty with budget management. In order to avoid problems at the end of the budget cycle, they purposely underspend significantly in order to ensure that they have not overspent. Some managers also labor under the false notion that a sign of good budget management is to turn funds back in each year. Parent organizations or boards rarely object to an agency underspending its budget. Depending on the culture of the parent organization, the administration may even count on some units underspending in order to balance the parent budget. A number of library directors have reported that upon taking a new directorship, they have discovered that their predecessor routinely underspent the budget and that the parent organization had begun to count on this in order to balance its own budget! This type of situation can place a new manager in a difficult position.

While underspending a budget is a fairly common phenomenon in libraries, there are some managers who consistently overspend. Again, the local culture will determine if this is acceptable, but it is less likely to be acceptable than underspending. Overspending or in some other way mismanaging the budget often leads to other problems as well. If the library manager is having some difficulty communicating with the board or faculty, a serious budget problem at this time often provides the perfect excuse for the manager's termination!

Managing the budget so as to match expenditures closely with allocations is in many ways a unique feature of nonprofit institutions. Managers who achieve this balance gain greater respect than their colleagues who either over- or underspend. This respect often translates into greater support for the mission and goals of the information place because it is one of the clearest indications of good management practices.

Achieving Maximum Benefit from a Budget

What should a budget do for a manager? What information should it give the manager? It should guide but not control her in the accomplishment of the library's mission. It also should help her to know where she is or is not spending funds. While it is conceivable that she could operate within a single line budget, this would not give any information on how funds are spent. Rarely do managers develop budgets with too many lines of detail. In setting up the library accounting system, the manager typically has a great deal of flexibility. For example, the parent organization may assign all book funds in one budget line. The library manager may choose to use the library's accounting system to allocate expenditure of these funds among a variety of constituencies. A public library may divide them between reference, children's, fiction, and nonfiction. A college or university library may divide them among the disciplines taught, e.g., English, psychology, philosophy, and history.

The library manager has much less flexibility in working with the system used by the parent organization. That system is set up to work across a number of diverse departments. Thus it cannot be tailored specifically to the library's needs. However, the university or city hall financial affairs office is usually willing to work with the library manager to create a new line, which meets a well-documented need, e.g., electronic materials, within their accounting system.

In setting up the library accounting system or in modifying it, consider the requirements of the parent organization. Consider the statistical reports submitted to such agencies as the state library, the U.S. Department of Education, and accrediting agencies. Accrediting agencies frequently ask for information on what percent of book funds were spent in a particular discipline during the last three years. The accounting system should be able to provide this information quickly and accurately. Consider reports that should be made to the library board or to the faculty assembly library committee. There are usually follow-up questions whenever reports of this type are presented and the manager should be well prepared with information, whether with information from the library's accounting system or with justification for how certain expenditures support the mission.

A good budget manager will respond to needs as they arise and find ways to meet the need, even if the budget does not specifically address the need. The budget projects the amounts that need to be expended in particular areas during the budget period. But unexpected things happen and the budget manager should be able to use the budget to respond adequately to the unexpected. Interlibrary loan expenses may increase dramatically and unexpectedly, a database vendor may increase prices in mid-year, a piece of expensive equipment may break and need to be replaced immediately, or a heating bill may skyrocket because of a natural gas price increase. It is often possible to use funds from other budget lines to cover unexpected increases such as these. Sometimes it is not possible. In that case, the parent organization should be informed as soon as this is discovered.

The following situation describes an event that may occur and be overlooked easily because it does not appear to have the immediacy of the situations mentioned above. Your library is located in a transition neighborhood. Shortly after the beginning of the current budget year, it comes to your attention that over the past several months a significant and new migrant population has moved into the area and that you have few materials to support their transition into modern American culture. This is obviously a budgeting issue as well as a political one. How do you respond? You could certainly include support for programming and materials in your budget proposal for the next budget cycle. But reviewing your current budget and programs for possible immediate response may be your best strategy. Creating programs, buying new materials, reallocating staff resources, developing outreach and partnerships with other social organizations early in the game may be critical in ensuring that the library is a player in responding to this new clientele. Having taken action at the time it is needed may be a factor in the budget hearing as well. Taking immediate action will have provided some indication of what can be accomplished and also creates the impression that the library is an action-oriented place.

References

Magazines for Libraries. 11th ed. 2001. New York: Bowker.

Stueart, Robert D., and John Taylor Eastlick. 1981. *Library management, 2nd edition.* Littleton, CO: Libraries Unlimited.

Stueart, Robert D., and Barbara B. Moran. 1998. *Library and information center management.* Englewood, CO: Libraries Unlimited.

Wasserman, Paul, and Mary Lee Bundy. 1968. *Reader in library administration.* Washington, DC: Microcard Editions.

Chapter 8

Learning about Management from Experience

Ways We Can Learn

We can learn a little about management from reading articles and books. Good teachers can teach us about management, and we can learn quite a bit from shadowing able managers on the job. Mentors can help. We can learn by doing, also. Until such time as we can shadow or be mentored, however, we have to rely upon what we can learn from texts, teachers, and each other.

Lectures and articles can appeal to our senses of sight and hearing and can contribute to our learning, but there is another kind of teaching device that appeals to additional senses—the sense of touch, and the sense of feeling or knowing. That other device is the experiential learning episode, the one which provides experience in a relatively safe environment where the rewards of success are modest but real, and the penalties for failure are minimal and phantom.

The most important job of the manager is to decide and then deploy. Experiential exercises give the manager-to-be a chance to ponder an issue, make a decision, and subject that decision to scrutiny—even vigorous disapproval—without risk. The budget episode in this chapter provides participants the opportunity to consider intelligence, make decisions, and then defend and/or adjust those decisions based upon what they learn from subjecting their choices to the marketplace of ideas. This kind of learning can take a firm hold in the participant's arsenal of responses. It is anchored there more securely because it results from personal experience and is based upon appeals to seeing, speaking, hearing, touching, and feeling. One of these exercises even appeals to the sense of taste. Serve pizza while doing them and they both can.

Each of the exercises presented here has been employed on numerous occasions as a learning device, and each has been honed as a result of critiques issued by participants. Personal observation, augmented by reports from the field years after people have done these, teaches us that they work as learning tools.

A Message to Facilitators

We issue a major caveat at this point. In order for these exercises to succeed, facilitators, teachers, or in-service educators *must*

- Clearly brief the participants
- Ably guide the processes and act as referees
- Artfully and compassionately *debrief* each one, especially the budget exercise

Briefing

Brief the participants well. Tell them what the exercise is about and what it is supposed to accomplish. Tell them that when each exercise is completed, everyone will have an opportunity to comment on the procedure. When scheduling an event, make sure that there is ample time for thorough debriefing. In fact, draw up a debriefing plan.

Guiding the process requires leaders to focus upon the issue, the welfare of participants, the process involved in completing the exercise, and the clock. In the case of the budget exercise, the Director shares some of that responsibility. In every instance, the leader of these sessions must be prepared to take questions and to respond decisively. For example, to the question, "What color are the walls in the room where the server is?" the answer may be,

- Industrial gray, if they are.
- Industrial gray, if it does not matter.
- What color would you like?

The facilitator who responds, "Gee, I don't know. The exercise does not say. I hope that is not important," torpedoes the exercise and erodes participants' confidence by inviting them to complain, "We do not have enough information."

Debriefing

Debriefing is crucial. For some participants this will be the first time they ever have led a meeting. For others it will be the first time they have ever subjected a work decision to the scrutiny of peers. For a few it will be the first time they have ever had their work decisions or opinions criticized in public. Some never before have made a managerial decision. Debriefers must provide these people the opportunity to express whatever thoughts and feelings they may have, including that they disliked what they just did. The debriefer who does not probe for impressions and feelings runs the risk of allowing participants with deeply felt personal issues to leave the exercise with exposed psychic bruises. One need not be a psychologist to conduct a solid debriefing, but one must prepare and one must watch and note. A hurried or sloppy debriefing can reinforce some negative learning. Specific debriefing instructions accompany the budget exercise presented in this chapter.

The Leader's Job and the Gatekeeper's Job

The leader of any group with an assigned task has to make sure that

- The group understands its charge
- The group shares understandings of key terms and concepts
- The group stays focused upon its mission
- He or she periodically summarizes and explains the group's progress toward its goal
- He or she obtains closure, completes the task, and adjourns the meeting

A leader who is doing this job well will probably direct full attention to the task at hand and may be so focused upon it that the important gatekeeping function goes unattended. In group settings, gatekeepers have two essential duties:

1. Make sure that every participant has a chance to voice an opinion
2. Make sure that the group dynamic does not permit a few to monopolize air time

The leader who attempts to do the gatekeeping as well as the leading will probably shortchange one or both. We recommend that the leader appoint a gatekeeper, who then does the job by issuing questions like this: "Fred, we have heard from everybody else about the wall color. Do you have an opinion?" This gives Fred an opportunity to respond. He may be shy or may not have said anything because he felt prevented or discouraged by the group dynamic. He may or may not have an opinion. Whatever the case, the gatekeeper gives Fred his chance, and Fred exercises his option. He is included. Shy people may be very bright and have lots to contribute, and a group decision may suffer if members feel prevented from chiming in. Gatekeepers watch and listen, and gatekeepers offer invitations.

If, during the watching and listening, the gatekeeper notices that a few participants have taken most of the airtime, he or she should interject something like this: "Thanks, Fred and Mary, for your very useful comments. Who else would like to chime in? Chuck? Pamela?"

Chuck and Pamela may have deferred to Fred and Mary because Fred and Mary are the only ones in the group who have informed opinions to contribute. The gatekeeper's job is not to force everyone to participate equally but to make it possible for all who may want to contribute to do so.

There is divided opinion about the participation issue. Some believe that knowledgeable participants have an obligation to contribute, especially when asked. They view the decision not to contribute, to withhold useful information in a group discussion, as an act of aggression. Other observers argue a personal freedom position and claim that people should not be forced to participate. We side with the former position. We think that people who buy into participative method obligate themselves to contribute. We question whether participants have the right to withhold intelligence that could contribute to a sound decision. Gatekeepers do not interfere with rights; gatekeepers help create opportunities for all who wish to contribute. They issue invitations, not orders.

Leader and gatekeeper cooperate to maintain a focus upon the task and to ensure that all participants have an opportunity to contribute. They work as a team to run a meeting.

Preparing a Group for Experiential Learning

Much of what we know about experiential learning we have gathered from the work of Martha Jane Zachert (1975), special librarian, master trainer, and distinguished professor at several major universities.

In our own training sessions we borrow liberally from her considerable expertise.

Any group, but especially one with no or limited experience with experiential or simulated learning, requires some setup. A leader/facilitator has to put them at ease, make them comfortable, and convince them to invest some energy in the exercise to follow. The facilitator explains that simulated scenarios give people some experience with sticky issues. Simulated events take place within friendly, nurturing confines. Reality is suspended long enough to give participants risk-free opportunities actually to take risks and to see how they respond to the challenge. This gives them a taste of what it is like to cope with thorny issues, and it gives them a glimpse of how they behave when doing so. This is valuable learning.

The facilitator points out that the record shows that when people believe something is important, then that "something" takes on significance. People's perceptions become their realities, temporarily, and they benefit from the simulated reality. So if participants believe, temporarily, that choosing a wall color is the most important decision that they will make this week, then they will benefit from an exchange of opinion about that color choice. They may get a valuable opportunity to observe themselves in a conflict situation, one in which they take a stand for or against a proposal. Then when the exercise is over, and the facilitator explains this clearly during the briefing, they exit the simulated reality and come back to their chairs in the room. They talk about what they have just experienced and the decisions they made. They get a chance to tell how their actions and the actions of others made them feel.

A facilitator may then prepare the group by leading them in an exercise designed to demonstrate to all participants that they have a capacity to benefit from experiential learning sessions. We thank an anonymous author/trainer for this lemon.

Exercise 1: The Lemon

Briefing by the Leader

Group, the exercise we will do now is designed to indicate to us the power of the simulated experience. I think you will enjoy this. We are going on a very restful vacation. Please get comfortable. Observe the room around you and the people in it. Relax. When you feel okay about it, please close your eyes and just concentrate on your breathing. Enjoy a few deep breaths. Put aside today's schedule; our work will wait for us. Eyes closed? (When all eyes are closed) Okay, I am going to begin.

The Exercise

The leader tells the following story:

To escape some horribly inclement weather, you have rented a cottage in Florida for a week. On your first morning in your lovely cottage, you brew some coffee, retrieve the Sunday paper from the front porch, and retire to the back porch to sip the fresh brew, enjoy an orchard view, and read the paper.

The sun has already risen and it is quickly burning off a subtle hint of chill in the morning air. You remind yourself that you left two feet of snow back home to enter this paradise. Just as you prepare to sit in a comfortable stuffed porch chair, you notice something glistening on the lawn near the porch steps. At first you think it is a grapefruit, but you quickly realize it is a superlarge lemon, the largest lemon you have ever seen. The dewdrops on its rich skin glisten like crystals. You descend the steps and reach for the magnificent fruit. In your hand it feels cool. The morning dew mixes with the texture of the bright yellow skin and you think of cool lemonade and your mother's lemon meringue pie. You can smell the lemon and feel its considerable weight. You are sure this is the juiciest lemon ever, and you think of even more delicious uses for it. You cannot resist this gorgeous lemon's appeal, so you retrieve the sharp knife you used to snap the cord around the newspaper and very carefully slice the lemon in two. You were right! Rich juice literally pours from each half and the aroma is marvelous, the essences of delicious springtime. Nearly intoxicated with citrus goodness, you raise a lemon half to your lips and take a huge bite from the gorgeous fruit. What a lemon!

The leader should give the group ten seconds or so to react to this and then ask them to open their eyes and come back from Florida to the room.

Debriefing

The group has had their eyes closed, but the facilitator's eyes were wide open throughout this exercise. Here is some of what the facilitator saw when the group members bit the lemon:

- Frowning
- Scrunched-up faces
- Faces about to turn inside out
- Determination
- Delight

- Cheeks compressed
- Lips puckered
- Laughter
- Disassociated expressions
- Apparent indifference

Based upon this intelligence, the facilitator begins the debriefing.

Leader: Let me tell you what I just saw. When I told you to bite the lemon, I saw some frowning. What was that about? (The frowners will report that they anticipated sour trouble when they bit.)

Leader: I also saw some scrunched-up faces, some puckered lips, and some real contortions. Tell me about that. (The scrunchers, compressors, puckerers, and facial contortionists will report, probably with lots of laughter, that the damn lemon was sour.)

Leader: Sam, I saw real determination on your face. What was going on? (Sam may insist, "I was not going to bite that lemon! The hell with the exercise!") This identifies Sam as an excellent candidate for experiential learning. He can imagine!

The facilitator saw some passive indifference, too, which he or she may choose to ignore. If the facilitator asks about the pleased or delighted expressions, some may respond that they *like* lemons!

Leader: All of you please hold out your hands. I do not see a single lemon, yet I saw frowners, scrunchers, compressors, laughers, and refusenicks who steadfastly elected not to bite a lemon that was **not** there. The happy news is that for every one of you who salivated just a bit, or experienced a sour reaction, or maybe even enjoyed the bite, the message is you can learn and gain experience from simulated events. You can create a reality, learn from dealing with the creation, and then come back to a *real* reality, having learned something about you. You are excellent candidates for simulated management episodes because you can suspend disbelief long enough to benefit from an invented scenario.

Those of us who bit and felt nothing, we can still learn from observing ourselves and others in simulated situations. If our wiring hooks us up to learn in different ways, so be it.

Give everyone an opportunity to comment on any aspect of this exercise. Respect the people who may think it was silly. Explain without condescension that it takes a certain childlike abandon to participate, and our processing adult ego states may prevent us from abandoning reality or pretending. Make sure to reinforce the good news that even the slightest reaction to the lemon is a favorable forecast about our ability to learn from simulated experiences.

The Budget Exercise

This is an experiential exercise that involves role-play. It includes a director and several other managers and employees of a public library. The director has called the group together to achieve a 10 percent reduction of a bare-bones budget submitted only last week to council. Each of the players has a personal stake in the budget, and each had participated in constructing the previous budget that the funders have struck down. The director has one hour to achieve this cut democratically or make a personal decision to cut if the group cannot.

The payoff in learning can be great if the players understand what role-playing requires of them. The leader will have to sell the idea. Players adopting assigned roles take on the opinions and characteristics assigned to them. They must stay in character. If their assigned position is to support the color blue, then that is what they do. They speak for blue and against red or any competing color. Even if they personally abhor blue, staying in character requires that they speak for it.

If the player speaks for blue, but prefaces these remarks with a disclaimer such as "I hate blue but this role says I must support it, so I vote for blue," he or she departs from character and disrupts the mood of the exercise. The leader must reassure everyone that during debriefing all players will have a chance to say anything they wish. If during role-play someone had to act out a rude behavior, during debriefing that player may explain that at her job she would never behave like that.

Players who take the assigned stands will quickly discover that their actions and statements trigger responses from others. That is another reason for staying in character and executing one's role. The pieces fit, and they form a picture. The payoff for the player who is invested, who buys into the belief that this is a very important decision opportunity, is a wonderful opportunity to observe

- How one acts when one has to make a decision based on limited information
- How one reacts to deciding under the gun when time is short
- What it feels like to give in
- What it feels like to win
- What it feels like to lose
- How to, and maybe how not to, run a meeting
- How to maintain focus
- How to deal with disagreement, even personal remarks

Provided everyone remains in character and executes his role, and provided the debriefer skillfully helps the group process the information about the exercise exchanged during debriefing, this can be a great lesson in managerial process.

This exercise takes about two hours: fifteen minutes to introduce, fifteen minutes to allow each player to commune with the assigned role, one hour to execute, and thirty minutes to debrief.

The essential participants/characters are: The leader who introduces the process, consults with the director, and referees the exercise.

1.	Director	10.	*President of Friends
2.	Assistant director	11.	Maintenance supervisor
3.	Young adult librarian	12.	Public relations librarian
4.	Public services librarian	13.	Children's librarian
5.	Adult services librarian	14.	Systems librarian
6.	Volunteer coordinator	15.	Technical services head
7.	Stack supervisor	16.	Branch librarian
8.	Extension/bookmobile librarian	17.	Periodicals clerk
		18.	Business officer
9.	Technical services clerk	19.	*Reporter

The roles of *reporter and *business officer may be dropped to achieve a smaller group, and the assistant director can make the announcement from the *Friends if the leader decides that sixteen is an optimum number. In twelve years of leading and revising this exercise, we have never found the large size of this group to impede its progress.

We recommend that the leader prepare title placards to display with each player so all may know which departments are espousing which positions.

Debriefers sometimes learn that some players would have preferred to have had more time to review and get comfortable with their roles—that having only fifteen minutes to get in character was not enough time. Leaders may opt to make getting into character an overnight assignment. We prefer the shorter period.

We encourage leaders to instruct players to read only their roles in advance of the exercise, but we assure them that with one exception foreknowledge does not contaminate the exercise. That one exception is the technical service head's note to the director. The pace of this exercise is so quick that peeking at another's role hardly gives one an unfair advantage or interferes with spontaneity.

If all the players are working with this text, then the temptation to read other roles may entice some to do so. Some leaders may choose to prepare single role sheets for distribution to individual players, along with budget and organizational information. Readers will note that general instructions to players are repeated with each role description. The indented portions of the following briefing indicate the text of the leader's instructions.

Briefing by the Leader

> Group, today we are going to do a budget exercise in which we have to make some important decisions. In a few moments I will distribute some packets on which you will find your name and your role or job title for the exercise. In the packets you will find sheets explaining your character's positions on budgetary issues and also indicating some specific actions for you to take or points to raise. You will see an organization chart, a "Things You Need to Know" chart, and a copy of the budget.

> If you will invest yourselves in this project, you will have a wonderful opportunity to observe yourself in a decision-making activity and you may get to see and feel how you react when you speak up for your point of view or defend an idea that is dear to you.

> Please stay in character once the exercise starts. This means that you must stay true to your assigned role. If your assigned role is to promote pasta, then do so, even if you do not care for pasta. Your support of pasta is required to make the exercise work. When we are finished, I will give you the opportunity to inform the group that you really do not care for pasta and would never support it so adamantly.

The Magic If

Actors refer to this act of staying true to one's role as achieving the magic if. If you can

- Understand and need what your character wants,
- Know what action will accomplish your objective, and
- Do that action,

then you can achieve what the great teacher Stanislavski called the magic if; you can do the role (Benedetti 1999). In this budget exercise, the understanding and the knowing are provided for you. Let your character do what it takes to make happen what you want to happen.

Here are your packets. Take the next fifteen minutes to read your packets and get familiar with your role. Do this privately, perhaps off somewhere, and return in fifteen minutes.

Spend some of these fifteen minutes with your director and assistant director, for these are the players who will run the meeting and they may require some extra assistance and reassurance from you. It might be a good idea to ask the director to assign gatekeeping duties to the assistant director, who may also post and tally the group's progress toward its goal—paring nearly $93,000 from the budget.

When the group returns, ask for questions, and answer any which do not compromise the exercise. Inform the group that you will act as referee, should the occasion call for a ruling.

Ask players to post their job titles in full view of all participants.

Tell them that once they begin, they stay in character for the hour.

Hand the session over to the director.

Start the Exercise

The director will explain what has happened—that the council has ordered a budget reduction. That is the purpose of this meeting. The director has some choices to make with respect to process, but very soon the exercise dynamic will take over and things will start to happen.

The leader will watch and listen. If the assistant director does the assigned task, the leader will not have to interject. If no progress has been made and the hour draws late, the leader may observe, "We have thirty minutes left and we have only cut $9,000 of the nearly $93,000 we have to find."

The leader may have to rule in the case of an information request for which the exercise does not provide a response.

The leader calls a halt upon completion of the exercise, or one hour, whichever comes first and will acknowledge that the group has done its job or that the director is now faced with making a decision. If the group has found $50,000, ask the director what cuts he or she will make to reach the required 10 percent. This may take a few minutes.

Director

> For this experiential exercise to work, each of us will have to do two things:
> 1.   Remain in character.
> 2.   Execute his/her role; do what the role indicates.
> This exercise will give us a chance to test our ability to make contributions to a group process. It can also help us deal with disagreement and with the feelings that sometimes accompany a failed or ignored suggestion. Other participants will play off our suggestions; some will respond directly to a position we take, so it is extremely important that we take and communicate the assigned points of view.
> When we debrief, we will tell how this exercise affected us—how it made us feel.

The Assigned Points of View and Attitude: What the Director Must Communicate

- I have just come from an emergency meeting of County Council where all department heads were told to shave 10 percent from their budgets by tomorrow.
- This comes to us just as we are about to begin our new budget year at the end of next month.
- I am calling this meeting to cut the budget by 10 percent.
- I would like to do this democratically, but if the staff cannot agree, I will decide.
- I want their input. I would prefer not to make these decisions myself.
- I must lead this discussion. I have one hour.

I Must Find a Way to Make This as Visual as Possible so Staff Can Follow—See Progress.

- I prefer to do this by priority, not across the board.
- Last year the staff cooperated in preparing this budget; now it must be cut today.
- Our major expenditure is personnel. There the greatest economy can be achieved with the simplest moves.
- We have to trim $93,400. Let's find it.
- Personnel, Xerox, new system, travel, books, periodicals, salaries, postage, dedicated items for branches, and PR are all candidates.

I Know That the Public Relations Librarian Is the Cousin of the Chair of the County Council

- I know my main job is to keep the group focused upon the cutting. I do not have the option of dragging this out. Keep looking for the dollars. Suggest compromise. Soothe feelings. But remember, I do not have the option of not doing this. Either the staff helps or I do it. I cannot tell the Council: "We couldn't agree."

Additional Information for Director

- Small cuts in personnel will achieve substantial savings.
- I know that some staff may resign if their areas are cut or if promised allotments are cut.
- I need the new copier. And I need one new public access PC. That's what the $3,500 capital expenditure item is all about. Anyhow, cutting that would be nickel and dime activity. We need to cut $93,400, not $3,500.
- There are three support people at this meeting, LTAs from circulation, reference, and technical services.

Some Things the Director Needs to Know:

- One technical services clerk is a niece of a councilman.
- You may cut 10 percent across the board, but you do not want to.
- You favor participation; the first budget was a group effort.
- The 10 percent cut is for all public agencies in the county, so this is an economy measure that affects everyone, not just the library.

- You do not have the option of delaying; you have one hour. You may ask the assistant director to do the boardwork and chart our progress toward our goal.
- There is professional/paraprofessional unrest; *paraprofessional rage*, some have called it.
- Periodicals clerk, stack supervisor, and one technical services paraprofessional are in attendance by your invitation; they are all clerks.
- PR librarian is half time.
- Technical services has a head (librarian) and three clerks, one of whom is here.
- Books arrive preprocessed with pockets, cards, dust jackets, labels: dollar cost is one dollar a pop.
- The new $55,000 system will provide access to the cataloging, transfer data to the electronic catalog, and provide processing labels—do some of the processing work in other words—save the one dollar a pop. It will also streamline circulation. We may also plug in our unreliable security system.
- The student liaison is a kid who regularly visits key teachers and finds out about upcoming assignments, and reports them to the public library.
- All the professionals have $1,000 travel/staff development allotment.

Director (You)	$1,000
Technical services	$1,000
Public services	$1,000
Adult services	$1,000
Public relations	$ 500
Branch (3)	$3,000
Extension/BMB	$1,000
Children's	$1,000
Young adult	$1,000
Assistant director	$1,000
Systems	$1,000

Government Appreciation Day is a day set aside for visitations by city leaders and politicians. Each takes a turn at the circulation desk, reference desk, or at a workstation in technical services. The purpose is two-fold:

1. It provides these city leaders with a view of important library functions and the quickness with which the library responds to customer demand.
2. It gives the customers a chance to see the human side of the community leaders.

Hint: You had better orchestrate this well. You do not want the Chair of County Council to languish for an hour at a very unbusy circulation desk. That would surely backfire.

Assistant Director

> For this experiential exercise to work, each of us will have to do two things:
> 1. Remain in character.
> 2. Execute his/her role; do what the role indicates.
>
> This exercise will give us a chance to test our ability to make contributions to a group process. It can also help us deal with disagreement and with the feelings that some-times accompany a failed or ignored suggestion. Other par-ticipants will play off our suggestions; some will respond directly to a position we take, so it is extremely important that we take and communicate the assigned points of view. When we debrief, we will tell how this exercise affected us—how it made us feel.

The Assigned Points of View and Attitude: What the Assistant Director Must Communicate

- I need to support the director, but I shall be persistent about my main point: We need to cut staff and we should begin with the clerks (LTAs).
- The director must achieve budget reduction and needs help managing the meeting.
- I need to be at the board to display a running account of what expenditures have been cut and what progress has been made toward the goal of a 10 percent reduction.
- I need to watch the time. If slow progress is being made, I must remind the director to speed things up. I will give the director the time check every fifteen minutes.
- While I can make suggestions to the director to help him/her achieve the goal, I must NEVER contradict or disagree with the director's approach.

- From a conversation with the president of the Friends, I learned that she might make an offer at this meeting. I must not anticipate this. When it comes, I will point out that council will not accept a *funny money* budget cut. They will not allow a budget with a pledge. I will tell my director this in private as soon as the Friends offer. I will ask the director to ask the staff to agree to cut $10,000 from the book budget. Then when the pledge is paid, we can restore the book budget. Privately, I will see if the director goes along with this and then get the director to suggest it.
- I wrote the Oral History Grant. This is my project, and I will defend it. It will collect stories from the community's aged population who will take history to the grave unless we capture it. Technical services clerks must go before this project is scrapped. This can't be done with volunteers. I will reject any such suggestion. The grant supports experts, not amateurs. That's the stipulation. Shall we return grant funds?

Young Adult Librarian

> For this experiential exercise to work, each of us will have to do two things:
> 1. Remain in character.
> 2. Execute his/her role; do what the role indicates.
> This exercise will give us a chance to test our ability to make contributions to a group process. It can also help us deal with disagreement and with the feelings that sometimes accompany a failed or ignored suggestion. Other participants will play off our suggestions; some will respond directly to a position we take, so it is extremely important that we take and communicate the assigned points of view.
> When we debrief, we will tell how this exercise affected us—how it made us feel.

The Assigned Points of View and Attitude: What the Young Adult Librarian Must Communicate
- This is the first money that has EVER been earmarked for YA.
- My YA collection has had zero growth in the last eighteen months.
- Any cut would be damaging to any department, but YA cannot stand a cut. We have been so poor for so long.

- What guides and motivates me
  - Righteous commitment to young adult services
  - Love of young adult literature and programming
  - Strong convictions that the library must serve young adults better
- If YA is cut, I might resign. I must hint at this without sounding too threatening.
- I have little respect for the catalogers; why do they need such an expensive system?
- Catalogers have too much staff; why do they need three clerks, especially if the new system is going to cut their time in half. If we get the new system for $55,000, then let's eliminate at least one $15,000 clerk position in technical services.
- How foolish to refuse grant money. Support oral history and adult literacy.

Public Services Librarian

> For this experiential exercise to work, each of us will have to do two things:
> 1. Remain in character.
> 2. Execute his/her role; do what the role indicates.
> This exercise will give us a chance to test our ability to make contributions to a group process. It can also help us deal with disagreement and with the feelings that sometimes accompany a failed or ignored suggestion. Other participants will play off our suggestions; some will respond directly to a position we take, so it is extremely important that we take and communicate the assigned points of view. When we debrief, we will tell how this exercise affected us—how it made us feel.

The Assigned Points of View and Attitude: What the Public Service Librarian Must Communicate

- Circulation is up a whopping 78 percent since September. We need student help, especially the student liaison.
- I do not think we can afford the new system. We can save $55,000 with one stroke of the pen; then we'd only have to find $35,500 more.
- I do not support the young adult librarian:
  - YA is the most underutilized area

YA is the most troublesome literature—always being censored

YAs are the most unappreciative, unruly clients

- If you do not like the student liaison, the student who checks on assignments and reports them to us so we can have advance warning about those assignments, then you help those monsters when fifty of them have to do a report on Hitler.
- Support oral history and adult literacy projects. They are what we are about.
- Ok, no one wants to cut, so let's do it across the board—everybody takes a 10 percent hit.
- I see tangible benefits of the PR program.
- We need a new Xerox, so that $3,500 should not be touched.
- I will support the stack supervisor, especially if the idea of stack maintenance is attacked. I love the order the stacks are in every morning and all that is because the stack supervisor has cleaned up at night.
- I have three clerks in circulation. They are busy all the time.

Adult Services Librarian

> For this experiential exercise to work, each of us will have to do two things:
> 1. Remain in character.
> 2. Execute his/her role; do what the role indicates.
> This exercise will give us a chance to test our ability to make contributions to a group process. It can also help us deal with disagreement and with the feelings that sometimes accompany a failed or ignored suggestion. Other participants will play off our suggestions; some will respond directly to a position we take, so it is extremely important that we take and communicate the assigned points of view.
> When we debrief, we will tell how this exercise affected us—how it made us feel.

The Assigned Points of View and Attitude: What Adult Services Must Communicate

- Let's cut by program, not across the board. We built this budget as a team; let's cut it as a team. Nevertheless, I need every penny of my $5,000.
- Adult programs are successful. Adult literacy is a must. I will

defend my grant. I wrote the $4,000 Adult Literacy Grant. Helping people read is why we exist.

- I support the new system of cataloging, but I oppose spending $1.00 on each new book for processing. Let the LTAs do the pockets, type the cards, and do the labels.
- I also think PR has paid off; look at circulation; it's way up!
- I must question the value of the student liaison. I oppose the concept. Don't let it go. I will claim it mixes mission statements when I am disagreed with. School libraries are school libraries—for students. This is a public library for everybody.
- Let the school librarians handle school assignment needs.
- If people at this meeting want to know what adult programming is, tell them. These programs help our community identify and support us.

Lectures	Computer literacy
Book talks	Play readings
Movies	Tours
Travelogues	Discussion groups

- I think we should cut the number of periodicals we buy. Maybe we don't have to bind them. There's a savings right there!
- Why so many on the maintenance staff. The supervisor makes more than I do and he only went to high school!

Volunteer Coordinator (Preprofessional)

For this experiential exercise to work, each of us will have to do two things:
1. Remain in character.
2. Execute his/her role; do what the role indicates.
This exercise will give us a chance to test our ability to make contributions to a group process. It can also help us deal with disagreement and with the feelings that sometimes accompany a failed or ignored suggestion. Other participants will play off our suggestions; some will respond directly to a position we take, so it is extremely important that we take and communicate the assigned points of view. When we debrief, we will tell how this exercise affected us—how it made us feel.

The Assigned Points of View and Attitude: What the Volunteer Coordinator Must Communicate

- If people start making suggestions for more uses for volunteers, I'll make sure I assert myself. We already have as many volunteers as we can use. We cannot solve every personnel problem we have around here by simply adding volunteers to do it for free.
- Interviewing, selecting, training, and evaluating volunteers is an involved process.
- Especially oppose any suggestion that volunteers do the oral history project.
- I think we should cut in cataloging, especially since the new system will do so much of their work. Why do we need so many clerks in cataloging?
- You know, I have never seen a single adult walk out of one of those adult programs and check a book out. So what, therefore, is the value of adult programming? They come in, they listen to a travel lecture, and they go home. They do not use the library. What's the value?
- Why don't we cut periodicals?
- PR is nice and I am for it, but can we afford it? I think we should vote on eliminating that half-time position. There's $15,000! Plus another $7,000! That's a $22,000 savings.

Stack Supervisor

> For this experiential exercise to work, each of us will have to do two things:
> 1.   Remain in character.
> 2.   Execute his/her role; do what the role indicates.
> This exercise will give us a chance to test our ability to make contributions to a group process. It can also help us deal with disagreement and with the feelings that sometimes accompany a failed or ignored suggestion. Other participants will play off our suggestions; some will respond directly to a position we take, so it is extremely important that we take and communicate the assigned points of view. When we debrief, we will tell how this exercise affected us—how it made us feel.

The Assigned Points of View and Attitude: What the Stack Supervisor Must Communicate

- It is not my place to say, maybe, but an across-the-board cut is not good.

- Two thousand dollars is finally in the budget to continue the evening assistant stack supervisor! Until recently there was no evening stack supervision from 5:30 on. This is a very busy time and the library is always in disarray afterward.

- Before we tried the evening supervisor, I had to spend my whole morning cleaning up from the previous evening's mess. Without this evening maintenance, order in the stacks goes to hell in a handbasket.

- With the new part-time assistant, there will be order every morning.

- When we get this permanent part-time assistant, we can
    Keep all the shelves in order
    Help with inventory
    Give better service to clients in the morning
    Assist reference and circulation with projects

- Cataloging has three clerks. Why? Baker and Taylor does their work.

- Why hire expensive professionals to do oral history? Get volunteers!

- If the hour grows late (half of the time is gone), and we seem to be getting nowhere, give in: surrender on the $2,000 evening person.

Extension/ Book Mobile Librarian

For this experiential exercise to work, each of us will have to do two things:
1. Remain in character.
2. Execute his/her role; do what the role indicates.
This exercise will give us a chance to test our ability to make contributions to a group process. It can also help us deal with disagreement and with the feelings that sometimes accompany a failed or ignored suggestion. Other participants will play off our suggestions; some will respond directly to a position we take, so it is extremely important that we take and communicate the assigned points of view. When we debrief, we will tell how this exercise affected us—how it made us feel.

The Assigned Points of View and Attitude: What the Extension/Bookmobile Librarian Must Communicate

- No cuts! None. Across the board or otherwise.
- We have $6,000 earmarked. That is
    > $2,000 for a reconditioned generator so we can air-condition the bookmobile;
    > $1,000 for needed lightweight shelving
    > $3,000 for paperbacks
- We have to have the new generator and we have to have the new shelving so we can double what we carry. That $3,000 for new paperbacks is so people will quit their constant complaining that we have nothing new and merely recycle old books.
- I put a lot of work in getting this to be a bare bones request. We cannot do with a penny less.
- I have been here for six years; this is the first time we ever got $3,000 for books.
- What in the heck is the big deal about messy stacks in the morning? Why does the stack supervisor need a special assistant just so there is no work to do in the morning? What do we have three stack clerks for if not to keep the stacks in order? I oppose the special stack maintenance student.
- PR is a joke. This is a library, not a movie studio. What do we need PR for. We spend $22,000 on salary and supplies for PR! For what? $22,000. That is almost a fourth of what we must cut. Cut it!
- Oppose oral history project as an expensive frill.

Technical Service Clerk— in attendance at this meeting

> For this experiential exercise to work, each of us will have to do two things:
> 1. Remain in character.
> 2. Execute his/her role; do what the role indicates.
>
> This exercise will give us a chance to test our ability to make contributions to a group process. It can also help us deal with disagreement and with the feelings that sometimes accompany a failed or ignored suggestion. Other participants will play off our suggestions; some will respond directly to a position we take, so it is extremely important that we take and communicate the assigned points of view. When we debrief, we will tell how this exercise affected us—how it made us feel.

The Assigned Points of View and Attitude: What the Technical Services Clerk Must Communicate

- I must say this without malice or resentment, but with confidence and a certain amount of pride. "We clerks run the everyday functions of the technical services department, plus lots of things you probably do not think about much of the time. In fact, my two colleagues are helping out right now in circulation and reference."
- We search and verify every single book order. We will continue to do this important collection development task even with the new system. We fix all the bugs and garbled citations before we order things and duplicate orders are now at .01 percent.
- We check every ordered item to make sure that we get what we order.
- We order preprocessed books, sure, but we still check every one for accuracy and placement of pocket and date slip.
- We verify call numbers and subject headings. We send this information to system.
- We bar code.
- We deliver stock in good shape to the circulation people for shelving.
- All our work is compartmentalized with each of the three technical services clerks having specific, compartmentalized responsibilities for fiction, nonfiction, and children's books.
- We work hard all day, every day.

*President of Friends

> For this experiential exercise to work, each of us will have to do two things:
> 1. Remain in character.
> 2. Execute his/her role; do what the role indicates.
> This exercise will give us a chance to test our ability to make contributions to a group process. It can also help us deal with disagreement and with the feelings that sometimes accompany a failed or ignored suggestion. Other participants will play off our suggestions; some will respond directly to a position we take, so it is extremely important that we take and communicate the assigned points of view. When we debrief, we will tell how this exercise affected us—how it made us feel.

The Assigned Points of View and Attitude: What the Friends Must Communicate

- I am at this meeting primarily as an observer.
- The director has invited me.
- One-half hour into the meeting, I will raise my hand and ask to speak on behalf of the Friends. I will say, "We in the Friends have been happy to support the library in the past. I propose that we have a fundraiser in July during tourist season. I can offer $10,000 from the Friends. Whatever we do not make on the fundraiser we will supply from Friends' funds. Currently our balance is $8,500, so this will be no problem."
- I will tell them that we will get the money to the library by August 15 at the latest.

Maintenance Supervisor

> For this experiential exercise to work, each of us will have to do two things:
> 1. Remain in character.
> 2. Execute his/her role; do what the role indicates.
> This exercise will give us a chance to test our ability to make contributions to a group process. It can also help us deal with disagreement and with the feelings that sometimes accompany a failed or ignored suggestion. Other participants will play off our suggestions; some will respond directly to a position we take, so it is extremely important that we take and communicate the assigned points of view. When we debrief, we will tell how this exercise affected us—how it made us feel.

The Assigned Points of View and Attitude: What the Maintenance Supervisor Must Communicate

- I must be prepared to hear maintenance functions questioned.
- I must react negatively to criticism and condescendingly to people who obviously have a limited view of what my crew and I provide in the way of services.
- I have a maintenance contract with the public library for $75,000.

My salary	$38,000
Salary for one full-time assistant	$15,000
Salaries for two part-time assistants @ $5,000 ea.	$10,000

Repair fund	$ 7,000
Supplies	$ 5,000

- I am on call around the clock.
- My assistant is a Tech grad in building maintenance.
- My two part-time assistants are building maintenance students at Tech.
- I serve the whole system, not just the main branch.
- I put in fifty hours a week in a "slow" week.
- I manage the repair fund granted by the director for my discretionary use.

> Toilets, furnace, air-conditioners are always in need of repair.
> Floors need waxing and buffing regularly.
> Rugs need shampooing and vacuuming constantly.
> Windows are cleaned biweekly.
> Trash needs to be emptied.
> Boxes need to be delivered.
> Bindery books need to be boxed.
> Bulbs need to be changed.
> Walls need to be washed down.
> Grass needs to be mowed.
> Snow needs to be shoveled.
> Vehicles (bookmobile) need to be washed.

- My crew and I are busy all the time!
- Cut maintenance and you cut service. If you cut us, what do you want to go? You cut us, and I have to let someone go. What do you want to do without?

Public Relations Librarian

> For this experiential exercise to work, each of us will have to do two things:
> 1.   Remain in character.
> 2.   Execute his/her role; do what the role indicates.
> This exercise will give us a chance to test our ability to make contributions to a group process. It can also help us deal with disagreement and with the feelings that sometimes accompany a failed or ignored suggestion. Other participants will play off our suggestions; some will respond directly to a position we take, so it is extremely important that we take and communicate the assigned points of view.
> When we debrief, we will tell how this exercise affected us—how it made us feel.

The Assigned Points of View and Attitude: What the Public Relations Librarian Must Communicate

- My $7,000 budget is bare bones; I need every penny. Any cut would destroy it.
- I need to keep our community informed about our fine library.
- Since launching our PR program last July
    Circulation has increased dramatically
    Cordial relationships have been developed with county council
    We did Government Appreciation Day and several council persons came.
- Last year we had only 20 percent of our population registered. I now have 30 percent of our community registered. I need to continue my registration drive.
- I have to get the message about our mission and role to the community.
- Support a cut in the periodicals budget.
- Volunteer my portion of the travel fund.
- Why so many clerks in technical services/cataloging? We pay Baker and Taylor $1.00 per book for preprocessing. Why can't technical service clerks do this? Think of how much we could save!
- Must we buy a NEW Xerox machine? How about a re-conditioned one?
- Support adult literacy and oral history projects.

Children's Librarian

> For this experiential exercise to work, each of us will have to do two things:
> 1. Remain in character.
> 2. Execute his/her role; do what the role indicates.
>
> This exercise will give us a chance to test our ability to make contributions to a group process. It can also help us deal with disagreement and with the feelings that sometimes accompany a failed or ignored suggestion. Other participants will play off our suggestions; some will respond directly to a position we take, so it is extremely important that we take and communicate the assigned points of view. When we debrief, we will tell how this exercise affected us—how it made us feel.

The Assigned Points of View and Attitude: What the Children's Librarian Must Communicate

- I will resist any cut in the $5,000 earmarked for children.
- Otherwise, I will favor an across-the-board cut as the only fair way. I will tell people this—an across-the-board cut is fair.
- If pushed, I will accept a 10 percent cut in children's allotment.
- I will offer this, be the first to give in. I'll take a 10 percent hit.
- I will support the YA librarian; I feel a kinship with the YA librarian.
- I will support the student liaison the instant it is attacked. I will be vocal. This is too important a job to cut or do without. The student liaison is the kid who checks with local teachers and reports to the library about major assignments that are coming up. This way the public library can know in advance about demands for scarce items. The library can gear up, load up to handle the demand. Formerly, the first few students depleted scarce assignment-related materials.
- Our entire book budget is $100,000. We pay the janitors $75,000, almost as much as we spend on books. What is wrong with this picture? What do we get for that $75,000. Good heavens! Couldn't we get volunteers to scrub floors and change bulbs. I say cut maintenance and train more volunteers.
- I will question the value of PR. Why do we have this?
- I will question the value of adult services programming. So we have lectures and travel movie programs. Do these ever have any impact on circulation? I doubt it. And what about in reference? Any activity there as a result of adult programming? I doubt it!
- Has anyone ever thought about how much money we could save if we processed our own books instead of paying $1.00 a pop? What do we have all those clerks in cataloging for if we are paying Baker and Taylor to do our cataloging clerks' work?
- My two clerks and I keep the department open for all its scheduled hours. If we cut personnel, we must cut hours. (I won't say this unless my staff is threatened.)
- Oral history and adult literacy are frills. Cutting them gives us about 30 percent of our required cut. At least eliminate the adult literacy program. It is nice but not essential.

Systems Librarian

> For this experiential exercise to work, each of us will have to do two things:
> 1. Remain in character.
> 2. Execute his/her role; do what the role indicates.
> This exercise will give us a chance to test our ability to make contributions to a group process. It can also help us deal with disagreement and with the feelings that sometimes accompany a failed or ignored suggestion. Other participants will play off our suggestions; some will respond directly to a position we take, so it is extremely important that we take and communicate the assigned points of view.
> When we debrief, we will tell how this exercise affected us—how it made us feel.

The Assigned Points of View and Attitude: What the Systems Librarian Must Communicate

- I have worked for a year to come up with the right combination of vendors and equipment to recommend the best possible system for $55,000.
- I know from twelve years of experience it is a bargain!
- Circulation will be speedier, more accurate, and we will be able to tell more things from the records the system will automatically give us:

    Who takes what
    What moves, what doesn't
    Print out overdues
    Many great indexes
    Global BIP
    When was the last time a book moved (instant weeding info)?
    Cost per book plus processing info (when people lose them)
    A preferred rate for CD ROM purchases
- A cataloging upgrade that will cut cataloging time by 50 percent.
- I am also in charge of the separate book security system.
- Our present system is fractionated and cumbersome; last year maintenance and repair of systems was $22,000; for slightly over twice that we get a brand new, superefficient system.
- We go to the 21st century or we go into the dumper!
- Anybody who opposes this has his/her head in the sand.
- I know this: If we do not get this system, I'm outta' here. My

skills will erode if I have to continue with the present anti-
quated and unreliable system. I have put a whole year into this
investigation and recommendation. $55,000 is a small price to
pay for our survival.

- When we get this system, we can do away with some clerks in
  technical services. There's a savings! Get rid of one TS clerk
  and that will pay for the system in four years.

- For very personal reasons, speak against the oral history and
  adult literacy projects. If they go, the new system has a better
  chance of surviving.

Head of Technical Services

> For this experiential exercise to work, each of us will have
> to do two things:
> 1. Remain in character.
> 2. Execute his/her role; do what the role indicates.
>
> This exercise will give us a chance to test our ability to
> make contributions to a group process. It can also help us
> deal with disagreement and with the feelings that some-
> times accompany a failed or ignored suggestion. Other par-
> ticipants will play off our suggestions; some will respond
> directly to a position we take, so it is extremely important
> that we take and communicate the assigned points of view.
> When we debrief, we will tell how this exercise affected
> us—how it made us feel.

*The Assigned Points of View and Attitude: What the Head of Technical
Services Must Communicate*

- Technical services head supervises acquisitions, cataloging,
  and serials.

- I will mention that cataloging is now operating very smoothly.

- When we order preprocessed books at $1.00 per shot, we have
  few errors.

- There is *No Backlog*! We are efficient.

- A new system will continue efficiency—$55,000—well worth
  it.

- Why do we even have books for teens!!? Don't the school libraries have books? Teens do not use the library for the right
  purposes. They are disruptive. They may not be bad kids, but
  we have little for them. Let them use the school libraries.

- I am willing to give up my $1,000 travel.
- I am opposed to across-the-board cuts. If the new system were cut 10 percent we couldn't have it, but if YA were cut 50 percent, they would still have money for books. If the system is cut at all, we cannot get it.
- PR! If PR is so great, how come we are getting cut? If our message is being communicated so well, how come the politicians are cutting our budget 10 percent? If the PR is so great, how come they are not increasing our support?
- Circulation may be up, but not because of PR. The community is growing!
- I will have to defend my department. People want to know why my staff is so large. They will propose cuts in my staff, so I better be able to justify this by explaining what they do, why they are necessary, and why we can't take a cut. I will huddle with the technical services paraprofessional on this. Below are some of our duties.
  > We search and verify every order:
  > We check for bibliographic accuracy
  > We check to make sure we do not already own a requested item
- We examine each book closely for condition.
- We inquire of OCLC.
- We check preprocessing.
- We do the work of a serials cataloger:
  > We classify;
  > We check in;
  > We claim;
  > We oversee bindery operations;
  > We maintain periodical shelves: current and
  > older ones shelved in stacks.

. . . .

- Immediately, right now, as soon as this meeting is called to order, detach the note below and give it to the director. Even if you must interrupt the director, give the director this note. If you cannot detach, write it out or hand over your copy. Get a response.
- Walk right up to the director and deliver it. Stand there and wait for an answer. Demand an answer now. Do not relent, unless you are given a direct order to take your seat.

. . . .

I deeply resent the presence of the stack supervisor and the periodicals clerk at this meeting. This decision should be made by the professional staff only. What is your answer to my request? Will you dismiss them and let us deliberate as a professional group? Nonprofessionals should not be here, except of course for mine, who does more library work than the PR person.

Branch Librarian— in attendance at this meeting

> For this experiential exercise to work, each of us will have to do two things:
> 1. Remain in character.
> 2. Execute his/her role; do what the role indicates.
> This exercise will give us a chance to test our ability to make contributions to a group process. It can also help us deal with disagreement and with the feelings that sometimes accompany a failed or ignored suggestion. Other participants will play off our suggestions; some will respond directly to a position we take, so it is extremely important that we take and communicate the assigned points of view. When we debrief, we will tell how this exercise affected us—how it made us feel.

The Assigned Points of View and Attitude: What the Branch Librarian Must Communicate

- I must argue against across-the-board cuts.
- None of us can stand a cut, especially branch A, which has the leaky roof. Last year we suffered a $2,000 book loss from rain damage.
- We need $4,000 just to return us to where we were before the damage.
- Willow branch can't even use the portion of the stack where it leaks.
- Why do catalogers and circulation staff have to have such sophisticated systems?
- $55,000 for a new system is OUTRAGEOUS! That's too much of our budget.
- Suggest cutting the oral history and literacy projects for an instant $29,000 savings. Right there we have about one third of what we have to cut!

- Come on! The stack supervisor gets a $2,000 clerk to do the stack supervisor's job?
- I must support public relations.
- If no one is budging, offer 10 percent of branch acquisitions ($600). Maybe that will start things in the right direction.
- As it stands now, Tommy, one of the half-time maintenance crew, spends a half day at each branch each week. How could he do less? Attack any proposal to cut maintenance. I know my branches will be the first to suffer if maintenance is cut!

Periodicals Clerk

> For this experiential exercise to work, each of us will have to do two things:
> 1.   Remain in character.
> 2.   Execute his/her role; do what the role indicates.
> This exercise will give us a chance to test our ability to make contributions to a group process. It can also help us deal with disagreement and with the feelings that some-times accompany a failed or ignored suggestion. Other par-ticipants will play off our suggestions; some will respond directly to a position we take, so it is extremely important that we take and communicate the assigned points of view. When we debrief, we will tell how this exercise affected us—how it made us feel.

The Assigned Points of View and Attitude: What the Periodicals Clerk Must Communicate

- As soon as the meeting gets underway, I will interrupt imme-diately!
- I will make sure I have everybody's attention. If people are talking, I'll say "EXCUSE ME" till I have their attention.
- I'll thank everyone profusely for allowing me, a clerk, to at-tend.
- I'll tell everyone that even though I do not have a master's de-gree in LIS, I am glad they think I have something to offer.
- From the beginning, I will oppose item-by-item review.
- I will favor 10 percent across the board cuts.
- I will consider no cut that exceeds 10 percent in periodicals because I know what the public complains about—"not

enough magazines." We are not binding everything we should bind. It costs more not to bind: (1) loss cost and (2) reshelving costs.

- Last year all nonessential periodicals were cut. I will remind anybody who suggests a cut in periodicals that I have already done that, been there, got the t-shirt.
- If we pay a professional salary to a volunteer coordinator, why don't we look into getting volunteers to do more around here. Volunteers could help out in cataloging. They could do adult programming, couldn't they?
- I will vigorously support the stack supervisor program.
- I will interrupt anyone immediately who questions books or services to YA.
- I will insist that preprocessed books are wasteful. What are we paying catalogers for!?
- I will preface most every contribution with "I may not have an MLS, but ... "

*Business Officer

> For this experiential exercise to work, each of us will have to do two things:
> 1.   Remain in character.
> 2.   Execute his/her role; do what the role indicates.
> This exercise will give us a chance to test our ability to make contributions to a group process. It can also help us deal with disagreement and with the feelings that sometimes accompany a failed or ignored suggestion. Other participants will play off our suggestions; some will respond directly to a position we take, so it is extremely important that we take and communicate the assigned points of view.
> When we debrief, we will tell how this exercise affected us—how it made us feel.

The Assigned Points of View and Attitude: What the Business Officer Must Communicate
- This office handles every systemwide payment of over $20.
- We issue all purchase orders.
- We manage the payroll function.
- We do the paperwork for all new employees

- We sell old equipment and furnishings.
- We track expenditures and supply printouts of accounts.
- We maintain inventory records (property stickers on items over $50).
- We prepare for the annual audit and send it to board and council.
- We send regular reports to board and council.
- We prepare bids for large purchases.
- We reconcile fine money, lost book money.
- We are funded separately by county government.
- We manage all grant accounting (state and literacy council grants)

*Reporter

For this experiential exercise to work, each of us will have to do two things:
1.   Remain in character.
2.   Execute his/her role; do what the role indicates.
This exercise will give us a chance to test our ability to make contributions to a group process. It can also help us deal with disagreement and with the feelings that sometimes accompany a failed or ignored suggestion. Other participants will play off our suggestions; some will respond directly to a position we take, so it is extremely important that we take and communicate the assigned points of view. When we debrief, we will tell how this exercise affected us—how it made us feel.

The Assigned Points of View and Attitude: What the Reporter Must Communicate

- Under state sunshine act provisions, I cover this meeting for the local newspaper.
- I will report the purpose of the meeting: To cut $93,400 from a $934,000 budget.
- I will follow the "journalist's model."
  WHO   WHAT   WHY   WHERE   WHEN
- I have a byline, so I may report what I think. I may editorialize. I will be asked by the referee to read my report as it will appear in tomorrow's newspaper. (We will then discuss

whether we think the report is fair, accurate, or biased. The "so what?" for public relations will be considered.)

Debriefing

The debriefer's first task is to thank the director and all the players. Then permit the director to talk about the experience and the choices he/she made about the process—about how to run the meeting.

Give all players a chance, probably by calling upon them specifically, to talk about how they executed their assigned roles. Probe for expressions of any personal preference that ran counter to an assigned role. Make sure people have adequate opportunities to talk about how it felt to disagree, to challenge another, and to be challenged.

Remind the group that had they prepared and submitted a zero-base budget in the first place, the trimming would have been much easier to accomplish. The trimming would have started at the bottom of the budget and moved upward until the 10 percent had been reached. Zero-base budgets are constructed in priority order, with the most essential items listed first and the least essential listed last. The budget they dealt with was the more common line-item type.

Then provide an opportunity for them to say anything, including what they thought of the exercise, how they did it, and what if anything they learned about themselves. Someone is sure to point out that she had to do this very task in her county last fiscal year. Someone may even volunteer that an agency had to submit two budgets last year—one that requested what they needed, and another that requested 10 percent less! Someone may apologize for his character's temper tantrum. "I'm sorry I yelled at you," he may say. The apology will probably earn a good-natured "No problem." Let these exchanges happen.

Give the group an opportunity to suggest how the exercise could be improved. Take notes. You may want to incorporate some changes the next time you conduct this exercise.

Chapter 8

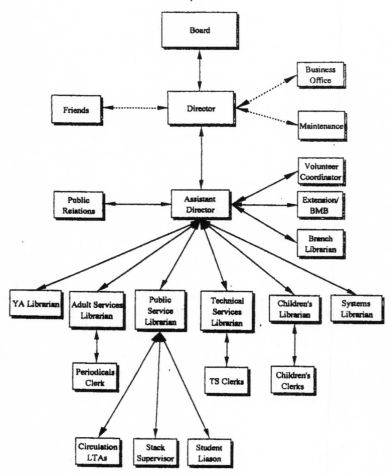

Figure 8.1. Library Organization Chart

Things You Need to Know

Budget 1

Staff	Cumulative No.	Travel	Salary LTA	Professional
Library Director	1	$1,000		$50,000
Assistant Director	2	1,000		32,000
3 Branch Librarians	5	3,000		75,000
1 Extension/BMB	6	1,000		25,000
Stack Supervisor	7		$20,000	
1 YA Librarian	8	1,000		25,000
1 Pub. Svc. Librarian	9	1,000		30,000
1 Tech. Svc. Librarian	10	1,000		35,000
3 Tech. Svc. LTAs	13		45,000	
1 Children's Librarian	14	1,000		25,000
2 Children's LTAs	16		20,000	
1 Adult Svcs. Librarian	17	1,000		30,000
1 ½ Time PR Librarian	18	500		15,000
1 Systems Librarian	19	1,000		35,000
1 Periodicals LTA	20		15,000	
3 Circulation LTAs	23		40,000	
1 Volunteer Crd.	24		25,000	
1 Eve. Stack Supervisor	25		2,000	
1 Student Liaison	26		2,000	
Totals	26	*$12,500	$169,000	$377,000
Salary Totals			*$558,500 w/travel	

Budget 2

Materials	Books, with $10,000 earmarked for YA and $5,000 for Children's	$100,000
	Periodicals and binding	75,000
	Paperback books for BMB	3,000
	Branch books	4,000
Salaries	Professional - $377,000 Clerical - $169,000	546,000
Operating	Postage	2,000
	Supplies	10,000
	Travel/CE for professional staff	12,500
	Maintenance contract	75,000
	Generator for BMB	2,000
	Repair branch roof	2,000
	PR program materials and supplies	7,000
	Adult programming	5,000
	Miscellaneous	2,000
Capital	New systems	55,000
	Copier	3,500
	Shelving	1,000
Special Projects Oral History	Materials/Equipment $ 3,000 Professional video crew 17,000 Hospitality/Transport 4,000 Historical Society Grant 5,000	19,000
Adult Literacy	Coordinator $5,000 Materials 9,000 Literacy Council Grant 4,000	10,000
Total		**$934,000**

References

Benedetti, Robert. 1999. *The actor in you: Sixteen simple steps to understanding the art of acting.* Boston: Allyn and Bacon.

Zachert, Martha Jane. 1975. *Simulation teaching of library administration.* New York: Bowker.

Chapter 9

The External Environment

No library is an island. Libraries exist as a part of a social structure. They are not ends within themselves. They do not operate in a vacuum. Libraries are perceived to be a common social good that adds value to the community. Relationships with other entities or forces within the external environment or community at large are thus vital to their success in fulfilling their mission. In order to enhance the library's value to its patrons and its community, forging and maintaining external ties is necessary and desirable.

External Entities

External entities are frequently some other social/political unit in which a common bond can be established for the benefit of both parties. Some entities exert a great deal of influence over the way libraries behave and have a direct bearing on their successful operation. Successful library administrators are very much aware of and in tune with the external forces such as consortia, Friends of the Library groups, civic and business organizations, and genealogical and historical societies, whose activities impact libraries. An external entity may also be another library or a group of libraries. Library managers work with a number of types of groups in order to achieve the highest levels of success for the library's mission.

External forces do not typically fall into neat categories. They may be primarily political such as the board of a public library or a faculty committee of an academic library. They may be social or intellectual

215

like the Friends of the Library or a genealogical association. They may be focused on technological concerns, e.g., automation network. Regardless of their primary purpose, they may often exert influence in varying degrees over library financial, technical, or service operations as well as public relations activities. For example, an external force may be primarily technological as is the case in many library consortia, but may also exert political and financial influence on a library's operation. The political influence may occur through a consortia's lobbying efforts while its ability to negotiate reduced costs for electronic products or obtain grants on behalf of the library have a financial impact. On the other hand, the external force may be primarily a support group such as Friends of the Library. But even friends groups often have financial as well as advocacy impact on the library. In many instances, friends groups can do some things which the law may forbid librarians to do. This may include selling souvenirs (Friends store), serving alcohol at social functions, and other fundraising or social activities. As a result, library managers cultivate and nurture these relationships.

Rationale for Relationships

Managers who seek to forge a relationship with an external entity should have a specific purpose or purposes in mind. For example, a library consortium may have as its primary purpose the purchase and management of technological enhancements that a single library could not afford, but is able to acquire in collaboration with others. Another example is a social organization that agrees to take on responsibility for funding a special interest resource (expensive art series, or genealogical resources) that the library decides supports its mission. Even a business or civic organization such as the Chamber of Commerce, Rotary, or Kiwanis may support the library's mission in specific and tangible ways. Sports groups may honor deceased members with memorial purchases of books on sports. A fraternity or sorority with a local chapter may purchase books in a collection area that relates to their purpose. These groups are sometimes interested in sponsoring a particular collection or service that parallels their own mission to the community. Regardless of the nature of the external entity, a relationship comes into existence because the parties perceive real benefits for the union. This chapter will explore the manager's role in relation to two of these external entities and offer some insights into how to successfully develop and nurture these relationships.

Consortia

Consortia come into existence because entities such as libraries perceive a need to collaborate.

> Collaboration is a mutually beneficial and well-defined relationship entered into by two or more organizations to achieve common goals. The relationship includes a commitment to: a definition of mutual relationships and goals; a jointly developed structure and shared responsibility; mutual authority and accountability for success and sharing of resources and rewards. (Mattessich and Monsey 1992, 7)

Over the past thirty years, one of the most phenomenal changes in the information environment has been the growth of library consortia. Although libraries in the United States have frequently participated in cooperative relationships since at least the latter part of the nineteenth century, the current information-rich environment and the enormous cost of accessing it have made membership in consortia almost pro forma for most libraries.

The standard and probably best definition of a library consortium may be found in the ALA Glossary:

> a formal association of libraries, usually restricted to a geographical area, number of libraries, type of library, or subject interest which is established to develop and implement resource sharing among the members and thereby improve library services and resources available to their respective target groups. Some degree of formalization of administration and procedures is required. (Young 1983, 131)

Consortia are catalysts for coordination, collaboration, and communication among libraries. They also even out the playing field for competition. They provide resources and expertise that do not exist in a single library. Automation systems for libraries are expensive to purchase and to maintain. Sharing those costs within a consortia environment makes it possible for many smaller libraries to participate and for larger libraries to reduce the costs of their participation in the technological revolution that has swept over libraries in the last quarter century.

Another reason for consortia is to lower the individual costs of purchasing electronic materials. Publishers and producers of electronic databases continue to struggle with pricing models. But one model that seems to work well for everyone is the one wherein vendors sell primarily to consortia. The Ohio College Library Consortium (OCLC), now named Online Computer Library Consortium, capitalized on this model in the early 1970s when it began to market its cooperative cataloging outside the state of Ohio. It reduced its costs of generating new business by selling its services primarily by marketing to large consortia rather than individual libraries. Publishers and other vendors of electronic information are discovering that this model works for them as well.

The Management Component

Whether stated explicitly or not, there is always a management function within consortia. This function differs contextually from the single library in that the frame of reference or environment will in some instances require that the manager act for the benefit of the group and not just the benefit of the individual library that employs her. We will examine some of the characteristics of consortia as well as factors leading to their development. This examination is intended to help clarify the manager's role within consortia. Many library directors wear the library director hat in their home library, but they must think and act in consideration of a larger group in the consortia setting. In a consortium, the manager is working with other managers. So how she operates in this environment will often differ from how she operates in her own library. Some decisions made in a consortia setting may be different from what might have been decided in a single library management environment. For example, the consortium may decide to jointly purchase a core set of electronic databases, one of which is not of any value to X library. The director of X library may vote for the purchase and support funding because she requires the goodwill of fellow members who may vote for the purchase of other databases that do help her library. Plus, joint purchase is still less expensive than purchasing each database separately. Or X library may be receiving unrelated benefits from the consortium, such as technical support, training, staff development, or other services.

Other management considerations are that in an automation consortium, an individual library may have to give up some of its decision-making authority related to cataloging and serials. What works well for one library may not be acceptable to a group or may just not be feasible within the system that has been purchased. Thus the director should try to understand the implications for her individual library when working within a consortium on the purchase of an automation system. In many cases the change in the way things are done is minor. Occasionally, it is a major cultural shift that does away with a procedure or service the library has provided for many years.

Factors Influencing the Development of Library Consortia

The desire and need to share sources for the benefit of users has usually been a central motivating factor in the development of library consortia. American library leaders in the last half of the nineteenth century and throughout the twentieth century frequently gave voice to the need for collaboration with one another. With limited resources, rising costs, and ever increasing demands upon those resources, collaboration rather than competition offered the most viable means of fully utilizing information resources. The earliest efforts were typically limited to rather small geographic areas. The lack of standardized cataloging rules and classification systems initially impeded collaboration. As these rules and systems were developed, often collaboratively, other collaborations such as interlibrary loan became feasible. This early cooperative spirit among libraries led to the development of a number of important shared bibliographic tools. A single example will illustrate one of the best of these early collaborations. The *National Union Catalog, Pre-1956 Imprints* came into being because of collaborative efforts among a group of major research libraries and the Library of Congress. After the initial collaboration, numerous libraries throughout the country contributed records to the catalog. Its existence then made collaboration in sharing of resources possible among large numbers of libraries who could now identify which libraries held which titles. Although OCLC now performs this function through powerful computer networks, it continues to depend on that collaborative model as the foundation for its success. The *National Union Catalog*, which predated OCLC, was a monumental effort in its time and a major breakthrough for libraries. It should be noted that this type of collaboration encourages cooperation at two levels. First is the cooperation needed for the shared input of records into the database. Second is the cooperation in resource sharing made possible through this collaborative database.

Recent Impetus

Several events occurred between the mid-1950s and the early 1970s that had a major influence on the management of libraries in the latter part of the twentieth century and into the twenty-first century. These include

- The explosion of information, particularly scientific information
- The advent of computers
- Passage of Library Services and Construction Act
- Development of the MARC record and other standards
- Development of cataloging networks

The Explosion of Information

Beginning near the end of World War II, the publication of information, especially that of scientific research, began to increase exponentially. This explosion in scholarly and scientific communication, most evidenced by the rapid increase in journal literature in the sciences, produced the need for improved distribution systems. As this journal and offprint literature (separately issued portions of a larger work) increased, the power of the computer was put to use in ensuring access through such services as Dialog and Bibliographic Retrieval Systems (BRS). Libraries became an increasingly vital part of the bibliographic management and distribution system for vast amounts of information, in particular scholarly and scientific.

The Advent of Computers

The primary event was, of course, the development of computers that could be utilized for a variety of business functions. The early computers were of great interest as well to institutions of higher education for their possible applications to research and to administrative tasks. It was but a short leap for a number of individuals to look at the paper-and-detail-intensive library to realize that computers might have major applications there also. Early efforts were directed toward processes such as circulation, cataloging, and inventory control. Management of bibliographic information appeared to present an ideal opportunity to exploit the power of computing. As large mainframe computers became more common on campuses, it was only a matter of time before librarians would discover ways to use them in managing library resources and in organizing information for retrieval and use.

Passage of the Library Services and Construction Act

A major impetus for the increased role of libraries was the Library Services and Construction Act. This act had a significant impact on libraries' ability to support the phenomenal growth in information that was occurring at this time. First passed in the mid-1950s, this act directed tremendous sums of money toward libraries and brought about a major increase in size of collections from small school and public libraries to large university and public research libraries. Many libraries saw their book budgets double, triple, and even quadruple in the space of just one or two years. Most of these funding increases were for material—not personnel. So the bibliographic management still had to be accomplished with little or no increase in personnel. Cataloging departments rapidly developed backlogs, and money was always difficult to secure for additional personnel positions. So the advent of the computer, which streamlined processing tasks at the same time as the materials increase hit libraries, was fortuitous indeed.

Development of the MARC Record

It is no accident that the Machine Readable Cataloging (MARC) record was developed between 1958 and 1964. The need to standardize bibliographic tools, evident from earlier collaborative efforts, led to the development of shared standards and protocols, thus laying the foundation for the MARC record.

New Age of Resource Sharing

Libraries often are early adopters of new technologies. With development of the MARC record concurrent with the growth in computing power, LSCA, and the explosion in information in the midpart of the twentieth century, libraries entered a new age of cooperation and resource sharing. This is most evidenced by the recent proliferation of consortia. Although consortia come into being for a variety of purposes, advances in technology have undoubtedly been the primary driving force during the past thirty years.

While a number of larger libraries attempted various automation developments on their own, undoubtedly the most successful utilization of computing power by libraries came about because of a consortia effort. The Ohio College Library Online Consortium (OCLC), created in the late 1960s for the purpose of sharing cataloging data, is today the Microsoft of the library world (albeit without the Microsoft baggage!). While OCLC is today's success story, there were numerous successful cooperative efforts launched during the latter part of the 1960s and throughout the 1970s. Efforts by individual libraries to develop major computing applications generally were not as successful as cooperative efforts.

Sharing

Underlying the development of consortia is the desire to share information resources and expertise as well as the need to share costs or the need to reduce costs through shared purchasing. Although these four needs are often interrelated in the individual library, few consortia attempt to be all-purpose organizations. Thus a library may find it necessary to belong to more than one consortium. Currently some consortia are looking beyond these basic purposes and developing a vision for the new information age that goes far beyond current practice. As a result consortia are increasingly sharing intellectual capital—valuable personal knowledge.

Even more areas of involvement for consortia appear likely for the future. Digitalization projects, shared portals, and an increased role in database license negotiation and pricing are all areas of possible future development for consortia.

Acceleration

In the 1980s, the involvement of libraries in consortia became much deeper. As automation systems matured and sought broader markets than large single institutions, consortia offered an opportunity for both the vendors and for libraries. A few vendors developed systems specifically for consortia, while others attempted to adapt their current systems for the consortia environment. By the end of the 1980s, it had become possible for even the smallest of libraries to automate their catalogs through membership in consortia. Thus consortia for the purpose of automation continued to be a large growth area. Buying clubs for supplies and services, such as equipment maintenance, permeated the library landscape to such a degree that there was little growth of consortia in this area. But automation consortia grew and flourished up through the late 1980s and early 1990s. In that period, there were still large numbers of smaller libraries without automated systems. Few had adequate resources with which to make that investment on their own.

Since the late 1990s, the market for new, first-time library automation systems in the United States has become exceedingly small. System upgrades and conversions to other systems sustain the automation vendors and continue to keep consortia busy. But in the 1990s a new consortia purpose began to emerge. For over two decades, libraries had struggled with horrendous increases in costs for journal literature. These costs far outpaced inflation or even, at times, the increases in health care costs. But the advent of electronic publishing in the early 1990s began to gently put the brakes on these runaway costs for scholarly journals. Although print journal prices are continuing to increase, the size of annual increases overall has decreased. In the 1990s, print journals in many scientific disciplines were increasing at rates of 15 percent to 18 percent a year. Currently, those science discipline journal rates are averaging closer to 10 percent a year. Numerous pricing models and ways of packaging and delivering electronic journal literature were attempted throughout the 1990s. With numerous library consortia already flourishing around the country, one of the most successful models for both publishers and information resellers turned out to be sales to large groups of libraries. As journal publishers and information resellers worked to gain market acceptance and share, they offered tremendous discounts to library consortia. Even long-time vendors of electronic databases discovered that new markets could be most easily developed though consortia.

Thus what began simply as consortia for automation of library catalogs has blossomed to a breadth of purpose far beyond the library functions originally planned. Numerous small consortia have collaborated with one another so that it is now often possible to offer opportunities for statewide or regional purchase and distribution of electronic journals and electronic databases. This has in turn created new opportunities for resource sharing and improved document delivery. Shared portals and a variety of digitalization projects are currently in planning and/or early implementation in many areas of the country. It is quite likely that as technology advances, many other collaborative opportunities will develop and take place out of the framework already established by library automation consortia.

The Manager's Role

Today, it is the rare library that does not belong to one or more types of cooperatives or consortia. Thus it is appropriate for managers to regularly revisit the reason or reasons for the original decision to join a particular consortium. How was the initial decision made? How does one go about evaluating either the original decision or a current opportunity? How does one make the decision on which consortia to join and whether or not a particular consortium is the best choice for a particular library?

Considerations for joining a consortium are always complex. A number of factors influence collaboration:

- Costs

- Benefits
- Politics
- Geography
- Purpose

Not all have to be present and or even fully present. There are usually very tangible results resulting from membership in a consortium. But intangible benefits are often quite important as well. Intangible benefits, such as improved communication among members and the increase in intellectual capital, should be evaluated in some manner so as to include them as part of the justification. With the formation of a new consortium in particular, specific costs and benefits may be unknown. What safeguards are available should the new consortia not meet the library's needs?

Costs

What are the costs? Costs should take into account actual outlay of dollars as well as staff time used to participate in consortia task forces and their governance. How rapidly are costs expected to increase? Are grant funds being used for the start-up costs and is the library expected to pick up full-cost share when the grant period expires? Do the costs create additional benefits the library could not otherwise obtain or could not obtain as economically? Thus a cost and benefit analysis is always an appropriate part of the process of considering whether or not to join a consortium.

Benefit Considerations

The essential question is whether or not the library (and therefore its patrons) receives any benefit as a result of becoming a member of a particular consortium. What does the library need that a consortium can provide? What are the potential benefits as well as the actual current and known benefits? The benefit may be tangible in actual dollars saved for a product or service the library already provides. It may be that the library needs to provide a new service or enhance an existing service. Will joining a consortium permit the library to provide a new service or an enhancement of an existing service at a lower cost than it could on its own? The benefits may be intangible in terms of opening new communication channels that facilitate services. Are the benefits understandable to parent organization administrators? When they question the cost, can a manager demonstrate the benefit?

Political Considerations

There are often political reasons for joining or not joining a consortium. A small college library of modest reputation may enhance its reputation by being associated with more highly regarded academic libraries. While this should not be the single reason for joining, it certainly can be an important one.

Often the political unit to which the public library is accountable plays a major role in whether or not that library may join a consortium. This is particularly true if there are expectations on the part of the consortium that are unpalatable to the city, county, or library district. A particular consortium may include a requirement that its members freely lend materials to each other. If there is not a mechanism in place for net lender reimbursement, a particular library may find that its taxpayers are providing a substantial amount of resources to non-taxpayers. It is less likely that the political unit would mandate that the library join a consortium than it is that the unit would prohibit it.

Considerations of Geography

Geography is frequently a major consideration in the decision on consortium membership. Because of the convenience of the Internet, this is somewhat less true now than in the past. Geography does exert a major influence on the success of the collaboration. For many libraries, it is easier to work through issues and develop protocols of cooperation if they are in geographic proximity. While geography continues to be important for most consortia, there are a number of successful collaborative efforts that are based upon some commonality, such as mission, without regard to geography. The Research Libraries Group and the Oberlin Group exemplify this type of consortia while OhioLink, Private Library Network of Indiana (PALNI), and Pennsylvania Area Library Network (PALINET) are contained within a specific geographic area.

Consideration of Purpose

What is the purpose of the consortium the library is considering joining. Does that purpose support the library's mission? Does the purpose meet a special need that the library cannot otherwise fill? The consortium may be strictly a technology-based effort in which a number of libraries join together to purchase a shared automation system. If a library already has its own system, there may not be a strong incentive to switch to a shared system. Thus, an examination of the purpose or mission of the consortium is an important part of the evaluation process. Ultimately, the best interests of her library and its users should guide a manager's decision.

After a manager leads her library into joining a consortium, the work truly begins. A board of directors governs most consortia. Although a variety of models of governance exist, all in one manner or another provide for representation by all of its members. This is a vital role for the manager, both to ensure that her own library interests are well served as well as those of all members of the consortium.

What is the manager's role in a consortia or collaborative? The following list contains only a few parts of that role.

- Initiate new projects
- Provide leadership for implementation of new projects
- Serve on the board and contribute to its deliberations
- Serve as an elected or appointed officer
- Serve on committees and task forces
- Commit individual library resources to support the consortium
- Search for new ways for the consortium to serve its members

There may be any number of other opportunities for a manager to serve in the consortium and to ensure its success.

Some collaborative or consortia efforts work better than others, while some simply do not work very well at all. Others seem to work well for a few years and then lose their sense of purpose. Sometimes this is because the external environment has changed and the consortium did not. At other times, there is simply a lack of good leadership. Sometimes the economic benefits envisioned do not materialize. The mission of the individual library may change in such a way that the consortium can no longer provide the particular benefits it needs. One academic library withdrew from a consortium when its parent institution decided to invest heavily in distance education. The consortium was unable to provide the services needed for their changed mission.

Your Turn: Are there times when a library manager may decide that belonging to a particular consortium is no longer appropriate and thus choose to withdraw? Can you think of changes in mission that might prompt this?

Types of Governance

There are several distinct forms of consortium governance and each consortium will have its unique way of implementing a particular governance structure. In general, governance falls into the following three categories. The first type is highly centralized. This type of consortium likely will hire an executive director and staff to carry out the policy decisions and directives of the board. All members will have representation (usually the library director) on its board. Decisions are binding on all members. For example, OhioLink purchases databases for all its members. Because it covers a broad spectrum of institutions, it often purchases databases that will be used heavily in one type of library (large academic) but may have little initial appeal to another type, such as a small college library.

The second governance structure is moderately centralized. There is some centralization of authority, but individual members may opt out on certain projects. This type also usually has a central staff and director. The board takes on more responsibility for decisions affecting members. Frequently in this type of structure, there is a core set of services that all members are responsible for financially supporting. However, many other services may be provided which serve only subsets of the membership. Members can easily opt in or opt out of noncore services.

The third governance structure may be classified as highly decentralized. In this structure, there is little or no central staff and the board takes on most of the responsibility for the operation of the consortium. This structure depends upon a good working understanding among the members. This type often proves to be as successful as either of the first two types. In this type of arrangement, however, the individual library manager must take on a greater burden in management of the consortia. This type of governance is rarely found in automation consortia.

While a top level library manager or director may delegate his role on the consortium board or collaborative effort to a midlevel manager, it is usually most appropriate for the library manager to be closely involved with consortia activities. This is because so much of what happens in the consortia is at a policy level that draws upon the resources or impacts the services of the individual library in such a way as to require a high level of decision making. Additionally, it is imperative that the manager maintain good communication and understanding at the highest level due to the budgetary and service impacts of consortia.

The library manager has a responsibility to commit funds and to enter into agreements such as interlibrary loan agreements, circulation agreements, and purchasing agreements. The manager also has a responsibility to work with other library managers to plan the direction of the consortium, to at times compromise her individual library's needs for the greater good of the group, and in general to think more broadly than she might otherwise do.

A library manager also has a responsibility to recognize when a collaborative effort no longer serves the needs of either its individual members or of the group as a whole and prepare to withdraw from or dissolve the effort. Only if good communication and understanding among the members has already been established can a manager make these decisions without discord or disruption.

Many library leaders agree that library consortia are becoming increasingly important in the management of libraries of all types.

> In earlier times, libraries were interested in consortia to reduce their costs. For example, through collective action, it has been possible for libraries to reduce the cost to purchase electronic information. However, libraries are increasingly turning to consortia to tap into a wider range of expertise, to share resources, and even to share the risk on projects that are larger than any one institution can afford. If libraries are unable to cope with and manage the process of change, then all of the other tasks that are before it will become insurmountable. (Hirshon 1999, 124)

Autonomy Issues

What do these developments mean for the individual library manager? Membership in a consortium always entails some loss of control for the individual library. This reduction in autonomy is often not well received by the individual library staff. They immediately recognize that many decisions previously made at the individual library level will more often be made at a consortium level. Previously, a library might have had several options for how it wanted to develop its local catalog or manage serials or acquisitions. In a consortia environment, there is much less flexibility for local options. Thus the individual library will give up some control.

In the mid-1980s, we worked for a library director who made the decision to join an automation consortium. After joining and investing a lot of time and money in the project, he learned that he would have to reduce library hours in order to accommodate the computer system's need for downtime each night to run reports for the consortium. He seriously considered leaving the consortium because he felt that with his own system rather than a consortium system, he would not have to make that sacrifice! Eventually, he did adjust the library hours to accommodate the consortium, but he certainly made everyone aware of how unhappy he was.

The manager then must be able to negotiate within the consortium as well as with her own staff to resolve these kinds of issues. The manager must determine if particular policies, procedures, or actions are truly important and, if so, at what priority level. He will often discover that it was simply a convenience to either the local library or to the consortium. This can prove to be a trying process.

On the positive side, the loss of autonomy may benefit library users. Many individual library practices will become standardized across all the libraries within the consortium. While such variations as length of circulation period within different libraries can be accommodated by many automation systems, other factors may compel the members to agree on a common circulation period. The effect on the library user is what must govern many of these decisions. The information place manager must continually conduct user-based cost/benefit analyses on this loss of autonomy that always occurs in a consortia environment.

The same loss of decision and control can happen with database licensing as well. Suppose a consortium is considering purchasing a suite of nine databases. Two libraries in the consortium discover that only seven of the databases meet their needs. If they attempt to opt out of those two, the vendor's pricing model raises prices, forcing the consortium to not purchase the databases. The pricing for the seven the two libraries do need is so favorable that they decide to purchase all nine for the common cause of the group. The alternative is more expensive and makes the situation a losing proposition for everyone.

Another autonomy concern is the surrender of collection development prerogatives. This happens in two distinct ways. The first is that the vendor often determines database content, albeit frequently with input from librarian-instigated focus groups or surveys. The second is that a consortium purchase of a set of databases may include individual titles the library might not choose on its own, but accepts in order to receive favorable pricing on materials it does need. So the individual library may make a different decision from one it would make if it were outside the consortium.

YOUR TURN: How might the manager help her staff redefine the professional role in collection development to incorporate such changes in the information environment as vendor-packaged collections?

Licensing Support

Many information place managers have little time to study or develop expertise in legal matters such as licensing agreements. Thus a consortium which has access to legal expertise may be able to relieve the manager of some of this responsibility. The consortium is assumed to have the best interests of all members at heart and thus will carefully negotiate the license. Even so, the manager must check to make sure that these assumptions are in fact true. It may be that some consortia will provide a license review service for their members, even for contracts negotiated by and for the individual library.

Friends of Libraries Groups

Friends of Libraries are what the name says—a group of people who help the library and provide direct financial support to the library as well as undertake fundraising projects and advocacy efforts. Friends groups are more frequently associated with public libraries and in some cases are responsible for the founding of a public library in a particular area. Although less frequently found in academic libraries, they nonetheless can be just as important to the success of the academic library.

While there is certainly a very tangible benefit to be gained from a Friends group, they also may require the library manager to expend considerable effort. Some Friends groups work independently of the library. This is the exception. Usually the library is very closely involved with the Friends both in governance and in activities. Although library staff may work with the Friends group on a number of projects, ultimately it is the manager's role with the Friends group that is key to its success.

In either an academic or public library setting, the manager's role is crucial to the success of a Friends group, whether in organizing one or maintaining it. The library director frequently leads the organizing effort in that he initiates contact with potential Friends group leaders and works with them in planning and organizing.

There are a number of other ways in which the manager can work with a group of people to organize a Friends group. She can

- Provide a place to meet
- Help with leadership/running the meeting
- Provide gentle guidance
- Discuss the library's mission and how a Friends group supports that mission.
- Ensure that they stay on target and consistent with library mission
- Suggest projects
- Suggest fundraisers
- Suggest sponsorship of programs

Individuals interested in working with a library director to organize a Friends group often forge a special bond with the library and/or books. In general, they are very much wedded to the physical entity of the book as well as to the ideal that reading is a societal good. Thus the manager's role may be to nurture and focus this bond in such a way that the Friends member receives the intangible benefits she is seeking and the library receives the tangible benefits it is seeking. The intangible benefits for the organizing group members may include special recognition, opportunities to serve, or simply the formal association with the library. Tangible benefits for the library include direct monetary support and the ability to utilize human resources not otherwise available.

If a Friends group does not currently exist and the manager wants one, she must identify a core constituency of potential members. Every library receives gifts of books, magazines, tapes, videos, music albums, and compact discs. Individuals making these donations are often one good source of a core constituency. These individuals in turn know others whose interests might coincide with the library's interests. Often, after a group has been formed, its programs will attract other people with similar interests.

In working with a core constituency, the library director should provide them with working drafts of ideas. These drafts might include such things as a suggested list of purposes for a Friends group, some possible projects and activities for the group to consider, or programs they may wish to sponsor. These should not be exhaustive and should be clearly presented as talking points and not as fait accompli. Most new groups need some ideas to get started and are able to proceed much faster if a few are provided.

Sometimes Friends groups are formed by highly sophisticated and able community leaders who are adept at management and group skills. A wise library manager will recognize this talent and allow more latitude to the Friends group. She can back off from the "running the meeting" or "setting the agenda" responsibility once she understands that the Friends group shares a commitment to the library mission within the community. Fortunate are those library directors who find themselves in this situation!

YOUR TURN: What other strategies or activities would you as a manager employ in your library to assist a new Friends group in getting organized?

Friends Maintenance and the Manager's Role

Friends groups need support and encouragement from the library in order to sustain themselves. The nurturing of a Friends group takes time away from other activities and tasks in a director's busy schedule. It is important to accept the idea that a Friends group will not be successful if it does not enjoy a high priority in the director's set of responsibilities. The library director must be clear in his desire for a Friends group and must be committed to its success. The success or failure of a Friends group is often directly related to the success or failure of library programming in general. A weak or ineffective Friends group may be an indicator of weak or ineffective programming on the part of the library. Thus a library is better served to not have a Friends group than to support a weak group or a group that ultimately fails.

In the maintenance of a Friends group, library staff may coordinate many activities. For example, the collection development librarian may serve as the liaison on the annual used book sale. The access services librarian may be the liaison with the docent program. But the library manager should always be involved with policy decisions and particularly with potential donors. Just as with consortia, it is important for the director to be involved in representing the library at the critical meetings and activities. While some of the work with Friends groups may be done by middle managers, it is quite common for the key people in the friends group to desire and even to demand that the director be directly involved, particularly with donor relations. We have witnessed occasions where Friends members/donors have specifically demanded that they have direct access to the director regarding their donation.

By being closely involved with the Friends group, the director can ensure excellent communication between the library and the group. If there is a single key to success, this is it. Regular, informative communication is essential. Bolstered by recognition of group efforts, most Friends groups are able to greatly enhance a library's programming and thus support its mission.

It is the responsibility of the director to clearly explain to the Friends group how they fit into the organizational structure of the library. She must also assist the group in defining and interpreting its role and in setting the limits of that role. She must help them understand how the fulfillment of that role enhances the library's ability to accomplish its mission.

Perhaps one of the greater dangers for a Friends group is that it becomes dependent on the library director for its leadership, programming, fundraising, and other activities. The director's efforts in communication, support, and recognition of the Friends group should be to foster a climate in which the Friends can take leadership responsibility for their activities while at the same time working cooperatively with the library to ensure that activities are aligned with the library's mission and needs.

Friends groups require a definite commitment of time and resources from the library. Successful Friends groups repay this commitment many times over with their ability to enhance the library's mission through fundraising, advocacy, and public relations.

Just as with consortia, friends groups encourage cooperation, communication, coordination, and collaboration. A broad-based coalition of support for the library will be critical as libraries change during the next decade. Thompson and Smith state that "friends groups will continue to flourish where they are embraced by the library administration, supported by the development staff, and honored by the community in which they reside" (Thompson and Smith 1999, 11). Friends groups will continue to be an important external force as the library's needs for funds, public relations, and support from its community grow.

The Future of External Relationships

Libraries need these relationships now more than ever. Rapidly changing boundaries of information and cultural institutions make imperative the need to nurture external supports for the mission of the library. Successful working relationships with external entities will continue to greatly enhance a library's ability to accomplish its mission. The examples provided in this chapter are basic descriptions of how these relationships get established and thrive. Local environments and the great diversity of human personality guarantee that there is no one right answer for every situation. The general principles and descriptions discussed here will always be modified, both by the director's personal views and inclinations as well as by the variety of people with which she interacts.

References

Hirshon, Arnold Hirshon. 1999. Libraries, consortia, and change management. *The Journal of Academic Librarianship* 25 (2): 124-26.
Mattessich, Paul W., and Barbara R. Monsey. 1992. *Collaboration: What makes it work.* St. Paul, MN: Wilder Foundation.

Thompson, Ronelle K. H., and Ann M. Smith. 1999. *Friends of college libraries*. 2nd ed. Chicago: American Library Association.

Young, Heartsill, ed. 1983. *The ALA glossary of library and information science*. Chicago: American Library Association.

Chapter 10

A Field Guide to Mistakes Managers Make

"Mistakes are nature's way of showing you that you're learning" (Mistakes 2005). That is a clever spin-off from the more familiar sayings, "We learn from our mistakes," and "Experience is the best teacher." Pithy sayings may be laced with truth, but they also may be loaded with error or danger. Unexamined mistakes may teach us nothing; and when the teachings come as the result of personal mistakes, mistakes *we* make, that kind of experience may carry a very expensive price tag indeed.

What Are Mistakes?

Mistakes are acts of commission or omission which directly result in some harmful consequence for the maker and/or the organization. Doing the wrong thing is often a consequential mistake, as is not doing the right thing. A harmful consequence is a serious negative repercussion. To some degree, the seriousness of the mistake may be in the eye of the beholder. The manager who fires Jim may think he is doing the right thing. Jim may consider his firing a mistake. A casual thoughtless remark which destroys a friendship with a colleague can have enormous personal ramifications; a similar remark uttered in public can derail a career or devastate an organization. Trent Lott will testify to this. Whether an act of omission or commission is a serious mistake may depend upon the circumstances, the audience or observer, and the nature of the issue. The key consideration is context. If managers could avoid some mistakes by examining a number of them which have been committed by other managers, might that not be a helpful thing? We think so, and we like the idea of learning from others before we encounter a much more severe teacher—our own experience.

We say "avoid some mistakes" because we believe no one is capable of mistake-free management. If someone has never made a mistake, he or she has probably never done anything either—never made a consequential decision, never solved a tough issue, never challenged a major problem, or never taken a risk. Managers pursue the values of an organization by doing, not avoiding. Although "mistakes" appears in the title of this chapter, its purpose is to focus upon taking advantage of possibilities, not just upon avoiding error. When it gets to be Your Turn, we will ask you to consider actions a manager might take to ensure more positive outcomes than the ones described in this chapter.

Why We Make Mistakes

We should examine why we make mistakes. Few rational managers and administrators deliberately make mistakes; their intentions are to succeed, not fail. One reason managers make mistakes is because they have not foreseen consequences of their actions or inactions.

This is very easy to do for two reasons:

- Few of us can predict the future
- Many of us misperceive the present

The future is an idea. It hasn't happened yet. Some experts in search of intelligence to help them make macro-decisions, on five-year plans for example, use tools like trends analysis, cross-impact matrices, and Delphi techniques. These methods can help them derive reasonable forecasts of the future. They cannot know, however. So they do the best they can. That can lead to mistakes, for possibilities may be limitless, even infinite. The capacity to select alternatives and list consequences is finite. Most choices are chancy.

Not only is predicting impossible in most cases, but some managers perceive their surroundings differently from the ways others do. Some of them don't get it. They report conflicting stories. There is a reason for this. The moment they begin to describe a fact, they begin a process of interpretation. They use descriptors derived from their individual psychological sets: those assortments of attitudes, beliefs, cultural backgrounds, educations, genders, language skills, and experiences through which they filter all stimuli in order to attach meaning to them. Abraham Kaplan has observed that people do not just record; they interpret. Observations are not contaminant free. Subjectivity creeps into even the most highly controlled experiments. The very act of choosing what phenomenon to study or how to study a phenomenon is a subjective act. How scientists ask the questions they ask often reveals their biases. A great German philosopher termed the notion that observations could be without bias "the dogma of the immaculate perception" (Kaplan 1964, 131). Kaplan would argue that the dogma has been disproved.

Similar Observation and Dissimilar Conclusion

Warren Bank reports the case of a leader's assigning a manager to formulate and present a plan to lift a struggling organization out of the doldrums. When the manager presented the plan at a staff meeting, the participants were dismissed and charged with bringing back their recommendations. Bank talked with two participants, one who opposed the plan and one who favored it. They both responded with *identical* observations about the manager's presentation, but they formed *diametrically opposite* conclusions about it. Why? Bank states that it is because the two held differing values about organizational pursuits. One was concerned most with sagging morale, the other with lagging production (Bank 1995, 150-52).

Banks believes, and so do we, that followers follow leaders who succeed in learning employee values and folding those values into their practice. One of the respondents to our survey spoke of a new manager who systematically spent one-half hour with each of his new associates and supervisees, then promptly disregarded anything he may have learned from these meetings; and he never repeated the visits. We also would bet that this new manager read in a text or heard at a workshop that new managers should schedule private sessions with each new associate as a technique for "getting to know you." Chances are he asked, "What do you do around here? How are things?" He probably suggested that they come see him any time. He even may have said, "My door is always open."

Instead, he should have discovered what the employees thought was important, what vision they had for the enterprise, and what organizational values they held dear. Managers should align their plans with employee values if they expect enthusiastic followership. Unless they obtain these matches, managers will face the problem Bank identifies. They will make mistakes, one of which is to create expectations among staff and then fail to follow up on what is perceived by them as a request for their input.

A Framework for Reporting and Discussing Mistakes
Information Managers Make

Because there is general agreement that managers plan, organize, staff, direct, coordinate, report, budget, represent, and communicate, we have chosen to use this list of responsibilities as a framework for presenting mistakes which have been reported to us and some which we have observed. Since most people are reluctant to display their shortcomings, and since the literature of information agency management reports far more "how I do it good" stuff than "how I really messed up" stuff, we are indebted to the managers who responded to our call for examples of managerial mistakes.

We chose this framework for another reason. It enables us to report about the people aspects of the mistakes described. A central theme of this book is that management is a people enterprise. For example, the budget is, to be sure, a thing, but the budget process is very much a people activity. All the mistakes reported here have affected a wide spectrum of people: the mistake maker, clients, coworkers, and the institutions or organizations they use and serve.

Planning, establishing a vision, setting goals, getting the agency moving ahead—

1. In the not-too-distant past, one information agency manager was instructed by the board to develop a plan for automation. The director did not agree that this should have been a priority, so she made a few phone calls, asked around, and decided to purchase a PC to be used by library staff to produce *printed library catalog cards*! That was her "plan."

Consequences: The decision to eschew computerization except for the rather low-level function of inventory control placed this agency far behind its competitors in the information transfer business. Clients lost respect for the agency. Demands went unmet. Good employees quickly realized that their skills would erode in such backward surroundings.

Qualified potential new hires chose not to seek employment there. The director's decision to procrastinate and her failure to update her own skills cost her her job. More importantly, the organization failed in its obligation to serve the needs of clients, and the employees, whose value systems strongly favored customer service, were frustrated.

2. An academic library director valued above all else the protection of the library's turf. So when he was invited by the computer science department to attend a meeting where he would learn about a new computer science curriculum and the department's needs for additional library resources, he declined. "Let them come to me," he reasoned, "and anyhow, computer science does not cooperate; it absorbs." His plan was to force them to come to him and to make their request. That way he could be in charge of the negotiations, and he could act as dispenser of resources. He would be in control. He knew how they operated over there. In order to get programs approved, computer science always understated costs by claiming they needed no new library resources. After approval, and after the new programs were up and running, they would show up at the library and claim they needed thousands of dollars worth of new journals and electronic resources. He would go to no meeting where library funds would be pirated; he would not be co-opted.

Consequences: Computer science leadership reported the librarian's refusal to the provost. Engineering got wind of the issue and communicated with computer science. They made the collective observation that they had a common interest in many of the same resources and a common stake in making them available to their students and faculty. So the provost, convinced by computer science's and engineering's need for collections that their respective students and faculty could access speedily, and angered by the librarian's failure to be a good team player, granted their request for a separate engineering, computer science, and information technology library. The librarian had valued power over information service and it cost him his most precious commodity—turf.

3. A director obtained permission to build a new library and to begin the planning process, which included submitting cost estimates. The director assembled an able team of librarians, faculty, and architects to help design the building and attach dollar figures to the specifications desired. They carried out this responsibility. Unbeknownst to the director, a capital campaign had been launched for which figures for library

construction had been set. These figures were much lower than the team's estimates, and the library had to settle for less, make all sorts of compromises, and wound up with a terrible building.

Consequences: Library capacity and service suffered. Being out of the communications loop made the director vulnerable to decisions which cost him dearly but about which he had no knowledge. When the planning started, he had not asked the right people the right questions. Users suffered because the library was not structured to accommodate traffic flow, automation needs, or seating. Staff morale dipped because they could not provide in the poorly designed building the kinds of user services they had hoped to offer in the originally planned building. Form had not followed function; it had followed the suggestions of people who knew little about library facilities construction.

Organizing, establishing a structure for achieving goals, creating policy, empowering staff—

1. In response to a client complaint, a director removed a book from the agency's collection. Even after numerous requests from clients and staff, the director refused to return the book for use. The agency used a selection policy that involved staff in acquisition decisions, but they had no formal policy for review. This enabled the director—one person—to make an arbitrary and ad hoc decision about a book that had been acquired through collective review and selection.

Consequences: The decision irritated clients and staff. The director's inflexibility prompted staff to avoid reporting subsequent client complaints, and this led to additional censorship problems. The staff valued service; the director valued a smooth, censorship-free and conflict-free organization. Neither got the wanted outcome because the organization was not equipped with a workable comprehensive policy. Clients suffered too. The only winner was the one complainant.

2. A director of a very large and prestigious university library had definite views about how professional staff should behave, views that went far beyond coffee break policy and dress code. He decreed that professional and nonprofessional staff should not comingle—not at lunch, not in the staff room, not socially, not at all. He maintained that professional status in large measure was established and maintained by observing this distance. Professionals and support staff were to communicate only about matters that involved the performance of their jobs. Professional supervisors were empowered to teach, train, evaluate, and reprimand. They were forbidden to joke, chat with, or otherwise engage

their inferiors. Sadly, many people who should have known better went along with this, so firm was the director's control.

Consequences: This policy was so restrictive and it was enforced so strenuously that it created a rift that lasted for years. Even as support staff assumed more and more of what formerly had been considered the domain of degreed workers, the "glass partition" remained. It endured years beyond the director's retirement. It only did damage to professional status. The director valued separation, the limits of which were seldom tested, and an encompassing collegiality never took hold in the corporate culture. It hung on as an impediment to a systems approach to information provision, an enemy of niceness and collegiality, and a major contributor to paraprofessional rage. Clients felt this when they entered the building.

3. A director became convinced of the arbitrariness of separating technical and public services. Maintaining the distinction was dysfunctional. The distinctions between technical services, where they acquire, classify, and construct the tools of inquiry, and public services, where they manage the tools and interpret client inquiry about the tools—were artificial. So she reorganized the information place so that information officers who made the tools of inquiry also spent time in information service departments where clients and other workers *used* the tools. Similarly, she scheduled information service employees to work in acquisitions, serials, and cataloging and classification departments, so that people who used the tools in the trenches could see how materials were acquired and described and how inquiry systems were made.

Consequences: Despite the conceptual attractiveness of the reorganization, it was a managerial nightmare. It violated whatever is useful about the principles of span of control and unity of command. Middle managers instantly acquired new trainees. Some of the new trainees had little knowledge of the operations in the departments to which they had been dealt. Some data-oriented people, who had picked technical services precisely because they wanted to serve behind the scenes, hated public service work. Some relationship-oriented people, who lived for the drama of question negotiation with clients, loathed what they considered to be the tedium of technical work. Scheduling became Byzantine. People adjusted poorly to reporting to two or three managers—one in their main area, and perhaps two in their inherited ones. Renamed departments lost elements of their identity, and the managerial morass negatively influenced service. The director valued a commitment to a concept that had serious operational shortcomings; the staff coveted stability and their chosen specialties, a value that the director's dream assaulted.

Staffing, recruiting and selecting people who can carry out the goals of the agency—

1. A circulation manager hired a dyslexic person to shelve materials. The shelver never caught on, could not do the work, and was continued in the position.

Consequences: Materials remained in constant disarray, clients could not find wanted materials, and the staff wondered if the manager knew about relationships between dyslexia and the capacity to place items in alpha-numerical order, an essential skill in the operation of classification systems. The manager valued compassion and opportunity for the disadvantaged citizen; the staff valued order and competence. These values clashed in this instance.

2. A manager hired an employee for an important post after reviewing a resume and conducting an interview in which he asked the stock questions like "Where do you want to be in five years?" and "What is your philosophy of information management?" The letter of reference from the applicant's current employer was glowing. The manager believed he had a real find. What he found was a dud whose current employer had been eager to be rid of this poor performer; ergo the testimonial letter. Instead of discovering at the interview how the applicant communicated, his views on and accomplishments with team projects, and how he approached problem solving, his new employer discovered only that resumes can exaggerate and current employers can have selfish reasons for stretching the truth.

Consequences: The agency acquired a thorn in their side, a performer who neither pulled his own weight nor worked well with others. He lasted six months. This set the organization back and required it to engage in another round of recruiting, interviewing, hiring, and training. The manager's preference for a smooth, conflict-free interview produced the phenomenon of the "closed window." At a point in an employment interview, the interviewer makes a yes or no decision about the interviewee and then closes the window on information exchange. Through that closed window the interviewer filters all subsequent information exchanged and force fits it to support whatever decision he or she made. Inept, unprepared interviewers habitually close the window too soon. The organization placed high value on team approaches, but hiring the dud thwarted these efforts.

Directing, training and supervising, evaluating, delegating, developing potential, guiding staff in the pursuit of organizational goals—

1. A weekend staff member in an information agency, when he did not know how to deal with a request or simply did not feel like doing so, frequently told clients to "come back on Monday," and he also mistakenly referred them to other agencies such as archives or planning commissions when materials at his agency would have helped the clients. His all too common message to clients was "We don't have anything on that."

   Consequences: Local agency administrators eventually called the staff member's boss and asked why clients erroneously had been sent to them. The boss had no idea of the problem until managers of sister agencies complained. The boss had placed a low priority on training, supervision, and evaluation. The weekender had placed a high priority on personal comfort and avoiding work.

2. When a clerk informed a client who had paid a fine on a book he wished to renew that he would need his library card to do so, a supervisor intervened and allowed the client to renew the book even though he did not have the card. Afterwards, the clerk fumed, "You made me look like an idiot by coming up behind me and waving your magic wand. You made me look like I did not know what I was doing." The supervisor responded that the library's first obligation was to service and that she was not going to let that client leave the library disappointed.

   Consequences: The clerk's feelings were severely bruised. He questioned the wisdom of enforcing policy when management was so quick and public about disregarding it. The way in which the issue was handled inflamed resentment and added to the rift between professionals and support staff. Paraprofessionals often develop strong proprietary interests in performing well the duties of their specialties. When they enforce the rules, when they do what they are supposed to do, they often deeply resent what they see as a cavalier disregard for their dedication. The supervisor valued flexibility over rigidity, customer service over rules, the big picture over the snapshot, and so she relaxed the policy. The clerk did not realize that managers see their role as exercising such a prerogative and questioned why the library had policy, seeing as how "they never stuck to it."

3. A school library media specialist instructed her two aides that their main responsibility was to keep order and discipline in the often

crowded media center. As many as four teachers at a time would deposit their classes in the media center and then exit to enjoy their planning periods, often leaving the aides with over eighty chatty undirected middle schoolers to supervise. The principal sanctioned this practice because it was the only way he could fit the mandated planning period into the school schedule. The aides were charged with keeping the children productively occupied, but except for suggesting that they be good and keep it down, they had no authority to dismiss the unruly, bar mischief makers, or report misconduct to school disciplinary officers or even to teachers.

Consequences: The aides quit, leaving the media specialist with no staff. Order and discipline deteriorated even further. The media specialist could employ little of what she had learned in her master's degree preparation, so overwhelmed was she with sitter responsibilities. The principal valued keeping the teachers happy and at bay. The media specialist had dreams for the information program, but the teachers coveted their free period. The students liked their extra recess.

Coordinating, achieving a mesh among staff and units in order to meet system goals—

1. When the agency acquired a windfall $100,000 bequeathal, the spend-it-or-lose-it manager ordered the acquisitions department to consult want lists, identify multivolume and other expensive purchases, and commit the money immediately. They did so. Inundated by the surprise and a copious flow of new items, the catalog staff fell behind.

Consequences: A massive backlog ensued, creating havoc in acquisitions and cataloging, chaos in stack management, and resentment among clients whose requests were buried in the overabundance. The money was spent but staff morale dipped. Also, some of the expensive large sets acquired in haste gobbled up the bequeathal, but did not fit the agency's mission, and this angered the catalogers.

2. After consulting with key personnel in cataloging, an academic library director decided to switch from Dewey Classification to Library of Congress Classification. Since the college's chief curriculum was education, the catalogers decided to begin the reclassification with the materials in that broad subject area. So they set out to convert all the 370s, a portion of the collection of books, periodicals, pamphlets, government documents, videos, nonprint and electronic items that topped 100,000 and which were dispersed throughout the library.

Consequences: No one had figured out where to place the newly classified items. Library of Congress Classification clashed with the numero-alphabetics of Dewey, managers in the curriculum laboratory were confused about placement of teaching aids and texts, and faculty complained about not being able to find anything in education. Students who had finally learned Dewey were befuddled by Library of Congress classification. Public service personnel were unable to explain the reason for the conversion process to inquirers and could not say what materials were next in line or when the project would be completed. All the players in this drama had to deal with eroded access, most of which was caused by information deficit.

Reporting, informing in timely fashion those in the need to know, publishing progress toward goals—

1. Faced with an overflow of in-house business one evening, a manager instructed the telephone reference specialist to direct all incoming calls to automatic voice mail and then come to assist in the information services department where clients were lined up to get personal service. This worked and the people who came in for help eventually got it. So when the same volume of in-person demand occurred two nights later, and again in the next week, the manager made the same decision. He decided, time permitting, to let the director know of his successful deployment at the next staff meeting in two weeks.

Consequences: The director began to get calls from angry and impatient clients who complained about the new policy. Why was the agency no longer taking telephone requests? Was the director not acquainted with e-mail possibilities? The director had no idea that the problem existed and could not explain anything to the callers. She vowed to seek some explanations from the staff at the meeting in two weeks. As a rule she did not like staff meetings, and neither did the staff, and she held them as infrequently as possible.

2. An administrator was good about reporting to internal constituencies. She kept fellow administrators informed. She spread vital and useful information laterally to division leaders and to all middle managers on a need to know basis. She communicated often and in writing to those whom she supervised and saw to it that her messages got distributed in the organization. On the other hand, she avoided contact with political decision makers and controllers of purse strings. She thought it best to be invisible politically and only sparingly accessible to the board, in

whom she had little trust. The lament that "they [the public and the funders] do not know what we do" was accurate, as the public seldom heard about the information place their taxes supported.

Consequences: Funders were reluctant to increase support for an organization they knew little about. Voters were unlikely to approve referenda for library development. The general public held dated views about how this agency fit into the Information Age, and many, because they could access the Internet in their homes, saw little purpose in paying all those superfluous employees and maintaining all those unnecessary buildings. When they were trying to attract industry to the area, local civic leaders were unable to say much about the library because they did not know much about it.

Budgeting, translating the agency's goals into dollar figures, influencing the award process, accounting for expenditures—

1. One planner in a knowledge management enterprise failed to notice that a major information provider had mistakenly given the library free access to several online data bases. So he canceled several thousand dollars worth of duplicated standing orders in paper format. Everyone in the agency enjoyed the free access, and no one questioned his decision to cancel the paper copy subscriptions. He also chose not to inquire about the free access when finally he did catch the provider's error. Almost a year later the provider noticed its ooops! and notified the subscribing agency that it was eliminating the agency's access to the online resources.

Consequences: The manager had to reinstate many titles in paper format, fill gaps in the standing orders, and rob the current fiscal year's budget of dollars never intended for this purpose, thus reducing the agency's capacity to add needed new materials and services. This budgeteer should have been suspicious of the free lunch, but he was seduced by the something-for-nothing value. The price for recovery was dear.

2. Newly placed administration in a government agency informed the manager of its special library that every major category of expenditure had to be considered for budget reduction. The manager responded that no area of current expenditure—not staffing, purchasing, subscription services, or any information service could be reduced. He made the additional demand that computer operations expenses should be borne by another department, even though the library supervised training and

access, and also assisted with research in the subscribed-to data bases. The library manager held fast to this stand.

Consequences: New administration immediately lost confidence in the manager's judgment and turned to others in the organization to make recommendations about library management, staffing, and budgeting. Administration deemed the librarian's position as resistant to change and insubordinate. The library lost face. More than that, it lost its place as the center for information provision, a function its charter had specified and its mission statement had asserted. Faced with having to manage with less, the librarian decided not to play a part in paring the budget. This decision neutered the information place and reduced the role of librarian to custodian of materials.

Representing, standing for the library, taking the message to the people, schmoozing, seeking support for agency goals—

1. A public library director is active in the community and knows all the important people. This director also believes that poetry, especially Elizabethan poetry, is particularly uplifting and communicative, particularly for clients in the semi-urban community served by the library. She has been especially eager and remarkably successful in winning donations of poetry-dedicated dollars and has inspired a floodgate of donated poetry volumes, most of which reside uncataloged in the library basement. Still she persists in her drive for poetry books.

Consequences: Donated books clog the shelves and inundate an overtaxed technical services department. There is no money to augment the catalog staff. Donors grouse and complain that their donations are buried in an avalanche of uncataloged materials. What started as a fundraising coup has turned into an embarrassment of riches and a public relations nightmare. This is a prime example of a librarian superimposing her values upon a community, and of squandering her talent for convincing people to support the library.

2. An administrator/manager of an urban public library has refused all invitations to attend Rotary or join the Kiwanis. He perceives little in common with the grocers, hardware store owners, financial planners, clergy, and social service providers who attend meetings and waste time at lunch together. He thinks if they see him at the lunches or meetings, they will conclude that he does not have enough to keep him busy back at the library. Moreover, when historical societies, garden clubs, little leagues, or religious groups request his presence at their functions,

he always declines. Sometimes he does send a delegate to these events, which he finds boring and irrelevant to his purposes.

Consequences: Ignoring the absolute fact that the librarian stands for and represents the library to its community, this manager has lost many a golden opportunity to communicate with clusters of constituents on their turf, maybe to attract their support and patronage. Moreover, by refusing the company of influential community leaders he has systematically excluded the library from participation in the decisions that affect support for the library. His value system does not include being identified by the public as a spokesperson for the library. For him it is not whom you know, it's what you know. The trouble is, he doesn't know what either.

Communicating, exchanging information about the management of progress toward goals—

1. This one has planning and communication ingredients. A new children's services librarian planned a large and complex kickoff party for a library summer reading program. What he did not do was show the plan to coworkers involved in its execution. They got no preliminary information and had no opportunity to give or get any feedback. So by the time they got their instructions, they quickly realized that the plan would not work, mostly because some concurrent programs were scheduled for the same space and because the same facilitators were scheduled to be in two different places at once.

Consequences: The program limped through, some children were disappointed, and the librarian lost the respect of his coworkers. It had occurred to the children's services librarian that all he needed to do was draw up a plan and then present it to competent staff for execution. It had not occurred to him that the plan had flaws or that it was either necessary or beneficial for him to provide opportunities for explanations and feedback prior to the event's scheduled time.

2. An academic librarian was invited to give a speech to a group of information scientists at their annual conference. In an effort to explain how successfully she had introduced innovation in a potentially hostile climate, the librarian made references to "a barbarian student body of physical education students who were majoring in towels, a faculty of clueless Luddites in shiny blue trousers and white socks, and an administration defiantly dedicated to the status quo." The audience laughed nervously at these references. Unbeknownst to the librarian, the transcripts of the conference presentations were published, and

staff, administration, and students at the librarian's college read her comments.

Consequences: They did not laugh at the college. The faculty issued a no confidence in the librarian vote, and the administration and board sought her resignation. Her inclination to go for laughs and to bite the hand that fed her collided with her college's fierce pride and thin skin. Disloyalty is a dangerous value. Few observers honor it when they spot it in others.

Your Turn: Select any of the decision errors listed. Speculate about how the manager could have done a right thing and avoided negative consequences. Hint: Avoid the temptation to use the expression, common sense. Common sense is a very uncommon commodity. Consider instead overt activity like planning, communication, and other actions. How do values factor in? Suggest behaviors. What could managers do?

Your Turn: Critics of the POSDCORB—RC approach to understanding management process argue that the list can mislead one to think that each activity is a discrete one to be performed and then set aside. Respond to this observation by pointing out that all of the episodes presented above contain elements of several managerial activities and that planning, for example, permeates all of them.

Mistakes to Avoid

If there are any givens in the management of information business, one of them is that people will make mistakes. So our goals reasonably might be to know what is a mistake, to recognize opportunities to avoid as many mistakes as we can, and to correct our mistakes. One manager's mistake may be another's triumph. It all depends. One size does not fit all. Managers should not interpret this advice as the equivalent of the "there's no one right answer" cant. There are right and wrong answers. We just do not find them in lists of rigid, unexamined, unqualified absolutes.

True, it is probably always a grievous mistake to publicly criticize and berate a paraprofessional who is interpreting company policy to a client, even if the paraprofessional is misspeaking. There are more appropriate, mistake-free ways to manage this situation. It is probably always a grievous mistake to fail to reprimand or counsel an employee whose ongoing unproductive behavior is creating a morale problem on the staff. Not taking the right action can be as harmful as taking the wrong action.

So, what should a manager do? Isn't there a list or a sure-fire formula one can use to start doing the right things and avoiding the bad things. "Don't just sit there, do something!" sounded like good advice until a very wise person advised, "Don't just do something, sit there!" When an expert encourages one to align company goals with employee goals and move forward from there, is not that a pretty good idea, a real Theory Y maneuver?

A caution flag should accompany this apparently reasonable advice. This alignment of organizational and personal values may work for healthy organizations. Some values, either organizational or personal may be dysfunctional. In those agencies where this is the case, the manager should try to help engineer a cultural face lift before merging values that collide.

Wise Sayings and Conditions Specific to a Given Environment and Staff

Here is another reason to be wary. Advice often emerges from the context of a given environment and cast of characters. Moreover, the advice may be elaborations of their creators' special take on matters. Often they are simply explications of pet pious sayings, sayings that have opposites which the creators conveniently ignore.

What is wrong with this? Well, let us inspect some of these wise sayings. "Look before you leap" sounds like responsible advice. Certainly one could build a strong statement about examining one's environment before risking one's resources. All right, but what about nearly opposite advice: "Strike while the iron is hot" or "He who hesitates is lost"? Is it not a mistake to delay action to the point of tardiness? Might one not add such behavior to a list of mistakes managers make? One could, if one thought the best way to run a business were to operationalize a set of profound sayings, pithy goodies that sound like absolute and ironclad prescriptions for achieving success—or avoiding failure. We call that MBSB, management by sound bite. "Neither a borrower nor a lender be." How is that for a motto for an information place; for a sign above the circulation desk, perhaps.

Let's You and George Take Risks

Take risks. Consider the legions of teachers, authors of management texts, and writers of "how to do it good" journal articles who have intoned this precept and folded it into their pronouncements. Not a single one of them will suffer a nanosecond's discomfort if a reader takes the advice to heart, takes a risk, makes a mistake, and tumbles. Does this render the advice of experts invalid? No. It renders it iffy though. Whether a risk is worth the risk depends on a number of factors, all of which managers of information places must enter into the equation. "Take risks" might appear in our chapter if we were to add, "Figure out what business you are in first, and determine how will this action (risk) may advance your purposes."

We more confidently would suggest "take risks" if we knew managers had a reasonable plan for risk taking and had asked and answered some important questions. A promise to rush a package of searched, interpreted, evaluated, synthesized, and organized information, urgently needed by an influential corporate officer, might be in order if the manager has

1. Determined what other tasks he will put aside in order to meet the rush deadline
2. Figured the probability of being able to create the product and meet the deadline
3. Mitigated, or increased the likelihood of success and lessened the likelihood of failure
4. Anticipated the impact of failure on the information place
5. Considered a strategy to employ should the effort fail

It All Depends!

Harvey Sherman once asserted that "It all depends" (Sherman 1975). We agree. Whether our advice, or anybody's, has any value for the manager hinges on his or her ability to consider as many of the "depend" variables as possible, at least the important ones. Sherman's idea, and ours too, is that administrators and managers must develop a frame of reference in which to place their decisions, risks, and wise sayings. That frame of reference must contain personal values, the mission statement of the organization, its vision statement, staff matters, client needs, and resource availability. To a great extent, many people in the organization must share and understand information about these things, not just selected administrators and managers. If "take risks" survives being filtered through such a framework, take some.

So, with "know upon what it depends" and "examine all opportunities within the framework of our personal and organizational values" as our mottoes, let us examine further what some of the experts say about mistakes.

We like the way Warren Bank thinks about making mistakes. He points out that leading and decision making are by definition activities involving risk, and where there is risk, there is the chance for error. His point is to learn from mistakes; let them teach us (Bank 1995, 227-28).

Experience is an especially severe teacher when it is our mistakes which do the teaching. Better we should learn from the errors of others than from those which we commit. This could lead to an equal amount of learning with a reduced amount of suffering.

We are also impressed with the way one organizational subgroup makes the processing of information about mistakes a productive, group-learning experience. When a problem has been detected by agency staff or by a customer of a product, managers assemble for a causal analysis exercise in which they examine chains of events that may have led to the problem. They strive to identify root cause. Their aim is to prevent repetition of such errors and to improve processes. They deliberately avoid finger pointing and blame finding, and they deliberately seek to provide a forum where all can learn from the mistake. There is a great twofold benefit of this procedure: the study of the chain of events by the group is far superior to a time-consuming investigation by one manager who would have to conduct a person-by-person inquiry; and, even more important, the group gets to learn from mistakes. This makes maximum use of "experience" as the teacher.

We do have some suggestions to offer, but remember, "It all depends"; opinions vary; perceptions are not immaculate; bad stuff sometimes happens; and it is better to learn from someone else's mistakes rather than one's own. So we present a set of suggestions in do and do not couplets, each accompanied by a list of questions to ask and answer before doing or don'ting. The list is derived from our own experiences in information place management, Internet contributions, some examples contributed by library directors selected randomly and surveyed by mail, and the wisdom contained in books and articles, notably *Sacred Cows Make the Best Burgers* (Kriregel and Breandt 1996), and *Top Five Time Management Mistakes* (Whetmore 1999).

One might use a staff meeting, in-service event, or class session to gather additional questions which could affect the risks associated with the coupled actions or inactions.

Delegate.   **Do not delegate.**

- Do we have people who can/want to grow? Can we surrender some authority, responsibility, and a little bit of the glory?
- Do we believe that if we want a job done correctly, we have to do it ourselves?
- Do we understand that delegation refers to the handing over of important, growth-producing tasks, not the transferring of grunt work we hate?
- Are we at peace with the risk that sometimes delegatees, and therefore we, will err. Is it true that "Every-one in your unit will be better at something than you are" (Sowards 1999, 523)?

Change.   **Don't change; resist change.**

- Do we know that change happens, there is little we can do to prevent it, and that radio stations are now playing oldies from the year 2001, the New Millennium!
- Do we know that while some sages say that if it ain't broke, don't fix it, others say that if it ain't broke, break it?
- What do managers have in mind when they reject "change for change's sake"? Does that comment ever make sense?
- Do we realize that extinction is nature's penalty for organisms which do not evolve? Are we aware that we probably work in a bureaucracy, and that in bureaucracies the instinct to resist change is primal?
- Do we understand that the community we serve from our change-resisting bureaucracy may be in a state of constant, even turbulent change?
- Is the investment you and your clients have in a given successful product or service so substantial and so ingrained that disrupting it and the routines that accompany it would not move you forward and might even move you back?
- Homeostasis is a comfortable state for many in our organizations. How should this fact influence the extent of and speed with which managers, especially new ones, introduce change?

Recognize performance.   **Don't recognize performance.**

- Once people achieve minimum standards of personal financial comfort, do they begin to need and seek more intangible rewards—like knowing they matter? Study after study reveals that workers work for rewards other than monetary. What does this tell the administrator/manager?

- Many workers crave immediate feedback. Do we supply it?
- Do we realize that giving people more responsibility can be interpreted by them as a reward—or as a penalty?
- Are we aware of how deeply workers resent not being recognized and included? Is a pat on the back or a note of thanks for a job well done, if delivered and received sincerely, an inexpensive yet effective form of praise?
- Do we deflate the value of recognition if we reward that which is expected rather than that which is exemplary?
- Could the bestowing of rewards create prima donnas? If turn, rather than earn, becomes a criterion, does the award tarnish?
- When we recognize accomplishment, do we first consider the developmental stages of the worker and adjust our expectations accordingly?

Don't smile till Christmas.   Lighten up!

- Do we know that "having" a sense of humor does not require hiring a team of writers and developing a stand-up routine?
- Do we know that even the jocularly impaired can smile?
- Do we realize that developing a sense of humor, of tolerance for human foibles, is the first line of defense against the stress that mistakes can provoke?
- Isn't it better to be around people who can smile and cause the line between work and play to blur a bit?
- Do we know that all work and no play makes managers Jack and Jackie age more quickly?
- Do we hide behind humor to avoid addressing mistakes or issues?
- Do we realize that sometimes employing humor can cause others not to take us seriously or to feel that we are not taking them seriously?

Develop a plan   Do not straitjacket yourself;
for each day.   deal with things as they
happen.

- Do we believe that if we make the plan, we get to attend to our needs as a manager; but if we wait to see what develops, we may merely react to random demands?

- Do things come up that we just have to deal with, and isn't being a slave to an agenda rather dysfunctional?

Take a lunch break.   ## Be too busy; do not take a lunch break.

- Do we know that we need time off from the routine, and that we will be more productive if we take that break?
- Are we aware that our stomachs will thank us if we take a break and eat healthy food, and that we will feel better?
- Do we realize that all fast food is the same, that it is squeezed out of the same vat and just shaped and packaged differently to look like a salad, burger, or fry?
- Do we know that some people resent the working lunch and consider it to be a violation of the "communion" eating together is supposed to be?
- Are we aware that the noon hour is the only workday time that some people have free, and that to schedule a noon meeting because it is free time and convenient for us may rob others of the chance to recharge batteries?
- But couldn't working through lunch free us up to get to the power cocktail party on time or enable our coworkers to get to their kids' soccer tournament on time?

Be consistent.   ## Be flexible.

- Have you seen one or the other of these in lists of managerial do's and don'ts? Ever seen them in the same list before? That is exactly where they belong.
- Are these not opposite values? Is it possible that these two values demonstrate why management is as much an art as it is a science? If ever "It all depends" applies, does it not apply here?
- Do we believe that if we tell them about why policies exist, most employees will understand and agree when we bend them for the good of the individual and/or the organization?
- Do we realize that if we do not communicate these things well with all the staff, they will get cranky?
- No matter what we do, some may complain. But is it not a frustrating mistake to try to make our information places curmudgeon proof?
- Are not most people pretty reasonable if we clue them in and they understand?

- How can bending policy for a good reason avoid the "favoritism" tag? Does it? Can supervisors have pets? Should they? Are you sure of your answer on this one?

Provide easy access to copious quantities of material in demand.

Have a book for every reader and know that every book has a reader.

- Are we aware that the concept of the hard-core nonuser is a useful ingredient to factor into the collection management equation?
- Do we know that if we advertise in our public catalog that we own an item, we create a client expectation that we can provide it?
- Can we understand that if we create a display of interesting materials, and some people become interested in those materials, they may want to borrow them—now?
- Have we come to grips with this truism: Weeding dead wood results in increased use of materials by clients?
- Do we believe, as a librarian from Cal Tech told us, that access and pilferage are inversely related?

Rely on the architect, the state specifications agent, and the construction engineer to know what kind of building you need.

Get in there and protect your interests or those people will give you the building they want.

- Do we know that most state contracts have been awarded to the lowest bidder?
- Will the politicians who wanted us to have the old Post Office be supportive of our interest in getting a new building for the information place?
- Will we hire a consultant? Is there a list?
- Do we remember that facilities planning was the weakest component of our formal LIS training? Can we find good workshops on building planning?
- Are there enough electrical outlets to accommodate new technologies?
- Is it not true that architects and construction professionals know more about their business than we could ever know, and we should, therefore, stand back and let them apply their expertise?

Engage the politicians.

Stay away from politicians; they aren't good library users and politics is dirty business.

- Are we aware that since funding decisions are made in the political arena, we are by definition part of the process?
- Do we know that by remaining disengaged from the politicians, we systematically detach and exclude ourselves from the people and processes involved in our support?
- Do we think that the best way to intrude upon the consciousness and plug into the value system of a politician is to try to interest him or her in the latest mystery story?
- Do we know that most politicians are ignorant about the extent of our information sorting, seeking, and packaging prowess and that by working with city or county managers (to avoid partisan politics) to learn agenda items, we can anticipate need and supply information that politicians use in their decision making?
- Do we know that if we plan well, by picking a day and time we know will be busy, the so-called Celebrity Librarian Day, where the mayor, the police chief, a township supervisor, a sports hero, or some known CEO works at the circulation desk, can be a PR triumph!
- Do we believe that asserting ourselves with politicians and academic or corporate fiscal officers has to result in grudge matches, or that we are the only unit competing for scarce resources?
- Should we remain invisible and therefore an unlikely target of opportunity for grandstanding, budget-cutting politicians?

Nurture the board of trustees.

Ignore the board if you can they are political appointees who know and care little about the library.

- Do we know that our state library agency can help us plan ways to educate and work with boards and help them understand the purpose and needs of the library and how to promote it?
- Have we determined that if we forge good relations with appointing groups (city council), we may influence the appointment process and that council may involve us in the nomination of members?

- Have we discovered in school, academic, and corporate settings that faculty committees and corporate boards can provide crucial support for the information place?
- Should we not ignore advisory and regulatory groups as much as we can; the less advice and regulation, the better?

When making hiring decisions, talk with a candidate's previous employers.	**In this litigious era, nobody will level with you, so don't bother checking employee's references.**

- Yes, hardly anyone will write negative references these days, but do we know that people will say in person or over the phone what they would never put in writing?
- Are you as amazed as we are that so often employers do not thoroughly check even the references that are supplied by the candidate?
- What wisdom is there in hiring someone else's problem?
- Is not each new employee a "clean slate," and should not we form our own opinions rather than rely upon the observations of a previous employer?

Treat support staff as human beings.	**You made sacrifices and worked hard for your degree; they made other choices; separation maintains rightful distinctions.**

- Support staff often constitute the first line of contact for clients; how do we think their being ignored and called nonprofessionals by the professionals affects their attitudes?
- Who invented the term *nonprofessional*, and who is it that we know who likes to be called a *non-* something?
- We ask more and more of support staff, especially in the automation, customer relations, and business ends of our information enterprises, so how does disrespecting them as persons square with this?
- How does giving support staff full privileges to play in our sandbox in any way diminish the professional status of degree holders?

- How would it be if we sent support staff to training sessions, and even went with them if they had fears about the process? Might they in turn become trainers in our organizations, even our systems?
- Speaking of training, do we provide any for support staff? Do we just assume everyone knows how to answer a phone politely?
- Who will help us find training opportunities?

| **In schools, aggressively market your products and services to teachers and principals.** | **In schools, let the quality of products, your displays, book talks, and user education do your talking for you.** |

- If study after study reveals that it is the teachers who have the most influence on student use of the media center, who do we think our primary clients are?
- Do you know that if you are in a school where teachers "dump" students for day-care sitting services in the media center, your opportunities for marketing the media center to the teachers will be severely diminished?
- The curriculum which school administrators study probably includes absolutely zero about the purpose and value of the media center. Guess whose job it is to do the training and convincing? Guess whose side a principal will take if he or she perceives an issue to involve the interests of one media specialist versus those of a mass of teachers? Is it clear that you must befriend and convince teachers?
- Should school library media specialists learn to frame their requests in terms of what is good for the whole school, not just in terms of what is convenient for them and the media center?
- We repeat: The clients are the teachers.
- Are we aware that unless we partner with some teachers, unless we become intimate with instructional development, some teachers will equate information literacy (IL), which is the survival skill for our era, with library lessons and the librarian's job, and IL will never achieve integration with the curriculum where it belongs?

So Where Does This Leave the Manager?

In many instances the buck may indeed stop here, right at the manager/decider's desk.

It makes many stops along the way, however, so the decider is not without help.

Assistance exists in the form of lucid vision statements, clear mission statements, and carefully conceived and constructed policy statements. It exists in the form of sound planning, solid and systemwide communication, strong personal and professional networks, and good friends and mentors. "If you want help, ask someone" is sage advice.

Deciding is your job. Expect to make an error now and then. Learn. Recover. Move on.

References

Bank, Warren. 1995. *The nine natural laws of leadership*. New York: American Management Association.

Kaplan, Abraham. 1964. *The conduct of inquiry: Methodology for behavioral science*. San Francisco: Chandler Publishing Company.

Kriegel, Robert, and David Brandt. 1996. *Sacred cows make the best burgers: Paradigm-busting strategies for developing change-ready people and organizations*. New York: Warner Books.

Mistakes are nature's way . . . 2005. Google (accessed 19 July 2005).

Sherman, Harvey. 1975. *It all depends: A pragmatic approach to organization*. University: University of Alabama Press.

Sowards, Steven W. 1999. Observations of a first-year middle manager. *C&RL News*, July/August, 523-25, 41.

Whetmore, Donald E. 2001. Top five time management mistakes. www.canadaone.com/ezine/august99/time_management.html (accessed 5 April 2001).

Chapter 11

Managing the Paradoxes

What Is a Paradox?

A paradox is an apparent contradiction. When conditions appear to contradict a set of assumptions about the world around us, we describe that situation as a paradox. How can what appear to be mutually exclusive conditions coexist? Nature provides an example.

When gray clouds obscure the sun and deliver rain, the sky darkens. During this time, however, if the sun should poke through, there is light *and* darkness. Two apparent opposite or contradictory conditions coexist. Nature observes this inconsistency and delivers a beautiful rainbow, sometimes two of them.

Nature teaches managers a good lesson, for paradoxes abound, they do not go away, and managers have to deal with them. We believe the message of the rainbow story is this: When conditions appear to collide, managers must address them. The result can be very productive, but the paradoxes will not disappear.

They or new ones will return. Paradoxes will not go away; they cannot be managed away. They are a fact of business life. They are "inevitable, endemic, and perpetual" (Handy 1995, 12). Some paradoxes are complex and opaque, such as the principle that "positive change requires significant stability" (Price Waterhouse 1996, iii, 37-58); and some appear on the surface to be quite simple, such as the warden wants to keep the prisoners under control and confined in the prison, and the prisoners resist order and long to escape, at least to be paroled from the prison. Prison management must confront these cross-purposes, this paradox.

261

The rainbow does not signal the end of darkness forever. The challenge of the organizational paradox is to confront it, take advantage of what it offers, and blunt some of its negative effects.

An Information Place Paradox

Managers ameliorate; they do not solve the paradox. They make the best of an apparent dilemma. If some of their books fail to circulate, they place the ignored volumes in a used book sale. People who rejected the items when they were free will snap them up at fifty cents a pop! They will buy what they refused to have for free. This is one of LIS's more curious paradoxes. Purchasers may use the turkey of a book to prop up the couch with the missing leg, and we clear the shelves for newer, more in-demand acquisitions. The circulation problem will repeat itself when additional books purchased because managers thought they would move, don't. There is room in the book sale bin.

Libraries collect to disperse. Do they solve this paradox? No. They address it, and in so doing they fulfill their purpose. Managing paradoxes is not a parlor game; it is what information professionals do for a living.

A People-Management Paradox

Managing people is difficult. Managers have to recruit staff, hire them, train them, supervise them, discipline them, pay them, reward them, promote them, and sometimes fire them. The conventional wisdom about this is that since hiring and training require such an investment of managerial time and effort, it would be good if the staff stayed long enough to return the investment. Excessive turnover is dysfunctional. Well, it all depends. In the fast-food industry, management encourages rapid turnover, which rids the organization of cranky minimum wage employees and those who might lay claim to expensive company benefits were they to remain. Hire them and fire them, or hope they quit. That is the corporate strategy (Schlosser 2001, 72-75). Hire them to fire them? Is this not a paradox? It is, and it is one of a number of apparent contradictions with which many managers wrestle. Many managers of information places would argue that their hopes and strategies for retention differ markedly from those of the burger joint managers.

In the following few pages we list and discuss a number of paradoxes confronting managers of information places.

Paradox 1

Managerial perceptions of quality may conflict with client demand. Managers get into trouble when they are lured into a discussion of quality *versus* demand, as though the two were antithetical and a collection could not contain some of both. Clients may demand escape literature. Giving them some Gothic junk food does not require managers to ignore current events, scientific inquiry, pop psychology, Sartre, Shakespeare, or the latest in electronic information delivery.

So the issue is quality *and* demand, not quality *versus* demand, and the question for collection managers is "How do I achieve a useful balance between providing supply-driven information products and services on one hand, and demand-driven information products and services on the other hand. If managers eschew needs assessment and insist on determining on their own what it is that the clients need, they may find themselves riding dinosaurs. If managers cater only to expressed need, they may preside over collections that quickly lose their value and their currency. So a perceived quality/demand paradox is not solved by admonishing each other to avoid the either/or position, but the problem is addressed when managers conduct community analysis and needs assessments and fold those findings into a sound collection development policy that is anchored in a mission statement and flexible enough to respond to identified, sometimes shifting, client need.

Knowing what business we are in is essential here. Supplying mystery novels may be precisely what some information places are supposed to do. For other information places where supplying up-to-date market research to busy research and development and sales staffs is the business of the information manager, those mystery novels may be irrelevant. Whose job is it to determine good or bad, trash or treasure, crucial or trivial, current or obsolete, useful item or shelf sitter? It is the job of the information manager. Managers must get comfortable with the reality of having to deal with the tensions that competing values create. "Who am I to judge?" is not merely a naïve cop-out, it announces an abdication of responsibility. Managers are paid to judge and to decide, and to base those judgments and decisions on sound intelligence gathering and a firm grasp of mission.

Managers of information places are currently discovering that the quality/demand issue is nearer the bottom of the list of problems. At the top of the problem list now is this issue: How do we pay the bill required to meet client expectations and demand for expensive automated services and still afford to grow the traditional collection? *E*ven this question displays a bias and suggests *a priori* that it is necessary to do both. Not only do paradoxes not disappear, they can emerge and loom just from the way we perceive our environment and ask questions about it.

Paradox 2

The instinct to acquire may be in conflict with the requirement to disseminate. Collecting things comes naturally to those people with pack rat instincts, and they become overly possessive of collections. Some prefer the orderliness of precisely shelved pristine volumes, and they resent the disorder that use of their treasures creates. Preservation may trump dissemination. The information manager who complains, "Inventory reveals that *they* stole fifty-six of *my* books last year." has two major problems to deal with:

1. Theft
2. The inner turmoil created by what appear to be conflicting purposes—acquiring and giving away

With regard to theft, chances are it is the good stuff, the new and in-demand material, that disappears. No detection procedure will catch the determined thief, but good electronic surveillance and detection can identify the forgetful client and the more casual thief. Sound, selective inventory exercises and careful monitoring of unfulfilled requests for owned items can identify replacement needs, or in cases where owned items are shelved improperly and not found by clients, stack maintenance needs.

We recommend a proactive response to replacement needs. Managers save time and money when they establish a replacement budget and instruct bibliographers to make immediate decisions about the replacement or nonreplacement of items judged to be missing. Each information place will determine what constitutes permanently missing, and each will determine whether to replace or not. We recommend a speedy process for this. If a lost item were to appear later, this would result in the agency's having two copies of an in-demand item, which is far superior to having merely a "missing" note in the catalog for the only copy of a popular item. This identify-and-replace regimen accomplishes three useful purposes:

1. It recovers useful, needed information more quickly

2. It reduces bindery time lag, for it identifies and replaces before, not after, collating in preparation for sending off, thus
   speeding up expensive claiming procedures for periodicals
3. It helps maintain the library's reputation for having what
   clients want

With regard to the ownership/dispersal conflict, shelves made un-
tidy by searchers and browsers, and circulation files, card or electronic,
made to bulge by eager borrowers may be among the most reliable indications that information places are doing their jobs.

Paradox 3

Managers should find a way to count in-house use of materials.
Information workers who only count out-house figures (circulation) are
noting only one third of usage. In-house use often doubles out-house
use. Often a client will examine a number of journal articles before
selecting the two he or she chooses to use for a project. The nonchosen
items are not necessarily off-target or irrelevant. On the contrary, they
are part of a corpus of materials of varying importance, and each of
them has been instrumental in helping a client pick and choose.

True, what information professionals are about is collecting and
preserving, but they are also responsible for retrieving, interpreting, and
using that which they collect and preserve—and they are responsible
for helping clients retrieve, interpret, and use. Collecting and disseminating are really not conflicting notions; they are enabling ones. When
people use what managers acquire, they signal that the managers are
doing their jobs.

We also suggest that managers be wary of the sour grapes assertion
that "you can not be sure people are reading the things they check out"
or that circulation "doesn't mean anything." Our assertion is that in-the-
place and outside-the-place usage is a significant and useful indicator
of important information place activity. We may not conclude from the
numbers that every client's spirit and IQ soar with each circulation
event, so we strongly suggest that managers develop a number of ways
to demonstrate that they are conducting well the business they are in.
Funders often conclude from the numbers, however, that the counts
demonstrate concrete evidence that the information place should be
supported. Circulation does not "mean anything"? We beg to differ.
Studying what does and what does not circulate gives us a useful picture of client demand. So does studying and then responding to requests
for unowned information resources.

Paradox 4

We claim that support staff constitutes the organizational back-bone; we pay them as though they were the appendix.

Many information agencies operate with a personnel structure that divides the staff in two and then subdivides each portion into graded categories. There may be, for example, a librarian category with three to five graded levels ascending from Librarian I to Librarian V. The I category is for new hires in entry-level professional positions, and the V category is for directors at the top of the scale. Similarly, there may be a support staff or library technical assistant (LTA) category, with the LTA I designation for new hires and LTA V for top-level support staff.

While there is wide variation in the classification rules with regard to who can be designated a professional, the most common credential required for that status is a preferred degree such as the master's of library and information science, its equivalent, or the master's of public administration, each a terminal professional degree. Some systems, including federal civil service, award "professional" status to bachelor's degree holders in certain information-related occupations. In some organizations there is tension between the two groups—the preferred degree holders in higher paid positions of authority, and the rest of the staff who may be hardworking employees in highly important jobs but who lack the certifying credential, the preferred or required degree.

Sometimes professionals put distance between themselves and support staff by referring to them as *nonprofessionals*. Occasionally the professionals disrespect them by contradicting or reprimanding them in the presence of clients. Professionals often exit the information place to attend meetings, seminars, and conventions, leaving the support staff to run the business. Professionals may create a work environment wherein support staff do not know or understand the full range of the degreed managers' administrative/managerial responsibilities, how their jobs contribute to the organizational mission, or how the units of the system function together to achieve organizational goals and objectives. Without consulting them, professionals frequently make decisions which affect their jobs and livelihoods. Professionals may ignore support staff development and see only to the continuing education needs of professional staff. When degreed managers permit them to attend staff meetings, it may be to inform them, not involve them. Professionals are much more flexible with their own schedules than with those of the support staff. The professionals may even enforce no fraternization rules, or the corporate culture may discourage any kind of non-occupational-related intercourse. Overt unfriendliness may reign, or maybe just an off-putting snobbishness. Degreed information workers may pay themselves 100 percent or even 200 percent more than the non-degreed staff who work side by side with them.

Yet when it comes time to squeeze more blood, to do more with less, who gets squeezed and bled and asked to do a little more? Who gets reminded about that backbone metaphor but treated like the appendix? Who gets paid minimum wage plus carfare but assured "that the business just could not run without you"? When degreed information professionals look down their noses, the objects of their offensive gazes may be hardworking support staff.

This disrespect is even more troubling these days when professionals assign support personnel not just the grunt work, but often place them in crucial technical service and systems positions. Paraprofessionals at database terminals frequently make the initial determination of how an acquired item will be classified, marked and parked, and made available for user access. They may be ace debuggers, the only ones in the building who can prevent a system crash or launch a recovery. They are frequently the meeters and greeters, the first line of business/client contact. They may be the last to learn about decisions and the first required to implement them.

Paraprofessional rage! Is it any wonder that some paraprofessionals have quickly and angrily asked, "What is wrong with this picture"? The record clearly shows that they are demanding to be included in the decisions that affect them. They want more opportunities for development, career mobility, and service in information organizations. They want to be eligible to hold office in those organizations and associations (Mayo 2000).

Let us quickly and happily observe that not all and probably not even most of these examples apply in the organizations currently served by the readership. In many of these agencies, enlightened information place managers promote cooperative interaction and discourage divisive separatist behavior.

Methods employed by sensitive, intelligent managers include

1. Praising in public, reprimanding in private
2. Telling staff where they go and why
3. Using in-service training sessions to give employees the opportunity to tell others about their jobs, to explain how they contribute to the cause, and to listen to others do the same, so that each can develop a bigger picture of organizational purposes and a firm grasp of how each contributes to the greater good
4. Consulting staff when making decisions that affect their work lives

5. Making sure that paraprofessionals have opportunities for growth
6. Involving key paraprofessionals in staff meetings
7. Extending opportunities for flexible scheduling
8. Encouraging friendliness
9. Pressing for adequate compensation for support staff

All right, managers cannot close the information place and send the entire staff to every meeting or workshop. Managers cannot give every staff member a vote on every issue. Managers should know that "It all depends" and "either/or" cautions should operate in these matters. The artful manager will determine when and whether and how much of these measures apply to sound practice.

Paradox 5

Intellectual freedom conflicts with parents' rights to monitor their children's reading. Many information professionals have and subscribe to codes of ethics. The librarians do; so do information brokers. Librarians also have produced a "Librarians Bill of Rights" (Library 1996). These codes often define intellectual freedom as the absolute, unrestricted right to know, to inquire, and to express one's beliefs and thoughts.

Comforted though they are by the absolutist stands they champion, these champions frequently collide with champions of decency and children's protection who can *identify filth when they see it* and who condemn librarians and teachers for condoning abomination. The more fanatical of the latter group delight in portraying librarians as snaggle-toothed pornographers who cannot wait to corrupt the naive and defenseless. They often become censors.

Censors seek to cause the removal of owned items from an information place because they object to content. Information professionals often do not initiate censorious acts, but they frequently participate in censorship-like behavior that has the identical effect—denial of access—as censorship. Censorship-like acts are labeling, locking, requiring special permission, transferring to other less accessible collections, and, most frequent and easiest of all, simply not acquiring an item that is a potential target for complaint. Timid selection produces vanilla and very safe collections.

Tempting though it is to explore the whys and wherefores of censorship, the most important concept for managers to grasp is that when intellectual freedom collides with censorship, the problem calls for intelligent management of the information place. Intelligent managers will

1. Understand that censors do not seek information about what offends them. They seek to remove what offends them. So supplying them with information that an item has been favorably reviewed will have zero effect on their quest. They do not seek to be informed and convinced; they are already informed and convinced. What they want is the removal of an offensive item. Only the most casual of censors will balk when presented with favorable reviews or recommendations.

2. Realize that the people whom managers must convince that information place selection practice is sound are the governing authority, advisory groups, and the general client base. Target them for rational explanations about collection development. They can be in the information place's corner when censors call.

3. Understand that censorship is a power move that requires a powerful response. Know that power resides in collection development policies, selection policies, challenge policies, gift policies, and weeding policies which have been signed and endorsed by governing authority.

4. Realize that the word "appropriate" in item No. I of the librarians Code of Ethics provides wiggle room and permission to exercise judgment (Code 1995).

5. Commit to the idea that parents have a right to oversee what their children read, but they do not have a right to oversee what other parents' children and the community read.

6. Understand that when like-minded censors unite, they can present a formidable challenge. They know how to marshal appealing arguments. They play on the fearful. They are eager for public forums. Many are accomplished organizers and spokespersons. They may form a community. They may claim to represent the larger community. They may in fact do so. They may be government, as in the case of the threat to withhold aid to information places which do not install filters on public access computers. Know that censors wear many uniforms: governmental, religious, special interest, right, and left. Political correctness, occasionally a most virulent strain of repression, comes from the left, not the right, thought erroneously by some to be the authors of all censorious acts.

7. Respect the censor.

8. Some censors will not have read the item to which they object. This will not confuse them half as much as it does management.

9. Understand that the more casual censor may be put off by the challenge form, or merely may want to vent and will abandon the attack after having done so. Others will comply fully, list each offending expletive or idea and the page on which it occurs, and answer the all the challenge form questions that are supposed to weed out the faint of heart: What do you think is the theme of this work? and What other books on this theme would you recommend?

10. Realize that compromise does not always require compromise, as in compromise one's principles. Strategic retreats and withdrawals may be the best managerial practice in some circumstances. Concede a skirmish; come back well armed to fight harder, and better, the next time.

11. Above all, as managers, reject the proverbs and cute sayings. They are odious and unhelpful. On the surface, they seem to absolve us of having to use our training or employ judgment. What are some wishy-washy wise sayings?

Our Turn: If you give in now, you will have to keep on giving in and pretty soon everything will be gone. Nonsense!

Our Turn: If a portion of your collection does not offend at least somebody in the community, you have a lousy collection. That is a "Let's you and George fight" pronouncement.

Must you have material that presents all sides of all controversial issues. No! Your job is not to promiscuously provoke every sensitive client about every conceivable issue. The balanced collection of which many speak should instead be quite imbalanced to serve the expressed needs and wants of clients. This way the collection is in balance with demand, not with a decimal classification system that predicts how many items should be in each category.

Managers, examine your consciences about events like banned book week. What are you trying to accomplish? Celebrate freedom? Promote inquiry? Rub the censors' noses in a mess and invite them to attack other titles they had not known about until you waved the list in their faces? Are victories over the censor best savored more discreetly?

Asserting the library's commitment to intellectual freedom can be most satisfying for the information professional who understands that access to information is an imperative for free people who wish to remain free. No other organization or profession, not churches or governments, not the journalists or the teachers, can lay claim to as full a commitment to providing access to as wide a range of information as librarians can. Library managers may fall short of making rainbows every time it rains, but they surely can shine a bright light.

Paradox 6

Before the Internet, the information professional was in charge of selection; after the Internet, the client is substantially in charge of selecting some of what the information place collects.

It used to be that information workers would consult reviewers' opinions or publishers' lists and select items for the information place. This is called *selection* and it was the information workers' domain. Sometimes they placed blanket orders for everything on political science from publisher Y or standing orders for every new almanac or handbook from publisher Z. They may have established a profile of need and turned this over to a jobber who automatically would send items published in the declared areas of interest. Some even urged and honored client suggestions for acquisition. The information worker remained in control, however. As gatekeeper, he or she passed judgment on what the information place acquired and made available.

No longer is selection the exclusive domain of the information worker. Every time a client consults the Internet, the client becomes the selector. He or she determines in that instant what the information place shall acquire, and in the case of a download or a printout, what the information place shall disseminate!

So instead of controlled access to approved sources, the information place now provides unfettered access to the information rummage sale, that global flea market that is the Internet—treasures, gems, warts, and all.

Are the inmates in charge of the asylum? Maybe they should be, but the answer is partly. Here a major problem for managers surfaces, and it is in this area that some have, with all good intentions, dropped the ball.

Some managers sought to head off all problems by installing filters on the public access computers. What these filters were supposed to do was block the porn goodies and admit only legitimate items. Research into their effectiveness reveals that they do neither very well. They admit the salacious and block the legitimate. Inventive pornographers have discovered ways to link legitimate sounding search terms to their sites, while some of the filtering devices deny access to information about Vice President Cheney of the United States because of his first name. Other managers dealt with the problem by adopting the American Library Association's absolutist stand on intellectual freedom and installed no filters. Concerned individuals and organizations have entered the conflict on both sides, and the government and the courts have intervened too. Congress passed the Children's Internet Protection Act (CIPA), intended to protect children from indecency. On the other hand, Virginia courts have ruled against filters. Minneapolis librarians complained that downloaded porn created a hostile work environment. Managers might hope for a final solution to this problem, this paradox of intellectual freedom and intellectual restriction. As with all paradoxes, however, the contradiction will not go away even though many managers find ways to deal with the contradictions. We recommend several excellent readings on this issue: (Sykes 1998, Bowman 2001, and Marshall 2001).

In our opinion, the managers who have been least successful in this area have been the ones who misperceived the issue. They saw the problem as either related to intellectual freedom, censorship, or protection of the innocent. It may have been about some of that, but it was a managerial problem first and foremost. It was a decision issue.

Wise managers who saw what was about to happen anticipated the problem and headed it off at the pass. They provided both camps a victory, and in the process avoided messy public relations disasters. They provided some filtered machines; they provided access to other unfiltered machines. Citizens and parents could choose.

In the case of the parents, the managers cooperated with them and gave them some power of choice. In the case of the average adult citizen, they provided uncensored access. Certainly by permitting some filtered access, these managers angered intellectual freedom purists. On the other hand, the thought police were not happy about the unfiltered public access computers, but in the filtered machines managers provided for children, they got to enjoy a victory too. Compromise worked. Without the compromise, offended parties may have gone to war and created such a stir that automation budgets could have suffered and the whole community would have lost electronic access.

Managers who saw this only as an issue of intellectual freedom, or who trotted out lame "we do not serve in loco parentis" arguments, and especially those who whined the outrageous complaint that they could not oversee what goes on in their own businesses, encountered lots of unnecessary trouble. Managers who fought this battle more adroitly continue to serve the interests of intellectual freedom in their information places. They have dealt with the paradox by understanding the competing influences and managing responses which serve and placate both.

Paradox 7

Change-resisting bureaucratic organizations must respond to change in the environments they serve.

"Red tape" is the most frequent response in a word association test in which the test word is "bureaucracy." Others are "inefficient," "delay," "impersonal," and "incompetent." The negative responses far outnumber the positive or neutral ones.

Some callers measure the efficiency of a bureaucracy by the number of times they are placed on hold before reaching a party who can help them. Some never reach any party and instead get stuck in a continuous loop of irrelevant-to-them recorded messages. Department of motor vehicle and post office jokes are legion, sometimes ghoulish. If people think bureaucracies are so bad, how come they do not make them go away?

How come? Number one, they are not so bad; number two, there are so many of them; number three, they do not want to go away; and number four, people need them. One, bashing bureaucracy is a popular pastime, but the fact of the matter is no one has manufactured an alternative organizational format that can handle the volume of transactions, numbers of people, and complexity of issues that bureaucracies deal with constantly. In certain instances flatter, less hierarchical structures may manage well. In others, where cooperation and communication are required for instant application to certain creative and decision processes (research and development, interior decoration), bureaucratic structure may impede progress. In short, however, bureaucracies work. They do what they do better than any other organizational type. Their champions claim that the delays, chains of command, isolation, impersonality, and the volumes of written regulations are not bad at all and that they help ensure that the right job gets done by the right employee for the right client.

Two, there are many, many bureaucracies. Government, schools, public services and utilities, churches, armies and navies, and information places are mostly bureaucratic in nature. Most of the readership serves in or will soon serve in a bureaucracy. They will work in departments with defined responsibilities, observe chains of command, note that authority travels more swiftly downward than communication travels upward, deal with a lot of by-the-book management, and witness the Peter Principle in action. The Peter Principle states that in a hierarchy, people rise to a position of incompetence, and there they stay. A corollary states that in a hierarchy many who have risen do not believe in the Peter Principle (Bloch 1977-82, 1980, 1982). There are so many bureaucracies. Where would they go? What would folks do in the meantime? Until managers can answer those questions, the sheer numbers of bureaucracies, both the bloated, inefficient ones and the sleek, competent ones, virtually guarantee their continued existence.

Three, they do not want to disappear. Armed with job descriptions, protected by tenure and civil service, skilled in their respective specialties, protected from harassment, paid a living wage, enjoying generous numbers of holidays, sheltered from inclement weather, and in most cases performing a needed service of some kind, most employees of the bureaucracy want to keep things the way they are. Progress makes them suspicious and worries them; petrifying does not. The very organizational structure and corporate culture of the bureaucracy stiffens itself against change of any kind. Volumes of rules and regulations nourish the beast. Brittle to the point of almost cracking, the bureaucracy embraces the status quo and resists innovation. For all the retiring or burned out employees, there are legions who willingly take their places. The bureaucracy loves being a bureaucracy. It likes things the way they are. An applicable motto might be: It is not broken; but even if it is, do not fix it!

While this may be just fine for the employees, how about the clients—the ones served by the complex bureaucracies. These clients work and live in communities often in a state of flux. Opportunities flash. Troubles surface. Priorities change on a dime. Demographics shift. Needs, made more urgent and abundant by prodigious change, may suffer if the organizations charged with serving them are rigid and unresponsive. The good news is they are not so rigid and unresponsive, and they can and do respond to demand, sometimes with great speed.

How can this happen? So much depends upon the leadership and vision of the people who head and manage the bureaucracy that is the information place. In bureaucracies where enlightened management constructs forward-looking client-focused mission statements, change can happen. In organizations where management commits to the essential principle of marketing—satisfying client need—change can happen. Change can occur when management discovers need, develops products and services that address that need, tells clients about the products and services, delivers them to the clients, stands back and measures the performance and the product, and then feeds that intelligence back to the organizational decision apparatus.

Change can happen in bureaucratic information places where the commitment to find out is operationalized. When administration and management establish a community relations staff, they begin this operation. They strengthen it when they emphasize consumer service functions. When they empower public relations officers, research and development teams, and marketing departments, they honor a commitment to change and be responsive. If information professionals who see the need to adjust and respond report to managers and administrators who welcome innovation and provide a hospitable infrastructure, change can happen. If leadership within the bureaucracy values change and, above all, places the power of their offices behind new ventures, change can happen.

Sometimes presidents of the United States discover to their great disappointment that the massive federal bureaucracy is substantially immovable. They use appointive and other powers of persuasion to nudge the behemoth, but the result is often inertia. Fortunately, most managers of information places face more modest versions of the giant hierarchies. Managers who understand the decision structures in their organizations, and who win the support of leadership, can become change agents. It all depends on how the bureaucracy views itself. New hires and managers in transition can make important discoveries about corporate culture and change by walking around the place to see if anybody talks to anybody else and by asking the right questions at the job interview.

1. What department oversees client needs analysis and to whom do they report?
2. To what extent do you budget for needs analysis and public relations?
3. Who is responsible for planning and executing responses to identified need?
4. What are some things you do differently today from yesterday?
5. What plans do you have for change?

By the way, someone who takes over the management of a small organization may discover that most of these responsibilities are his or hers! If the bureaucracy is to change, it may be the new manager with the new broom who must lead.

Making Change Happen: Some Tips for the Would-Be Change Agent
The literature of innovation and change agentry is rich and helpful. It presents a lot to think about. Eventually, the person who wants to introduce a change has to do something with those thoughts. Then the

would-be change agent may run into resistance from the guardians of the status quo, the people who are comfortable with the way things are.

We say understand this; then act. Understand the force for keeping things the way they are and construct a plan to reduce the resistance and increase the willingness to accept and adopt a change. Daryl L. Conner provides invaluable assistance with his assimilation metaphor (Conner 1992, 74-85). He speaks of assimilation capacity, calling it the process we use to adjust to the positive or negative implications of a major shift in our expectations (Conner 1992, 74). We have a finite amount of resources to spend on the assimilation of change, and we spend those resources on dealing with the changes—global, organizational, and personal—that confront us. If a person exhausts these finite resources to deal with major personal or organizational change, he or she will not have the assimilation capacity to accommodate a change introduced by a would-be change agent.

Therefore, a senior manager whose support the change agent must have, who is distracted by a divorce and a need to retool corporate systems, may have too few assimilation points left to accept our new plan for marketing service to an underserved population. The plan may be a brilliant one, but it will fail to get a hearing if the innovator chooses the wrong time to introduce it The change agent who knows the environment, and who factors in the conditions which distract the attention of all those players whose support the agent requires, increases the likelihood for acceptance. The odds become even more favorable if the innovator can demonstrate that the change can help solve some of the organizational, even personal, issues upon which the players spend assimilation points.

The Decision Style of the Leader—the One Whose Support Is Most Needed

Knowing the environmental conditions is essential. Also, knowing the decision-making style of the ones who must hear, accept, and support the change is equally essential. Suppose a leader's agreement hinges upon advice from a cadre of department heads, without whose advice to go ahead the leader will not act. The change agent will have to convince them, probably before approaching the leader, that the innovation is a good one. Incidentally, the leader who knows that the agent has gone under his head with a proposal will not resent this. The issue for this kind of decider is not chain of command but support from advisers.

Suppose the leader is less democratic and more of an autocratic decider. In this case the change agent will want to appeal to the leader's sense of control. Demonstrating how the change fits with and contributes to a leader-authored vision statement may make such an appeal.

The Importance of Control

More advice from Conner: One can improve a plan for change if he or she factors in the effects of ambiguity on the control we all seek, devises a plan for achieving control during the introduction and management of change, and manages the speed at which the change happens to match the pace of change in the environment (Conner 1992, 84-85).

Paradox 8

Managers are advised to be consistent and flexible, at the same time.

Consistency implies uniformity, a steadiness, and a reliability. People tend to rely on a manager's consistent response to certain issues and questions. They may take comfort in knowing that the manager will consistently respond in specified, known, and predictable ways. Many consistent managers go by the book. Everybody can know what the book says, and everybody can forecast how a book decider will decide. By-the-numbers managers contribute few surprises, and they can provide reassuring balance. What could be bad about this?

Flexibility implies the capacity to change, to go with the flow, to take advantage of opportunity. Change agents like to work with flexible managers because they appreciate the managers' willingness to take risks and bend policy. Flexible managers examine issues before pronouncing decisions to steady the course or modify the course. Flexible managers may be intolerant of the status quo, and they may be quite loose with the book. What could be bad about this?

What kind of management and supervision is better—consistent or flexible? The answer is probably both. Employees trust managers who consistently enforce company rules, who show no favoritism when it comes to rewards and discipline. Managers who behave this way may count on employee loyalty and cooperation. Employees equally may be comforted to know that a manager will bend policy to take advantage of opportunity. Flexible managers may find their employees more excited about change if they know the boss does not march in lockstep to the book.

How does the manager know which stance to take? A firm grasp of what is the business of the information place helps. It is also essential that staff shares this understanding. Knowing why the manager decides what the manager decides helps employees avoid the organizational or departmental vertigo that results from mysterious moves by management. Artful managers who want staff to know why they make the moves they do take the time to explain them.

Your Turn: How would you respond to the following decision opportunities? What questions would you want answered before you respond with a decision?

---

1. Ginny is the new head cataloger. She wants to go to a database workshop, but the policy manual states that employees must have passed the probationary period before they can attend workshops on company time.
2. Frank, the circulation clerk who opens the station each morning, was late twice this week. Personnel from technical services had to fill in.
3. Information services personnel in the public library you direct are limited to twenty minutes per client, owing to volume of business and staff size. A local corporation has offered to pay for some service that will require several hours to complete.
4. A company in town has suggested that they sponsor your fiction collection.
5. Your two best marketing professionals are new mothers who want to change their two full-time jobs into one full-time job which they will share in a.m./p.m. shifts. You have never done anything like this before.
6. Two scientists want personal, not mail or fax, delivery of journals. No one else seems to mind coming to the information center, or downloading copies on office computers. You are concerned about the effect on staff who have to make deliveries and the effect this is likely to have on other users.

Paradox 9

Cooperation is a good; cooperation is very expensive.

Cooperation is such a nice word! Is there any concept more in keeping with what the information place is about than cooperation? When people who join the information professions examine their reasons for doing so, they often discover that the inclination to want to help others—to unite them with the information they seek—is a driving force. Working with each other, with producers and providers, and with other information places, to connect request and response—that is the fulfilling event. Cooperation makes that happen.

And why not cooperate? Information agency A discovers that client B needs something that A does not own but information agency C does. So A borrows from C and gives to B. It is simple, easy, and beautiful. That is why network is such a magnificent concept. See the network run. Run, network!

When Ken Beasley addressed a preconference on performance measures at the annual convention of the American Library Association in Las Vegas, Nevada, he was booed and nearly run out of town for what he said. He told librarians that they had better study this cooperation thing before pouring so much psychic and monetary investment into it. He said that they better stop and smell the costs associated with cooperation. He said information places might be moving too quickly into unknown territory.

That was an unwelcome message for card-carrying cooperation enthusiasts. For them, in 1972, there was no higher calling than to cooperate. For them, in 1972, the major problem was finding a way to standardize entries, for everybody to name information the same way, so that when agency A wanted to borrow from agency C, A could be sure C named the item the same way A did.

We know differently now. We know that all the C agencies grew weary and impatient with the A agencies, who under the flag of cooperation, instead of developing their own collections, preyed upon the C's. Many of the early cooperative systems and federations encountered enormous unanticipated managerial surprises when they discovered that these new entities required funding and governance. They were shocked to discover divided loyalties of some agency A and C staff who were employed by their respective agencies but who also served in the new cooperative.

Shortly after listening to Dr. Beasley, one of the participants in that 1972 preconference made the happy discovery that an Ivy League library held a volume needed at the participant's library. Soon he made an additional discovery. The holding library would gladly process the loan request (not necessarily send the book, just officially set out to look for it) for $7.50.

No one from the Ivy League library had attended the preconference, but the Ivy League agency had already decided that if cooperation meant the small prey upon the large, they would institute their own equalization formula long before the rest of the information profession caught on that cooperation costs money. Such formulas are now standard ingredients in cooperative arrangements. They have to be! Interlibrary lending and borrowing is big business. Once just an ancillary department that a library budget carried, interlibrary loan departments now reside in major budget categories and may employ sizable staffs headed by several professionals. Some information agencies employ staffs whose main responsibility is to search and snatch from the collections of other information agencies. Some of the others will play . . . for pay.

Paradox 10

Free is not without cost (the free lunch?); charging fees disenfranchises the poor.

It is important to note that some information agencies, mostly of the public variety, by law may not charge for anything other than things like postage, copying, or the processing of requests for owned but in-use items.

It is equally important to note that some information agencies, mostly of the public variety, are being directed by their funding authorities to recover costs. Tax money is in shorter supply, demands from competing agencies mount, and the politicians are saying, "There is no likelihood of increased tax support; find alternative ways to support yourselves, public agencies."

So managers of information places acquire grant-writing skills, seek corporate sponsorship, promote referendums, and with the green light from authority, embark on entrepreneurial ventures like day-care visitations and Herculean information service for a price. They contract to serve business or they establish search services and offer them for sale to individuals and groups. They charge nonresident fees.

It may say "Free Library" on the agency letterhead or above the door, but information is not free. Information may be paid for by tax money, tuition, donations, or from corporate coffers, but information is not free.

Information may be available on the Internet, for the taking from library shelves, and merely by asking for it at an information agency, but information is not free.

Information explodes and becomes more expensive. Clients expect libraries to be totally wired. Information workers who demand to keep their skills current drive investments in the new technology. The steady availability of new electronic products also requires information place managers to invest heavily in electronic hardware and software. Traditional acquisition budgets suffer. Information is not free.

Nevertheless, images of the free library and the peoples university persist. Some people believe their tax money has already paid for the materials and services they seek from the information place. Little do they know about the intricacies of licensing restrictions, obsolescence deliberately sewn into products produced by those who do understand the business of the information business, and the enormous costs associated with just trying to keep up with the steady flow of new, in-demand products. The concept of the costs that accompany a manager's decision to commit to a CD-ROM version of a periodical index never crosses their awareness. Information is not free. Even Information Age electronic philanthropy may lock a manager into selecting a given manufacturer's product and require frequent, expensive upgrades, especially of software.

Getting extra support and recovering some costs are absolutely essential if information agencies are to continue to offer automated services, even at the level available to many people in their homes today. Few budgets can handle the electronic onslaught. Charging for some kinds of services appeals to some managers of information places, but there are people, including spokespersons for librarians' organizations, who claim that charging fees disenfranchises the poor.

The disenfranchisement argument would seem to have some surface logic to go along with its appeal to our instinct to want to help others. People who cannot afford soup or housing or tuition are unlikely to be able to afford even some of the cost of a computer search and printout of articles on relationships between osmosis and plant regeneration. One must ask, however, how many of the poor are lined up to make such a request.

Perhaps that question is insensitive, but it is necessary to drive home the point to managers of information places that social pronouncements require as much investigation as scientific ones. In the face of prohibitive costs, unless recovery is possible, does it not make sense to discover who and how many real and potential requesters really cannot afford a needed service, and might there be a way to spread and prorate costs so that more people who need access can afford it? If the issue were, in fact, recover costs or do not provide the service because it is unaffordable, otherwise, to anyone, would it not make sense to study how to effect some recovery? It may already be a requirement.

When some information places provided free copying services, many clients determined that they must copy copious amounts of material. When some of these agencies decided to institute even modest charges for copies, many clients became more selective about what they needed to copy. Costs have a way of helping people establish priorities. This we know. What we do not know is how many people suffer a knowledge or power deficit because we recover some costs. Just as true as "the person who does not have a dime for bread does not have a dime for a photocopy" argument, is the fact that some organizations have found a way to spread costs, prioritize, and serve a greater number of clients.

Some managers question the validity of the "fees disenfranchise the poor" assertion. They argue that the absolute right to all information is not guaranteed by the Constitution of the United States, and they protest that borrowing terms like "Bill of Rights" is a corruption and infringement upon the ten amendments. If constitutionality is claimed for every privilege, they say, then rights lose their unique status. If everything is a right, an entitlement, can real rights survive? They judge as specious the argument that the poor have absolute rights to information based either upon their poverty or their membership in the human race, a stand popular among some in the helping professions. The readership will have to decide whether arguments are meritorious, compassionate, without compassion, or merely politically correct or incorrect. One thing is for sure: Managers will face this free or fee issue.

Paradox 11

Practice, or reality contradicts theory. "That is okay in theory, but it does not work out in practice." This is a favorite anthem of many among us who think of themselves as practical. They are sometimes correct. Their veracity lies not in their understanding of things theoretical, however, but in their general mistrust of them. So they are sometimes right for the wrong reason.

Theory strives for what is true, for what can explain relationships. What is true today can change tomorrow. What is true of an environment today may be modified tomorrow when the environment changes and circumstances shift. Theory must change to conform to the realities change poses. It is not static. Sound theory helps us manage situations with which we have had little or no previous experience, for it consists of bundles of ordered observations that form the basis of the creative response. For a theory to be useful, it has to help us deal with the circumstances that apply in a given moment. Not appreciating this, not realizing that bad theory is not the equivalent of theory, invites the suspicious among us to belittle theoretical explanations.

"Sure, be nice to people and they will reciprocate in kind sounds great in theory; but some people will take advantage of you, so it does not work out in practice."

Does this render invalid the theory that people generally respond to the way they are treated? We think not, but we recognize that critical incidents—departures from the rule (theory)—can modify thinking. They should! A theoretical construct that predicts unwavering niceness in response to consistent niceness is as faulty as one which posits that people will always take unfair advantage of pleasant treatment. So the problem here is with the theory—it is bad theory—not with theory or theoretical approaches in general.

A better theory might pose that most of the time most people will respond positively to respectful treatment. Of what value is such a theory? Well, this theory reflects a number of observations over time, observations of human interaction that support the theory that niceness begets niceness most of the time. It also acknowledges that occasionally we will be disappointed. We need another theoretical construct for handling departures from the norm. We do not need to scrap the original theory unless or until it begins to miscalculate the relationship of niceness to response. Until that time, the niceness theory may serve as an excellent guide to organizational behavior toward bosses, coworkers, and clients. That is the value of good theory. As a very wise person once said, "There is nothing so practical as a good theory."

Paradox 12

Elaborate organizational charts contradict those of the one-person information place.

This contradiction is not in the same league as the classic paradox. It has more of the properties of irony. By this we mean that people who work in one- or two-person information places often scoff at hierarchical charts that show directors, associate directors, department heads, support staff, systems people, human resources divisions, interlibrary loan sections, and volunteer coordinators. "I am the director, head of technical services, chief of information services, shelver, and janitor in my store," they point out. "I do every one of those jobs shown on the diagram that looks like a pyramid. I *am* the pyramid."

Indeed they are right. In many school library media centers, special libraries, and entrepreneurial operations, one or two people run the show. Both your authors serve in academic institutions whose information places employ more people in one tiny department—acquisitions—than work in the majority of the smaller organizations.

Here is the problem, though. Even though the small libraries and information centers may not employ people in the slots identified in the tables of organization that apply to the larger agencies, they still have to perform most of the functions listed on the charts. In the larger ones, designated people develop vision statements, establish policy, develop the collection, classify and catalog the collection, and retrieve and interpret the collection for clients. Several different departments will manage marketing of services, user education, interlibrary loan, and the circulation function. In the one and two-person shops, a mere pair of people will manage all of those functions. More likely, they will short-change some important ones, and this can pose a great problem for the understaffed information place. For example, the marketing function is as important in the management of the school media center as it is in the large public library, research university resource center, corporate library, or knowledge management agency. School media specialists must market information services to their main clients—the teachers—just as corporate information service workers must market their ser-vices to their main clients in research and development or sales depart-ments. This is hard for one manager to do, especially if he or she must deal with classes of children sent to the media center so teachers can have their mandated daily planning period.

Paradox 13

Marketing is manipulative and it mocks all that is good and noble about the information service professions.

It may surprise and shock readers to discover that some people drawn to the LIS professions find the idea of marketing most distaste-ful. They envision the marketer as a huckster who cleverly makes a person feel smelly and insecure and then tries to sell him deodorant. To them the marketer is the advertiser who convinces people they need new cars, now, and in the process drives them into debt. They see Madison Avenue types figuring out how to package stuff attractively so people will buy it regardless of their need for it. They were scandalized by planned obsolescence. They bristled when Vance Packard reported that manufacturers discovered how to increase the sales of potato peel-ers. The peelers were made with handles that blended with the colors of the newspapers on which folks peeled the potatoes, and so the folks often threw away the peelers with the peels (Packard 1957 and 1960).

Perhaps if marketing were defined humanely, all managers would recognize its importance. Marketing is meeting and satisfying needs. It is a strategy that consists of several important and interrelated steps. It is four Ds and an E, and it is in no way manipulative, evil, or dishonest.

The first D is discovering who is out there. This is accomplished through community analysis, a systematic method of learning the char-acteristics of one's community.

The second D is determining how those characteristics may indi-cate a need for information. This is accomplished through needs as-sessment, a systematic method of finding out, mostly by asking the people in the community, what issues they face, what decisions they make, and how they recreate.

The third D is developing products and services which address the needs and preferences discovered during needs assessment.

The fourth D is delivering the products and services. This may be accompanied by advertising or public relations. Advertising and public relations are tactics which are part of a sound marketing strategy; they are not, as is commonly believed, synonymous with marketing. They do not mean the same thing.

The E is for evaluating. This is the process of determining whether the products and services designed to satisfy needs actually do. If they do, fine. If they do not, then managers must revisit community analysis or needs assessment, or they must investigate product development. Perhaps they must retool their public relations. Here it is important to note that some information managers mistakenly believe that the reason people do not frequent the information place is that they do not know what goes on there or what materials are available. Misguided ones love to trot out an anecdote, or an *n of 1* (one observation), as proof of the "do not know" theory. "Oh, I did not know you circulated art prints at the library!" The majority of people who do not use information places do not use them because their perception, sound or shaky, is that the information place is irrelevant to their needs. They will not trade their most valuable commodity—their time—for the products and services the information place provides. The problem is not just with publicity; the problem is with product and service development and delivery. The information place that does not market is not satisfying needs by providing demand-driven responses. Providing demand-driven responses, marketing, is not manipulative, but it is very intelligent management.

References

Bloch, Arthur. 1977. *Murphy's law and other reasons why things go wrong*. Los Angeles: Price/Stern/Sloan.

————. 1980. *Murphy's law, book two: More reasons why things go wrong*. Los Angeles: Price/Stern/Sloan.

————. 1982. *Murphy's law, book three: Wrong reasons why thing go more!* Los Angeles: Price/Stern/Sloan.

Bowman, Lisa M. 2001. Librarians fight porn in their workplace. CNET News.com. http://news.com.com/2100-1023-258403.html?tag=m (accessed on 28 January 2003).

Code of Ethics of the American Library Association. 1995. http://www. ala.org/alaorg/oif/ethics.html (accessed on 26 January 2003).

Conner, Daryl. 1992. *Managing at the speed of change: How resilient managers succeed and prosper where others fail.* New York: Villard Books.

Handy, Charles. 1995. *The age of paradox.* Boston: Harvard Business School Press.

Library Bill of Rights. 1996. American Library Association Council. http://www.religio.de/codex.html (accessed on 26 January 2003).

Marshall, Richard. 2001. *The polarizing effect of Internet filters: Should ALA take a position?* Mississippi Libraries (Winter): n.p. http://www.lib.usm.edu/~mla/publications/ml/win01/filters.htm (accessed on 28 January 2003).

Mayo, Elna A. 2000. They thought they could——. *Virginia Libraries* 46 (October-December): n.p. http://vn.web.com/hww/shared/shared_ main.jhtml:jes . . . (accessed on 29 January 2003).

Packard, Vance O. 1957. *The hidden persuaders.* New York: D. McKay Company.

——. 1960. *The waste makers.* New York: D. McKay Company.

Price Waterhouse Change Integration Team. 1996. *The paradox principles: How high-performance companies manage chaos, complexity, and contradictions to achieve superior results.* Chicago: Irwin.

Schlosser, Eric. 2001. *Fast-food nation: The dark side of the all-American meal.* New York: Houghton Mifflin Company.

Sykes, Rebecca. 1998. *U.S. Court: Library can't require porn filter.* http://www.thestandard.com/article/),1902,2662,00.html (accessed on 28 January 2003).

Chapter 12

Information Policy

Advocates who claim that information policy is an issue of crucial importance sometimes encounter skepticism or resistance from people who may not fully grasp the meaning of the term. Advocates have a responsibility to communicate the definition as well as their fervor. Managers need to know that information policy will influence a substantial chunk of their managerial ministrations.

Definition of Information Policy

Peter Hernon and Herold C. Relyea have supplied an excellent definition. Information policy

> is a set of interrelated principles, laws, guidelines, rules, regulations, and procedures guiding the oversight and management of the information *life cycle*: the production, collection, distribution/dissemination, retrieval, and retirement of information. Information policy also embraces access to, and use of, information. (McClure and Hernon 1991, 153)

Information Policy applies at international/global, national, and local levels. Efforts to convince a number of countries to observe copyright provisions are examples of international information policy activities. A federal government might pass a freedom of information type of act or take steps which result in the privatization of the publication of documents once produced and distributed by the government itself. Those would be examples of information policy at the national level.

When a corporation rewards its employees for sharing information, or when a public library doubles its fine rate or institutes a free reservation system, those are examples of information policy at the local level.

Information Policy Does Matter

Information policy matters because of what it aims to help accomplish—access to information. It has been described by the Council on Library Resources as a "common thread" that links six important information-related areas:

1. The description, analysis, integration, and organization of information
2. How government policies impact access to information
3. The impact of technology
4. Information economics
5. Information diffusion
6. Change agentry

(McClure and Hernon 1991, 152-53)

The life cycle of information—what information policy is about—is not important simply because the information goes 'round and 'round. It is important because of the stops it makes, and may not make, along the way. How do we manage the abundance? How do we see to it that people who need information get it? How important is access to information in a democratic society? Who gets to say what is information? Is it ever okay to deny access? Is it ever okay to reveal who has accessed what? Is it okay to charge for information, or does this disenfranchise the poor?

The Abundance

Information proliferates so quickly that it doubles at increasingly smaller intervals. No one can keep up with it or with the forecasts of its exponential growth. The good news is there is lots of it. The bad news is there is lots of it. Over thirty years ago Toffler described our being inundated by the then prodigious flow of information; we were choked with over-choice, he claimed (Toffler 1971). The abundance has hardly abated. If in the year 2003 one inquires by entering a common subject into a database, he may well get 15,000 hits. What is one to do with

15,000 hits? Who controls what gets into a database? Who establishes what kinds of inquiry/retrieval language shall apply? Which databases should an information agency purchase? What should an agency do about subscriptions to a print journal now being received online? May clients print copies and at what cost? Who, if anybody, will teach users how to sort through the abundance? Whose job is it to teach information literacy skills, without which clients will surely choke on the abundance, or almost as worse, settle for incomplete or faulty information? Information managers will deal with each of these questions, and many more, all of which are directly linked with information policy—guidelines for managing the life cycle of information and people's access to it.

People Who Need Information Get to Access It

What purpose is served by the information organization that owns 500,000 volumes but not the one volume a client needs? The agency that has made the information policy decision to join a consortium which can respond to requests for items which that agency may not own addresses the need issue. While that mechanism responds to requests placed to the system, what about unpresented client requests and unstated client needs? Does an agency have a mechanism for learning these? A library which establishes user profiles and delivers information in anticipation of demand exercises a proactive information policy.

Who Gets to Say, "This Is Information."

Do Joe's musings about smoking and health (His grandma lived to ninety-five years of age and she smoked two packs a day!) exist on the Internet side by side with the findings of the National Institute of Health? They well might.

Although his point was to comment on the possibility for more widespread electronic publication, consider this statement by Fytton Rowland in terms of its implications for who gets to say what becomes information:

> Virtually all publications exist in digital form at some time during their production and many publications are printed indirectly from the author's original keystrokes. The development of networks, particularly the Internet, means that it

is practical to send these machine readable files of *publica-tions* [emphasis ours] around the world by electronic means. The presence of the infrastructure has led to many people in the publication chain considering the potential for electronic distribution. (Grieves 1998, 21-22)

Anybody with a roll of dimes and access to a copy machine can publish locally; anybody with a PC and a modem can publish globally. Who gets to say what is information? Anybody? Consumer beware! Do we need information policy to guide a sensible approach to information management at all levels?

Who determines what war news will be broadcast? A network? A government? Which government—ours or theirs? If a federal govern-ment privatizes the publication of some government information, will private publishers issue only those items likely to earn a profit? What would happen to the published studies on beekeeping if the United States Government Printing Office opts out? These kinds of jurisdic-tional decisions affect what becomes information, and they have an impact on the majority of information managers.

Is It Okay to Deny Access to Information, to Reveal Who Has Used It?

When in the 1950s we worked as pages at the Carnegie Library of Pittsburgh, the books on martial arts and the sex manuals were given a blue dot and kept under lock and key. This information policy meant that if one wanted to read how to sneak up on someone and injure him with a toothpick or just make love, one had to ask the librarian. Some libraries restrict children to the materials in the children's room and forbid children to use young adult (YA) or adult materials. This may be denying access. Is that okay? Pharmaceutical information agency ABC is unlikely to welcome employees of pharmaceutical company XYZ to ABC's knowledge management font. That makes sense, does it not? Is not some information legitimately private and secret? It is legitimate and prudent for ABC to write policy to protect its interests. What about when the interests of corporations or private researchers are also in the public interest? What about access to research on disease control, espe-cially if that research has been funded by taxpayer dollars?

Is It Ever Okay to Charge for Information?

What a question! Is it ever not okay? But the question does get asked, and answered. Some claim that it is not okay for a public library to charge for services, and they argue two points:

1. Tax monies have already paid the freight
2. Charging fees disenfranchises the poor

While it seems clear that people who cannot afford soup or housing are unlikely to be able to afford a database search on Elizabethan costuming, opponents of fees for service have as yet supplied figures on exactly how many poor clients have lined up for such services and been turned away. Proponents of fees, at least of the cost recovery variety, argue that they will not be able to offer expensive new technologies unless they can charge fees. In fact, some public libraries have booked passage on entrepreneurial bandwagons and won board approval for charging for Herculean information services—those which require significant staff time to execute and deliver, and those for which clients willingly pay.

There is divided opinion about the ethics of charging fees for public library services. There should be no divided opinion about the need for information policy to guide the manager of the information place who will most assuredly have to deal with the economics of information transfer at some level.

Your Turn: Suppose your governing agency tightens its purse strings, tells you there will be no new money for electronic expenditure, and orders you to engage in cost recovery and find new sources of income. How might you respond, especially if you have no established track record of charging fees? What considerations would affect your creating new information policy? How would you prepare your clients?

Technology and Information Policy

Information in the hands of clever people can be a mighty source of power. Most information managers acknowledge and understand this. They know why the age has been named the Information Age and why our society has been named the Information Society. In the industrial nations, most people who are employed are employed to create, process, or transfer information. Information products constitute major portions of gross national products. Corporations recognize that intellectual capital—what they know—has value. They can put a price tag on it. Many people see information as a commodity, a utility.

The new technologies enable people to create and transfer new information—these new commodities—at a prodigious pace and with blinding speed. Issues of copyright, intellectual property, privacy, confidentiality, and public safety loom. Often they outstrip the capacity of the information manager to deal with them. Communicators are able to do so many things so quickly that they often do not comprehend the ramifications of their actions. They forge ahead without controls, without guidelines, without policy. Shall the marvelous Internet always be so economical a tool to access; what provisions have been established at the local level to archive electronic publications; what about the fine print in licensing agreements? Twenty years ago most information managers never dreamed of such questions. Today they grapple with them, and in the blink of an eye several more issues will surely surface—all of them ushered in by the electronic revolution, all of them crucial, and all of them requiring information policy.

Among the issues and questions which new technologies force managers to confront are

- Consumer demand for the latest information products
- Staff and client training in the use of acquired electronic products
- The shelf life of digitized products
- Whether traditional libraries shall continue to have a role in the digital age, or shall other agencies take their places?
- Shall *knowbots* and search engines replace librarians? Are librarians too conservative to adjust?

(Hobohm 1996, 1-4)

What Are Some Additional Issue Areas That Require Information Policy?

Readers will note that information technology influences these also:

- Information technology issues affect business, freedom of speech, privacy, democratic governance, and the accountability and efficiency of public administration
- The dissemination and promotion of research findings (Foundation n.d.)
- Copyright and fair use in the digital age
- Patient confidentiality

- Copyright and public domain
- Preservation (IFLANET n.d.)
- Information security and risk management
- Information flow and balance of power
- Information for social care
- Archive and preservation policy (United Kingdom 2003)
- Telecommunications
- Community networks (University of Texas n.d.)
- Database protection and the politics of knowledge
- The growth of the global Internet
- Ethical and human behavior issues related to information transfer
  (University of Maryland n.d.)
- Internet abuse; computer crime
- E-commerce and e-markets
- Information infrastructure
- Cybercommunications and mass media
- Increased competition for the global consumers' dollars
  (Information n.d.)

Government Influence

Certainly changes in the U.S. Government's information policies do impact libraries and citizens at the local level. When the Federal Government proposed the closure of the National Technical Information Service (NTIS), shock waves sped through the documents and government information community. What would happen to the dissemination of and access to information produced by nearly 250 agencies and funneled through the NTIS clearinghouse?

In particular, the passage of two laws at the federal level has had enormous implications at national and local levels for information agencies, information managers, and their clients. These are the Child Internet Protection Act (CIPA) and the USA Patriot Act.

In short, CIPA required mandatory filtering of the Internet in libraries receiving federal funds, under penalty of loss of such funding if recipients did not comply. An Eastern District of Pennsylvania appeals court ruled provisions of the act "facially invalid," and the case has moved to the Supreme Court of the United States (American 2002, 1). President George W. Bush signed the USA Patriot Act into law on October 26, 2001. "With this law we have given sweeping new powers to both domestic law enforcement and international intelligence agencies and have eliminated the checks and balances that previously gave

courts the opportunity to ensure that these powers were not abused"
(Electronic 2001,1). As one might expect, organizations such as the
American Library Association (ALA) have spoken out on this issue.
ALA has issued a resolution in support of information access and inquiry, free speech, free thought, user privacy, and oversight of Patriot
Act implementation. ALA stresses that librarians and all information
professionals should understand the law and be prepared to deal with
challenges to privacy and confidentiality. The organization does not
tout civil disobedience in any form, but it urges information workers to
operate within the law to help preserve client privacy and confidentiality. The Patriot Act comes into being in the aftermath of September 11
and in response to national resolve to protect ourselves from terrorist
attacks and other assaults. This resolve could threaten rights, according
to some advocates of intellectual freedom. One of ALA's points is this:
the Patriot Act is information policy at the national level; what policy
shall managers develop at the local level to guard both our liberties and
our safety?

Another federal law that is an example of information policy which
affects the local scene is the Freedom of Information Act (FOIA). Congress passed it in 1966 and amended it in 1974. It requires certain federal government agencies (but not congress, federal courts, and executive office staff) to disclose certain kinds of information. Public librarians, take note. The two kinds of information which these agencies must
disclose concern the activities of the agencies, and a biggie—records
that the government may have about oneself. The American Civil Liberties Union (ACLU) is heavily involved in monitoring FOIA activity
and offers counsel to citizens who wish to make FOIA inquiries
(American 1998, 1-28).

Information Managers on the Local Scene

Managers must create various kinds of information policy at the
local level. In order to render a good accounting for moneys spent, information managers in schools, public libraries, corporate information
centers, and knowledge management operations should grow their collections, print and electronic, systematically. A collection development
policy provides guidelines for such systematic growth. Good collection
development policies include a

- Sound mission statement
- Selection policy

- Weeding policy
- Challenge policy
- Donor policy

A good mission statement will remind everyone what the business of the organization is. Selection policy covers selection routines, who shall be involved, and what kinds of materials to select. Weeding policy reminds everyone that the garden requires weeding if it is to be a garden and usually asserts that the agency will weed systematically and regularly. Challenge policy informs both the agency and anyone who objects to the contents of agency acquisitions how to proceed, if at all, with a formal complaint. Donor policies are extremely important. Because they announce that the same criteria apply for donations as apply to selection, they protect information agencies from having to accept the contents of attic drives, somebody's 1927 chemistry textbooks, or the not quite publishable vanity press poetry by somebody else's Aunt Clernella.

Information managers must create and implement these kinds of information policies. Not having them invites disaster. Getting caught in a censorship battle, for example, without policy to guide a response and protect one's agency from unfriendly assaults can be very disruptive.

Information managers can placate child protection advocates when they initiate policy that provides filtered (against porn) Internet access to children and unfiltered Internet access to adult inquirers. This may not please the antifilter advocates, but it may assure managers that they can offer Internet services to all without fear of distracting, budget-threatening attacks by the censors. We believe such a move demonstrates a manager's grasp of politics of use and in no major way offends intellectual freedom. Considering what might happen if the censors march, this compromise information policy is enabling, not restrictive.

Information managers will face many questions which will surely surface in most information places and which will require information policy decisions. Operating with sound policy helps managers avoid treating every question as a new one and every decision an ad hoc one. Here are some of these questions:

- To whom shall this agency grant user privileges and what kinds of privileges?
- What shall be the lending periods?
- Shall we charge fines; may we ever forgive them?
- Who shall be responsible for helping and teaching clients?

- To what extent shall we assist, direct, and counsel clients?
- Shall we offer assertive or proactive information services such as document delivery?
- What hours shall we observe and who will provide coverage of information stations during these hours?
- Shall we outsource some of our functions; shall we hire an outside agency to do our cataloging, for example?

None of these issues is anywhere nearly as consequential as some of the access and safety issues addressed by information policy at the national level, but every one of them will constitute a thorn in the side of a manager who confronts them unarmed—without policy. Policies are guides, not commandments. They are not made to be broken, but they should be bendable. Getting caught without information policy is embarrassing and dangerous.

Your Turn: A division head sends fifteen of her people to your information center at one-half hour before closing with instructions that you should teach them the Internet. What would you do with those thirty minutes? What would you do first thing tomorrow? Do you think an information manager should have a policy in place which outlines procedures for requesting and offering user education? What provisions would you include in such a policy?

References

American Civil Liberties Union. 1998. Using the freedom of information act: A step-by-step guide. http://archive.aclu.org/library/foia.html (accessed 18 April 2003).

American Library Association. 2002. ALA CIPA website. www.ala.org/Content/NavigationMenu/Our_Association/Offic (accessed 16 April 2003.

Electronic Frontier Foundation. 2001. EEF analysis of the provisions of the USA patriot act. www.eff.org/Privacy/Surveillance/Terroism_militias/200110 (accessed 16 April 2003).

Foundation for Information Policy Research. About. www.fipr.org/about.html (accessed 10 April 2003).

Grieves, Maureen, ed. 1991. *Information policy in the electronic age.* New Providence, NJ: Bowker Saur.

Hobohm, Hans-Christoph. 1996. The impact of new technology on libraries: An introductory note. www.ifla.org/VII/s5/conf/62hobh. htm (accessed 16 April 2003).

IFLANET (International Federation of Library Associations and Institutions). Information policy: Copyright and intellectual property. www.ifla.org//II/copyright.htm (accessed 10 April 2003).

Information infrastructure, information security and information privacy. www.brint.com/NH.htm (accessed 10 April 2003).

McClure, Charles R., and Peter Hernon, eds. 1991. *Library and information science research: Perspectives and strategies for improvement*. Norwood, NJ: Ablex.

Toffler, Alvin. 1971. *Future shock*. New York: Bantom Books.

United Kingdom Department of Health. 2003. Information and IT for the NHS. www.doh.gov.uk/ipu/ (accessed 10 April 2003).

University of Maryland Center for Information Policy (CIP). The Center. www.umd.edu/ (accessed 10 April 2003).

University of Texas Telecommunications and Information Policy Institute. Reports. www.utexas.edu/research/tipi/menu.htm (accessed 10 April 2003).

Chapter 13

Knowledge Management

> *Lew Platt: "If Hewlett-Packard knew what it knows, we'd be three times more productive" (Crainer 2000, 207).*

> *"Who ya gonna call?"* (Ghostbusters *1984*)

Some Essential Considerations

If information were power, librarians would be the healthiest, wealthiest, richest, happiest, wisest, smartest, holiest, and best-dressed people around. They would be the most well-adjusted citizens, the most successful diplomats, the most insightful counselors, the most innovative scientists, the most brilliant raconteurs, and the keenest analysts. Surrounded by all that *osmosing* information, librarians should absorb even the most inadvertent seepage of knowledge orts. Wisdom's firm assimilating embrace should sustain and maintain the information workers at the highest level of skill and accomplishment. Isn't that the way it works? No, it is not. Information is not power; good information in the hands of resourceful people is a source of power.

If information not put to work is not powerful, and neither are people who merely sit next to it, what is all the fuss about knowledge management? From what we have observed, especially from the knowledge managers themselves, here is a seminal point: To make knowledge management kick in, to take information services out of neutral and shove them into high gear, managers must change the culture "from

299

'knowledge is power' to 'knowledge *sharing* [emphasis ours] is power'" (Skyrme 2000, 4). Knowledge managers engineer systems which encourage and reward users to contribute, share, and use information.

This pithy observation underpins two mighty messages: The first is that the very essence of knowledge management is the sharing of useful information. Somebody has to make that happen. The second is that teachers, practitioners, and information professionals in training should observe that it is the creation, communication, and use of applicable information that differentiates KM from its important blood relative, library and information science (LIS). Granted, many librarians care that clients learn to use information products, and many, most notably corporate and other special librarians, have constructed databases and devised assertive information delivery practices; but knowledge managers raise the information transfer process to different levels. They understand that what they do feeds organizational decision-making processes. They operate in intimate alignment with the corporate mission, especially its bottom line aspects. They identify information need more aggressively, they diagnose more courageously, they mine the know-how of users more inventively, they create more resourcefully, they deliver more rapidly, they monitor more closely, and they manage more carefully an information transfer process involving users as contributors than do their cousins the librarians. The information and know-how that they manage often resides in people rather than in books and journals.

The term *information resource management* (IRM) bridges a gap between LIS and KM. Like the knowledge managers of today, IRM practitioners hold that information is capital, that it has value, and that it should be shared. KM takes concepts of information creation, utility, value, transfer, measurement, and evaluation to extended heights; it is not just the terms that are evolving; practice is changing.

Naysayers and Hay Makers

While some ivory tower types gripe and moan that KM is just another fad, other information workers grasp the concept and run with it. While some skeptics grouse and complain that knowledge is an abstraction that cannot be managed, other forward-looking professionals manage it. While some theorists are knocked off balance by their inability to agree about the origins of knowledge management (Does it spring from computer science or management science? Is it a breath mint or a candy mint?), other centered knowledge workers earn a comfortable living by aggressively uniting corporate types with the information they need, even before they seek it, and most especially when they do. While some academics boast that they have no idea what knowledge management means, other insightful professors create syllabi and teach students how to merge their valuable computer, searching, and sorting skills with the communication, management, and marketing skills that make knowledge management, organizational sharing, and organizational learning happen. While one observer asks, "What's next . . . wisdom management" (Goodrum 2001)? We respond with a definite "Perhaps."

We may call knowledge management something else in ten years; but as long as information is the commodity, there will be those who want it, require it, and who will pay for managed, refined doses of information. That means there will be a need for those who deftly manage its creation, storage, and transfer. "The most direct and often most effective way to acquire knowledge is to buy it—that is, to buy an organization or hire individuals who have it," [and quoting Arthur Hugh Clough] "Grace is given of God, but knowledge is bought in the market" (Davenport and Prusak, 1998, 53, 25). We paraphrase and modify our colleague Robert Molyneux's observation: Knowledge management may well be the modern information worker's full employment act.

So where do today's students, teachers, and doers of management want to be? KM is nothing new? KM just means cataloging? We have always done KM; it's just a fancy term for what we have been about for centuries. Or is what we have done for centuries substantially different from what KM undertakes? Is KM what earns information managers release from the custodial role and a chance to be more than mere ushers in the temple of knowledge? We think the answer to the latter question is yes. Have some librarians for years engaged in many KM practices? Surely they have. We have no interest in posing chicken or egg propositions, nor are we eager to debate information versus knowledge issues that obscure what we adopt as our central purpose here: To introduce knowledge management concepts and practices.

For ages librarians have excelled at providing acquisition and descriptive services. They could get information, and they could mark it and park it. They could fashion retrieval systems that delivered upon request. They were masters of all the storage, retention, and, to some extent, preservation functions; they were champion providers of reactive service, service delivered upon request—a service response delivered only upon demand placed to the system by some requestor. They taught users how to use acquired materials and included some of the users in the selection process. All this is but a part of knowledge management.

Well, Then, What Is Knowledge Management?

> Knowledge management is the explicit and systematic management of vital knowledge and its associated processes of creating, gathering, organizing, diffusing, using, and exploiting. It requires turning personal knowledge into corporate knowledge that can be widely shared throughout an organization and appropriately applied (Skyrme 2000, 2).

Knowledge management "is a discipline that promotes an integrated approach to identifying, capturing, evaluating, retrieving, and sharing all of an enterprise's information assets" (Duhon 1998, 10).

Knowledge management "is the process by which the organization generates [value] from its knowledge or intellectual capital" (Bukowitz and Williams 2000, 2).

"Knowledge management is the systematic process by which knowledge needed for an organization to succeed is created, captured, shared, and leveraged" (Rumizen 2002, 13).

Knowledge management is "the practice of creating, capturing, transferring, and accessing the right knowledge and information when needed to make better decisions, take actions, and deliver results in support of underlying business strategy" (Horwitch 2002, 27).

The answer one gets to the "What is KM?" question will depend upon whom one asks. The term attempts to name the processes which aim at corralling and operating (managing) the creation, discovery, evaluation, acquisition/access, maintenance, packaging, delivery, and distribution of knowledge, and the measurement of the value of such procedures. Knowledge is interpreted information deemed relevant and applicable in a given environment or situation. That cobra venom is a deadly neurotoxin is information. That there is a cobra nesting in the company server is valuable knowledge, as is knowing that life-saving antivenin is stored in one's upper left desk drawer. The ability to administer the antivenin is know-how. The specific answer to What is Knowledge management? will vary depending upon who fields the question: the company librarian, the managers who oversee server operations, the software and hardware suppliers who may have inadvertently delivered the serpent, the scientists in research and development, or the herpetologist called to retrieve the snake and rescue the staff. The catch line, *Who ya gonna call?* from the popular Ghostbusters movie, interestingly asks an important KM question. Knowledge managers are determined to corral who knows what in the organization and to make that knowledge available to all who have rightful access.

Traditional information management may have resulted in the acquisition of phone books for the company library. Modern KM involves not merely the collection of recorded information but also includes the identification of communication/information-related company problems and issues; the collection of previously unrecorded information; the discovery, acquisition, retrieval and packaging of relevant information; the development of systems for tagging, storing, adding, subtracting, and transferring information; the delivery of that information to decision makers, perhaps in advance of their asking specifically for it; and the follow-up determination of whether the right information got to the right persons in a timely, cost-effective manner. Note the use of the terms *right, timely,* and *cost-effective.* They, along with the key KM practices of contributing, sharing, and participating, help elevate information to knowledge and make it a valuable commodity. In the effort to build and manage the knowledge base, modern knowledge managers attempt to involve anyone and everyone in the organization who has useful information and knowledge to contribute to that base.

Another take on "the definition of KM depends upon whom one asks" is supplied by authors writing from the business/LIS perspective. They observe that the term KM is unstable and in a state of flux. They label three kinds of knowledge management operations, calling them domains. In the LIS context, the first domain, KM refers chiefly to the management of information—of recorded information, like publications. Managing know-how is the second domain of knowledge managers in the business environment. The third domain is that of the organizational theorists and it "denotes a major conceptual shift, from knowledge as a resource, to knowledge as a capability, a readiness to respond that allows organizations to co-evolve effectively with a given environment" (Davenport and Cronin 2000, 294).

However the KM definition evolves, it does so within the specific context of the organization's mission, goals, and bottom line, to which KM is securely attached for accountability purposes.

Is Knowledge Management Real?

As important as it is to name a thing what it is, and to see it in its wholeness, it is also important to get on with the observation that it exists in practice—and that it matters. People who dismiss KM as a fad do so at their peril, and at our peril if we believe them. People who protest that knowledge is not a thing that can be managed need to wake up and smell the consultant reports, some of which reek, to be sure. Knowledge management has become a 5 billion dollar industry (Srikantaiah and Koenig 2000,10). Some notorious corporations have mismanaged information and knowledge to the point of fraud and have produced disastrous results. Harley Davidson, on the other hand, has managed knowledge about how to craft motorcycles, who rides motorcycles, and how to make motorcycles appeal to veteran and new riders, as well. Thwarted in their attempts to trademark the distinctive *potato, potato* sound of the powerful Harley engine, HD has instead managed knowledge so well that thousands of riders believe the only *real* bike is a Harley. Be leery of arguments claiming that knowledge cannot be managed. Some folks are managing it quite well. Be skeptical of prophets who foretell of the demise of the KM term. For sure, we may call it something else in ten years; but as long as information is *the* commodity, there will be those who desperately require it, and a need for those who deftly manage its creation, storage, and transfer. KM is just another term for something we have always done? Sure, and Ferrari is just another term for buggy.

The current record shows that people who learn how to manage knowledge (interpreted data applied by people to a given set of circumstances) can earn a living doing so. Information workers in training and practicing managers of information agencies, take note.

What Knowledge Management Is Not

Knowledge management "is not just about sharing all the information you can think of with everyone you can imagine; e-mail can do that" (Horwitch 2002, 27). Knowledge management is not just about disseminating standard artifacts of information, print or electronic, and KM is the absolute antithesis of custodial or supply-driven information service. Custodial or purely information storage and retrieval pursuits can result in precisely cataloged and superbly conditioned materials that lie in wait for potential users. Accurate descriptors and good hygiene are necessary ingredients in the KM equation, but they are not sufficient. Supply-driven service says, in effect, "We invite you to come use what we have." Custodial and supply-driven service begs the question: "Have you determined which of our encyclopedias, or which database in our inventory, answers your information need?" This is not an argument against having supplies, but it is a caution issued to would-be knowledge managers. Do not base service upon an on-hand collection of explicit print, micro, or electronic products alone. The information products many knowledge managers manage consist of the know-how and experiences of the work force.

What Drives Knowledge Management?

Aggressive or demand-driven service moves knowledge management. It is demand driven, not just supply driven. It includes, of course, the skills of describing, preserving, and retrieving required information. Instead of inquiring, "Which of the information items that we own— that we have in stock or access to—will suit your purposes?" knowledge managers ask: "What information do you need and use to operate? How do you prefer to receive, exchange, and dispose of information you need in order to cope, survive, succeed, and thrive? What do you do when a problem or information need surfaces, but you do not know whom to ask for assistance?" Knowledge Managers have to construct and bend their information services to meet the unique needs of personnel and the idiosyncratic natures of their organizational settings. Knowledge managers invent and create information products and services, sometimes from whole cloth, often in response to critical and unusual information needs. The repositories of the information that knowledge managers must discover, assemble, and provide are often tacit ones that exist only in the minds of people. Knowledge managers make house calls—they deliver.

People who seek clear distinctions between KM and LIS should consider this pronouncement: "people, not printed materials and online databases, are the organization's most precious information resources." (Choo 1995, 206) The knowledge manager's job is to discover who needs to know what, who knows what, and how to get needed information to the ones who need to know and use it.

An Explanation from the Field

"When knowledge is your product, you'd best be able to manage it" (Chait 1999, n.p.). The reporter is referring to the business of a consultant firm that employs over 3,000 people all over the world. Their aim is to connect every one of them to "the knowledge, skills and experience of 2,999" other employees. Whatever it is that is known by this organization must be made available to people who need to know it, when they need to know it, and where they need it. The virtual access/availability of and to the intellectual capital of the organization is achieved through a Web-enabled system which links both employees and clients. The KM effort provides information about employee skills, customer needs, and corporate protocols, "which allows us to deliver consistent service in an efficient and effective manner; [and] we have information about our practices and groups, which keeps everyone up to date even when they get to see one another only infrequently" (Chait 1999, np). This firm discovered that while the technological aspects of this connecting activity were important, other ingredients—the stuff of what was to be collected and shared, the corporate culture, and the actual processes involved in accumulating and sharing—were every bit as important.

Four Terms That Help Describe Knowledge Management

Four terms help describe KM and distinguish it from traditional library and information science. They are intellectual capital, information architecture (IA), leverage, and participation.

If one were to study Kat Hagedorn's excellent glossary of IA terms (Hagedorn 2000), one at first might conclude that the terms are familiar and not very new. Indeed, a very new message is announced by this compilation. Knowledge managers create, oversee, monitor, and evaluate the structures designed to deliver an organization's intellectual capital to those who need it in order to take advantage of present opportunities and create future responses to opportunities as yet undiscovered. Design is a key word here. The information architectures used to construct websites, intranets, and information transfer systems are key tools of information management. It is important for information architecture and knowledge management personnel to share a vocabulary, and the glossary helps them do this.

Intellectual Capital

Simply put, intellectual capital "includes everything an organization knows" (Rumizen 2002, 288). It is the knowledge that is shared and put to use, and which affects corporate profits. Imagine a corporation that suddenly finds itself without any knowledge resources to share. They were here yesterday; they are gone today. Nobody remembers anything: no history, no manufacturing processes, no marketing know-how, no customer list, no record of relationships among these things—*nothing*. Intellectual capital includes the skills of the work force, the goodwill of customers, and the stabilizing effect of established procedures. All these are gone now, and without its intellectual capital this corporation is helpless. This little exercise of the imagination can demonstrate the importance of accessing and sharing what the organization knows. Nasseri poses a telling question about the suddenly-no-resource example: What is this company suddenly devoid of all intellectual and human capital now worth? "The difference between the market values of the company before and after the blight struck is the value of the company's intellectual capital" (Nasseri 1996, 1). Consider how much would it cost to replace all that lost intellectual capital.

Corporations are making the effort to discover the specific value of this shared information within the organizations. The result has been a fresher look at what constitutes corporate wealth. They identify and measure the sharing. They identify and measure the impact of the sharing on the business—on the bottom line. Ives, Torrey, and Gordon list "five areas of performance: financial, customer, human, process, and renewal and development" (Morey, Maybury, and Thuraisingham 2001, 117) that demonstrate the value of managed, shared knowledge.

Moreover, some corporations have documented savings directly attributable to their KM efforts. Ford Motor Company reported a savings of over $160,000 as a direct result of sharing production information; Texas Instruments reported savings of $1,500,000 directly attributable to sharing performance information among plants; Chevron announced a dramatic reduction in operating costs—$2 billion dollars, the direct result of sharing and learning about successes of cost reduction efforts within the organization (Rumizen 2002, 12-13).

Information Architecture

Information architecture is about design. What an organization wants to design are the mechanisms for identifying all the things it knows and needs to know, marking them, parking them, making them accessible, safeguarding them, and managing their delivery upon— even before—request, and getting rid of them when they no longer serve their purposes. "Information architecture involves investigation, analysis, design and implementation" (Hagedorn 2000, 5). Information architects may employ two complementary approaches: top-down (which considers content and user needs) and bottom-up (which also considers content plus needed tools, like indexes). John Shiple breaks this down for us. "Information architecture is the science of figuring out what you want your site to do and then constructing a blueprint before you dive in and put the thing together" (Shiple 2002, 2). One has to consider and factor in the goals of the site, customer and staff opinions, content, and the skeletal construct for the design. His architectural products result from the confluence of top-down and bottom-up procedures. Information architects devise systems composed of the subsystems managed by data analysts, operations personnel, communications staff, Web designers, systems analysts, program managers, information officers, and use/user managers.

Information architects address this fundamental question: "What information infrastructure can be installed so that it can best facilitate creation, tracking, storage and sharing of knowledge to support strategic and operational objectives?" (Nasseri 1996, 4)

We have all experienced architectures that we liked and those we have hated. We have liked the houses that make living in them pleasant, and we have liked the websites that make searching and finding easy and effective. We have hated the buildings that are sterile or tough to navigate and the websites that are cumbersome and complicated to use. Might the bad houses or websites have been the products of consult-and-run architects who never had to live in those houses or work with those websites? Rosenfeld and Morville provide a strategy for the information architect, one which incorporates user input that should help protect the organization from installing a bad scheme:

1. Clarify the vision and mission for the site
2. Determine what content and functionality the site will contain
3. Specify how users will find information in the site by defining its organization, navigation, labeling, and searching systems
4. Map out how the site will accommodate change and growth over time

(Rosenfeld and Morville 1998, 1-9, 11)

Leverage

Leverage is defined in dictionaries as a way to accomplish something by lifting it, with a bar, perhaps. It is derived from words that mean *to raise* (Old French) and *light* (Latin). Leverage provides positional advantage and the power to act effectively. According to one observer, points of leverage are "places within a complex system (a corporation, an economy, a living body, a city, an ecosystem) where a small shift in one thing can produce big changes in everything" (Meadows 1997, 1). Dixon speaks of leveraging as transferring corporate "knowledge across time and space" (Dixon 2000, 17).

The extent to which knowledge managers tweak their systems to affect the bottom lines in their organizations is quite different from the ways in which traditional LIS managers make adjustments in their systems. Librarians frequently adjust hours of operations, acquisitions procedures, and ways of entering data into their electronic catalogs. Sometimes these measures can be shown to affect numbers of visitors, time saved in inventory control, or frequency of information hits. Knowledge managers claim that the acts of leverage they help engineer affect money saved and money earned—results more closely related to the organization's bottom line. Yes, knowledge managers perform acquisition and delivery functions. Their role does not stop with delivery; it continues through use and evaluation, and the creation of new information.

Another way to look at this leverage idea is to ask, What do corporations do with the information they create, store, access, and interpret? Whereas ancient warriors may have inserted a lever and tipped a supply of boulders upon the heads of their enemies, modern knowledge managers help their organizations tip the odds in their favor by providing access to research and development, manufacturing, marketing, or sales information, the use of which may reduce costs or increase profits. It is the measured and evaluated sharing and use of managed intellectual capital which substantially distinguishes KM from its cousin LIS. Knowledge managers care what happens when somebody takes a book out. Many librarians have convinced themselves that it is unnecessary, none of their business, or impossible to tell what happens when they provide an item, and they have focused instead on developing quicker methods for circulating books and other media, print and electronic. This is a worthy objective, but it stops short of concerning itself with the interpretation, use, and value of information, driving forces of KM.

Here's how leverage works. Somebody in an organization makes a discovery or notices a relationship, tests that discovery or relationship, and produces "common knowledge" (Dixon 2000, 20). The KM force selects an information transfer channel, massages the new information into usable form, and sends the new common knowledge to others who adapt it for use. That use itself may produce new common knowledge.

The leveraging takes place in the transferring. The warriors leveraged by transferring lethal rocks; knowledge managers leverage by transferring valuable knowledge. Valuable knowledge? Yes! Ford, Texas Instruments, and Chevron all credit savings in the multi-millions of dollars to the transferring of information—leveraging.

Participation

When information workers ask clients for suggestions, faculty for book or journal purchase recommendations, and coworkers for management or service counsel, they invite participation. Ideally, the collection mirrors in part what potential users want in the way of available publications and programs because some of the users have had their say in the composition and arrangement of the collection.

Knowledge management requires a different kind of participation, for in those cases where information, knowledge, and know-how reside in the minds of employees, the users *are* the collection. They must share, and they must contribute. They use what they learn, and they feed what they learn to the knowledge base. The knowledge managers manage the transfer of this learning and sharing. A public or university librarian may or may not know to what use the collection is put; it is the business of the knowledge manager not only to know how the collection is used but also to manage the communication of useful information and discovery to everyone who needs to know. Who needs to participate in that loop? The knowledge manager must know this.

Neither passive, nor merely reactive, knowledge management aggressively seeks to involve its constituents intimately in knowledge creation and exchange. In addition to participating by suggesting an acquisition or by taking an owned item from the information place, the participants in a knowledge management operation create some of the collection, respond to calls for more, use, share, collaborate, and help evaluate.

What Knowledge Managers Do

Stated very broadly, knowledge managers help organize and provide access to the intellectual capital of an organization whose goals include learning and adapting. They deal with the challenge of making this abstraction happen. In this chapter we have reported striking gains produced by KM efforts, but Crainer reports that less than 20 percent of KM programs make a substantial impact and almost a third are failures (Crainer 2000, 208). In addition, apparently some organizations are making the KM leap without fully understanding why. "In a recent Conference Board survey of 200 senior executives, 85% of companies with KM efforts underway conceded that their KM programs had no stated objectives" (Horwitch 2002, 30). So the challenge is indeed great, and one of the first things knowledge managers ought to do is determine why they are about to do KM and if and how whatever it is they will do aligns with the goals and objectives of the organization.

The KM process consists of six nonlinear and interrelated cells/activities:

- Information Needs
- Information Acquisition
- Information Organization and Storage
- Information Products and Services Development
- Information Distribution
- Information Use

(Woo 1995, 24)

We add a seventh activity:

- Evaluation

Information Needs

The term *information need* is very familiar to LIS practitioners. Generally, they know, or think they know, what they mean when they use it. When they ask others, "What are your information needs?" they often befuddle those whose definitions of the terms differ from theirs. More resourceful KM practitioners instead ask questions like these:

- What problems do you face on a daily basis?
- Who is available to help you with these problems?
- When issues arise, who should be involved in addressing them?
- Whom do you contact on a regular basis and how successful are these contacts?
- What kinds of decisions do you make?
- What is it that you need to know in order to do your job?
- What would make your work easier?
- Upon what kinds of resources—personal, print, or electronic— do you rely?
- How successful have you been at solving organizational issues?
- What are this organization's chief challenges, opportunities, and problems?

- Does this organization have any friends? Who?
- Does this organization have any enemies? Who?

Knowledge managers construct and use needs assessment instruments, formal and informal, subject specific, and open ended. They use surveys and interviews. They collect answers to these and other questions and they mine the responses for expressions which in any way relate to the information needs of the respondents. The employee who may draw a blank if asked, "What are your information needs?" might supply a volume of responses to the question, "What would it take for you to gain a competitive edge on your rivals?" These responses may contain a gold mine of information-related issues for the KM force, provided they have a good plan for dealing with the responses they get.

Burkowitz and Williams have created an excellent tool, the Knowledge Management Diagnostic, "designed to help you identify knowledge management areas in which your organization is weak" (Burkowitz and Williams 2000, 17). Inspecting this tool will introduce the novice to what KM is; using this tool will help knowledge workers do KM.

Information Acquisition

Some of the identified information needs can be addressed through owning and accessing available supplies of information in print, micro, and electronic formats. Knowledge managers acquire books, serials, models, maps, pamphlets, technical reports, indexes, abstracts, databases, and search engines. They collect directories of consultants, grant agencies, and manufacturers. They discover and assemble communications, procedural manuals, and intelligence reports from within the organization. They find out who knows what in addition to who needs what. They code, sort, organize, arrange, and store, not merely for archival purposes but mainly for dispersal and use purposes.

Knowledge managers quickly discover that the real issue may not be to get information but to avoid choking on the abundance. Here their cataloging, classification, and sorting skills assume great importance. It is relevant, useful information they seek, not just information. One can identify what is relevant only if he or she knows what the organization needs to know, and knows and asks the people who do know.

Knowledge managers must know and observe copyright law. They must know or have access to those who know the intricacies of licensing agreements, and they must thoroughly understand their organization's intellectual property policies. They must be skilled negotiators when they deal with vendors. They are acutely aware that a significant corpus of what they must assemble and transfer exists not in traditional packages but in the minds of people—in what they know and say.

Information Organization and Storage

Knowledge managers work with information architects, data managers, and Web designers to structure the best systems for acquiring, retrieving, and disseminating needed information. They place into these systems the precious intellectual capital of the organization. Again, we emphasize here the unique role of the user in an organization that would manage its know-how. Users will create a substantial portion of the knowledge database. This "what the organization knows" has to be available to legitimate inquirers, so the knowledge mangers and architects must fashion systems which preserve as well as respond. They must make inquiry language discernable and user friendly. They often must adapt systems to the capabilities and habits of diverse sets of inquirers. There are formidable unknowns to confront, and "if you build it there is no guarantee they will use it" (Morey, Maybury, and Thuraisingham 200, 121).

Information Products and Services Development

It is in the production of information products and services that knowledge managers begin to separate their functions from traditional LIS ones. Production often includes creation and it must result in measurable value added for the KM function to thrive. Knowledge managers often deal with raw data and with information from several units. They massage these resources. They make connections based upon content, context, and need within the organization. They interpret, analyze, combine, and repackage. They make information that did not exist in a given format until they intervened. KM staff aggressively link users with the acquired and created product.

Information Distribution

Part of the KM discovery mission is to determine who needs to know what and to get whatever it is to that person or persons. This involves the transfer and sharing of information, which is the core concept of knowledge management. KM staff must engineer inquiry systems that employees can and will use. The method of distribution must achieve a fit with technical needs and inquirer preferences. In cases where employees may not know what they need to know, the KM service must anticipate their needs and produce a product that helps.

To achieve this, knowledge managers employ survey techniques, tutorials, user profiles, and personal observations. They will discover during this distribution activity that the cyclic and interrelated properties of the nonlinear KM activities or cells manifest themselves. For example, during distribution, new needs and new information will surface, both of which will feed the identification and acquisition activities.

Information Use Is the *Kicker*!

The cell or activity that really separates KM from purely information storage and retrieval pursuit models is the use cell. KM is concerned with the measurable impact that created, acquired, distributed, and shared knowledge has upon the decision activity of those who use it. What is the mechanism for inquiring, for using the system? Has KM facilitated the process? Does the organization use the information retrieved? Does the information matter? How does the information contribute to what the organization needs to know and do? How do the applications of the shared knowledge impact the overall corporate welfare?

Evaluation

What numbers, especially budget figures, support the contention that KM activities influenced decisions that saved money, reduced costs, or increased profits? When investigation reveals a causal link between KM, specifically use, and something good, then KM has achieved its highest calling—a contribution to the bottom line.

The question is what kind of return is the organization getting for its investment in knowledge management? The costs for materials, hardware and software, people and time, distribution, and implementation are great. Are the expenses worth what they cost? Says who? How can they tell? The questions are easy to ask; they are more difficult to answer? Why?

Rumizen wisely points out that determining the value of knowledge management requires a sophisticated measurement technique (Rumizen 2002, 225-37). She touts the balanced scorecard as the best method she has observed for measuring performance. This technique joins the organization's purpose with monetary gain, customer goodwill, business activity within the organization, and perceived advances in learning and development. Profit sheets may reveal some causal value added if the evaluators apply the appropriate methods; so may responses to employee surveys which aim at discovering and attaching perceived value to knowledge management procedures. According to her, Siemens and Hewlett-Packard Consulting "measure the maturity of their knowledge management effort" (Rumizen 2002, 232) in these kinds of ways.

Who Hires Knowledge Managers?

Many organizations hire people to manage know-how. Some of them are familiar names with familiar products. Some of them are knowledge organizations whose product is information and knowledge. This short list is derived from four sources and represents only a portion of the organizations they include in their reports (Burkowitz and Williams, 2000; Dixon, 2000; Morey, Maybury, and Thuraisingham, 2001; and Skyrme, 2000).

Bechtel (engineering)	British Petroleum
Teltech (KM firm	Dow Jones Interactive Publishing
Ernst & Young (consulting)	Fairchild Semiconductor
Ford Motor Company	Hewlett-Packard Consulting Hoffman
General Electric	LaRoche (pharmaceuticals)
Heller Financial	Buckman Labs (chemicals) Chevron
Lockheed Martin (defense)	Pricewaterhouse Cooper's Financial
Steelcase (office furnishings)	Texas Instruments
3M	

Managing Knowledge Management

In a chapter on KM in a book about management, there should be some information about managing knowledge management. Managers manage by deciding and doing, so we think the best way to report on the management function is to describe what a manager of knowledge might decide, do, and face on a typical day.

- Think. Map. Develop a plan for the day.
- Prepare especially well for selling and demonstrating new ideas and technologies.
- Fight the temptation to believe, "I know exactly what I am going to do today."
- Do not expect your plan to work completely; interruptions will intervene.
- Get to work early; this will compensate some for the inevitable interruptions.
- Accept reality of frequent and seemingly endless meetings.
- Know that you will have especially important sessions with information technology (IT) personnel, the people who construct and run the organization's computer-based information systems.
- Know that you will be managing *show and convince* sessions with unit managers and that you may have to bring them along, one unit manager at a time.
- Work with library staff to integrate library resources with the learning and sharing activity.
- Target user groups and frontline personnel for training and demonstration.
- Make a special effort to sell the use of local area network (LAN) and wide area network (WAN) systems.
- Expect resistance.
- Get top management support; without it you must fold up the KM tent. Convince top management to encourage and reward participants and to punish the uncooperative.
- Listen.
- Teach.
- Cajole.
- Encourage sharing, which may be a new concept in the organization.
- Discourage hoarding, which may be standard operating procedure in the organization.
- Prepare to deal with reluctance. Some naysayers will hold back or wait until their advantage is sealed, then jump onboard and claim credit. Live with this.

> **Your Turn:** Will you let us get away with that word "punish"? Do you find the concept of disincentives offensive? Do you think the knowledge manager has the juice to demand compliance or cooperation, or do you think the manager needs support from the top to succeed?

In many respects management is management, so the knowledge manager will plan, decide, train, supervise, coach, teach, evaluate, and reprimand. All managers achieve results largely on the basis of how well they ply their interpersonal skills, so they must acquire and practice good communication skills, especially powers of persuasion. Managers should expect an endless blur of meetings, actual and virtual.

How Soon Will a New Term Replace Knowledge Management?

Before the toner dries on these pages, opportunists will have invented new terms, maybe even new processes. In the frantic and often amusing process that is one-upmanship, someone will have added a wrinkle or two to KM practice and righteously renamed it. "What KM overlooks," they will intone, "is such and such." They will add the such and such that addresses an issue they claim KM cannot handle, and come up with the new name: Corporate Cyber-Cerebellum. They will conveniently ignore the fact that their new orthodoxy incorporates 90 percent of KM canons and tenets, just as early total quality management (TQM) gurus blasted management by objectives (MBO) and then structured a management tool that was as focused upon measurable outcomes as MBO was. Speaking of one-upmanship, TQM, and KM, one of TQM's central ideas was the concept of the next customer as the recipient of system or subsystem products. KM also focuses upon the next customer, the user, but brings him or her into the system as a participant. KM users are not out there; they are in here, even when they are out there.

Knowledge managers count on there being an evolution of method and nomenclature. They know there will be harsh skeptics and friendly observers who note drifts, shifts, cracks, seepages, and oversights. There will be critics of definition, concept, and practice. Knowledge managers know there will be holdouts who insist that whatever the knowledge managers think they are managing, it is not knowledge, for knowledge cannot be managed. Undaunted, knowledge managers believe we are all ticketed to ride on Six Flags over Cyberspace's greatest attraction: the information/knowledge ride, and someone will manage that ride. Right now, the knowledge managers aim to do this, and we can learn from them. We can join them.

Command and Control

Why do we include this military reference in our presentation of KM? Isn't command and control (C2) an environment-specific term that applies only to orders, execution, the defeat of an enemy, and accountability? We think KM is about knowledge, the application of knowledge to specific problems, the determination of who is in charge of managing the diffusion of knowledge, and whether the costs justify the expenses involved. That's pretty military all right, and the C2 model apes many KM specifics.

When organizations cannot determine for themselves who knows what within the organization, there is a need for KM and C2. The record shows this situation seriously afflicts many an agency and that within those agencies individuals often share information poorly. When personal emergencies take employees from their posts, what redeployment is triggered? Without missing a beat, who picks up the absent worker's project that is due at 8:00 a.m. tomorrow? When an insurance giant and major software customer complains to a provider that the provider's 3 million dollar software product is torpedoing the corporation's actuarial data and issuing payments to phantom policyholders, which of the software provider's personnel handle the complaint, fix the problem, placate the customer, and route the remedy to all the software engineers who need to know the composition and debugging particulars?

The Department of Defense defines command and control thusly:

> Command and Control is the exercise of authority and direction by a properly designated Commander over assigned forces in the accomplishment of the mission. Command and Control functions are performed through an arrangement of personnel, equipment, communications, facilities, and procedures which are employed by a Commander in planning, directing, coordinating, and controlling forces and operations in the accomplishment of the mission. (Diedrichsen 2000, 2)

Yes, knowledge management and command and control are strikingly similar in many ways. Both are about who is in charge, what needs to be known, and who needs to know what? To achieve success, they each require reliable intelligence (information) capabilities. Both depend heavily upon information *exchange*. Both concern themselves with accurate, precise information. Both involve possibilities, opportunities, accountability, risk, timely responses, and productive human interaction. KM and C2 operate in a context that includes the need to gain initiatives, to confront uncertainties, and to react to the actions of competitors. Both aim at the same outcome, the good decision.

Granted, most knowledge managers do not wear battle uniforms, nor do they fire surface-to-air missiles, but they do create, assemble, and communicate information to people who use it to achieve corporate victories.

Isn't C2 about Enemies; Do Nonmilitary Organizations Have Enemies?

Experts in competitive intelligence strive to keep their organizations competitive by gathering as much information as they can about competitors and their products and putting that information in motion within the agencies they serve. These efforts can and should be part of the KM strategy. Such efforts imply that an agency has enemies out there who are more than willing to weaken their competition. So the concept of enemy, part and parcel of command and control, is not so inappropriate in the corporate environment. The business community may include competitors who plan to market a rival product or who commission industrial spies disguised as journalists. LIS agencies operating in the public sector deal with private sector predators and with publishers who raise subscription rates to compensate themselves for the widened free access to their expensive products provided by libraries. Public and private sector organizations deal with clients and employees who will not play by the rules. Then ethical issues may surface, those involving intellectual property rights among them.

KM and C2 are not identical functions. We do not recommend that KM advocates adopt military uniforms and ways of behaving. What we do recommend is that knowledge managers study the military model and observe the need to construct architectures that incorporate intelligence-gathering strategies, assessment tactics, and stated lines of authority and supervisory oversight—all of which would strengthen an organization's KM effort (Diedrichsen 2000, 5). We agree that C2 "is about the management of conflict" and that "business management can be about the same thing at times" (Hitchins n.d., 2).

Opposition to C2 Concepts

Opponents of C2 notions claim that regimentation and order stifle creativity. Ironically, they have found an unlikely ally in the U.S. Army, which has run some "be an army of one" ads in order to attract creative souls to the ranks. We think, however, that army basic training will soon reconfigure the outlook of any recruit who opts for do-it-my-way approaches. Nevertheless, anti-C2 rhetoric is available for inspection: "Ultimately, we have to rely not on the procedural manuals, but on peoples' brains . . . . If they are acting by rote or regimen, they actually have lost the capacity for excellence" (Wheatley 1997, 6).

We invite critics to inspect a well-constructed disaster-preparedness policy and a stocked disaster-preparedness box and to answer a question. In a time of disaster and panic, who is the best choice to cope with the situation: an employee armed with a plan, or a creative thinker? Our answer is 'C'—both of the above.

We agree with JESSE listserv participants Claire McInerney of Rutgers and Mike Koenig of Long Island University who think we have a responsibility to help readers think critically and thoughtfully about what knowledge management gurus and practitioners do (McInerney 2001; Koenig 2001). About the term itself, it will most certainly morph, but that should not discourage us from examining the phenomena of information architecture, transfer, and use by knowledge workers within and beyond corporate structures. As Koenig notes, we "word process" every day even though those words have never really accurately described what we do when we word process.

A Knowledge Management Outlook?

Here is the way we think knowledge managers think about information and knowledge. Information is a utility, a thing that when applied by people to a situation can become knowledge. Information workers must manage data, information, know-how, knowledge, and solutions. None of these is static; they flow and change. They may reside in books, reports, tapes, or charts, and they may be tacit and they may reside in the minds of individuals in the organization or outside the organization. Knowledge managers acquire, sort, and organize information and knowledge, and they position it in systems which employees use to retrieve information they want. These systems may also aggressively disburse information in anticipation of employee need. Sometimes corporate employees do not know exactly want they want, and even if they do, they might not know whom to ask. As much as possible, the KM force builds and manages a KM function that accommodates the corporate culture, that is sensitive to the sociology and psychology of information transfer, and that embraces the user. For the knowledge manager, an inquirer is not an end user positioned where the information stops but a full participant/contributor in the KM process. The great challenge to KM is to make discoveries about the creation and dissemination of information, to discover ways to get people, some of whom may not be accustomed to letting go, to share information, and to feed the results to corporate players with decision-making responsibilities. Therefore, knowledge managers are as concerned with what people do with information as they are with the information itself. Knowledge managers measure their success in terms of how favorably the creation, learning, and sharing of information/knowledge affect the goals of the organization, including the bottom line.

What Does Any of This Have to Do with Managing a Library?

Maybe nothing, and that would be very sad indeed. Knowledge management is not better than library science; it is different from library science. Those differences may point to ways in which libraries can guarantee their places in the information society. A library science that results chiefly in passive collection, organization, and storing is not likely to survive the electronic era. Neither is a library science that is merely reactive—one which willingly helps out but only if asked. We think librarians must disengage themselves from the false assurances which captive audiences provide. Captive audiences are any students who must do library assignments; middle school students who earn points for reading specific library books and passing a test which asks questions like "What color was the ball the boy bounced?"; and teachers who assign tours and scavenger hunts. Librarians must educate faculty or administrators who think the library is the heart of the institution, but are not quite sure what that means, and treat it like the appendix come budget time. We think librarians should invest more energy in finding out what people want; in acquiring, creating, and delivering products and services aimed at expressed needs; and in evaluating the results in ways that impress funders.

We recommend a new way of looking at information and users—the KM way. Develop an interest in what people make of the information they get from us, what it means to them, and how to use it. Jettison puritanical rituals such as teaching classification systems to unsuspecting inquirers. The road to self-reliance as an information seeker is paved not with decimal blocks or alphanumerical codes but by productive encounters with user-friendly librarians. Cease the practice of loading mission statements with predictions about "lifelong learners" unless you are prepared to conduct rigorous and massive longitudinal studies of clients and their victories. Abandon references to awful terms like: end user. Information doesn't end when a user retrieves it; it may well enjoy a new and productive beginning. Graduate from thinking of users as the focal point of service, and instead consider them participants in the process of information sharing. Give them a role to play, perhaps not the crucial role required of participants in knowledge management operations but some active responsibility in the sharing of information and discovery. Keep fighting the battle to make information literacy, media literacy, oralcy, or however the new information skills are called, as crucial to curricula, corporate responsibility, and public awareness as they are to us in our information places.

Your Turn: Librarians, is this last paragraph disrespectful of your mission? Argue that you do all these things every day. Point out examples of very assertive library practice that you know about, and give evidence that what librarians currently do "works." Discuss the quality of that evidence.

References

Burkowitz, Wendi R., and Ruth L. Williams. 2000. *The knowledge management fieldbook*. Revised edition. New York: Financial Times/Prentice Hall.

Chait, Laurence. 2002. Creating a successful knowledge management system. *Journal of Business Strategy* (March-April): n.p. http.//us. f97.mail.yahoo.com/ym/ShowLetter?Msgld=3415_33060 (accessed on 6 June 2002).

Choo, Chun Wei. 1995. *Information management for the intelligent organization: The art of scanning the environment*. Medford, NJ: Information Today, Incorporated.

Crainer, Stuart. 2000. *Management century: A critical review of 20th century thought and practice*. San Francisco: Jossey-Bass.

Davenport, Elizabeth, and Blaise Cronin. 2000. Knowledge management: Semantic drift or conceptual shift. *Journal of Education for Library and Information Science* 41 (Fall): 294-306.

Davenport, Thomas H., and Laurence Prusak. 1998. *Working knowledge: How organizations manage what they know*. Boston: Harvard Business School Press.

Diedrichsen, Loren. 2000. Command & Control: Operational requirements and system implementation. *Information & Security* 5:1-16. mlpltp://www.isn.ethz.ch/onlinepubli/publihouse/infosecurity/volume (accessed on 16 July 2002).

Dixon, Nancy M. 2000. *Common knowledge: How companies thrive by sharing what they know*. Boston: Harvard Business School Press.

Duhon, Bryant. 1998. It's all in our heads. *Inform* 12 (September): 10.

Ghostbusters. 1984. Los Angeles: Columbia/Tristar Studios.

Goodrum, Abby. 2001. E-mail to JESSE Listserv. Accessed at JESSE@LISTSERV.UTK.EDU on 19 November 2001 (JESSE Archives).

Hagedorn, Kat. 2000. Information architecture glossary. Argos Associates. http://argus-acia.com/white_papers/iaglossary.html (accessed on 23 May 2002).

Hitchins, Derek K. Command and control: The management of conflict. http://www.hitchins.co.uk/CandC.html (accessed on 15 July 2002).

Horwitch, Robert A. 2002. Helping knowledge management be all it can be. *Journal of Business Strategy* 3 (May-June): 26-31.

Koenig, Mike. 2001. Re: Knowledge management. E-mail to JESSE Listserv. Accessed at JESSE@LISTSERV.UTK.EDU on 19 November 2001 (JESSE Archives).

McInerney, Claire. 2001. Re: Knowledge management. E-mail to JESSE Listserv. Accessed at JESSE@LISTSERV.UTK.EDU on 19 November 2001 (JESSE Archives).

Meadows, Donnella H. 1997. Places to intervene in a system. *Whole Earth* (Winter): 78-85.

Morey, Daryl, Mark Maybury, and Bhavani Thuraisingham, eds. 2001. *Knowledge management: Classic and contemporary works*. Cambridge, MA: The MIT Press.

Nasseri, Touraj. 1996. Knowledge leverage: The ultimate advantage. http://www.brint.com/papers/submit/nasseri,htm (accessed 24 May 2002).

Rosenfeld, Louis, and Peter Morville. 1998. *Information architecture for the World Wide Web*. Sebastopol, CA: O'Reilly.

Rumizen, Melissise C. 2002. *The complete idiot's guide to knowledge management*. Madison, WI: CWL Publishing Enterprises.

Shiple, John. 2002. Information architecture tutorial overview. http://hotwired.lycos.com/webmonkey/design/site_building/tutorials (accessed 23 May 02).

Skyrme, David. 2000. *Knowledge management: Making sense of an oxymoron*. http://www.skyrme.com/insights/22km.htm (accessed 29 January 2001).

Srikantaiah, T. Kanti, and Michael E. D. Koening. 2000. *Knowledge management for the information professional*. Medford, NJ: Information Today, Inc. for the American Society for Information Science.

Wheatley, Margaret. 1997. Goodbye, command and control. *Leader to Leader* No. 5 (Summer): 1-9.

Chapter 14

You Will Not See This in Other Information Place Management Texts

This chapter covers the kinds of things that are discussed or gossiped about in bars, in tiny groups in the staff room after most of the others have left, during one-on-one conversations with trusted mentors, and sometimes with veteran professionals and friendly support staff who have spent years in the information vineyards.

We present the following topics for conversation:

- Opting to have sex with a coworker
- The real reason they did not hire you
- Sh*t happens and things do not work out
- Are cliques okay?
- Do information places have enemies?
- Is it okay to be a little crazy?
- Can I escape management?
- Image
- Am I any good at this?
- Can I delegate and still hover a little bit?

Opting to Have Sex with a CoWorker

Most any management text will provide ample amounts of information about sexual harassment: tell what it is, what it is not, and what to do about it. Many organizations have template approaches to defining and dealing with sexual harassment. Wise observers ask several questions about affairs of the heart. Are the consenting participants of age? Is there a power relationship? Then these wise observers form their judgments, accordingly. What about just plain old-fashioned and high-spirited consensual sex between two consenting adults who happen to work on the same team or faculty group?

In this day and age of mobility, team approaches, and multiple opportunities for interpersonal relations, people meet, talk, work together, flirt, become infatuated with each other, and sometimes fall in love. At some point in this process, maybe five minutes after meeting, or perhaps after falling in love, which can take ten minutes, they decide to have sex with each other. Is this a good idea? Yes and no.

It is a good idea in the same sense that breathing, taking liquids, or getting a haircut are good ideas: It is necessary or it feels good, or both. There may be moral issues. Adultery can produce hurtful results; so can sexually transmitted diseases. Sexual harassment suits are disruptive and few winners win much, in the long run. Regardless of the potential for misery, coworkers often couple. This can work out badly for both parties, for coworkers, and for the organization, especially if there is a boss/subordinate ingredient or a real or perceived power or information advantage to be gained by one of the couplers. Even so, couples couple. Every manager should ask himself or herself this question: Is this a good idea for me?

It is a bad idea for many, many reasons. But first of all, it is important to describe specifically the issue under consideration. We are not talking about a classic boy meets girl love story where two innocent people meet at the water cooler, fall in love, marry, and raise one and one-half gifted children. We are talking about plain old lustful sexual congress of the wink-wink or even forbidden variety, the kind people whisper about, condemn, and maybe even fear because of the waves of concern it engenders. It is that kind Nat "King" Cole sang about when he crooned, "When love is forbidden, love is so sweet, love is so sweet" (Washington and Tiomkin n.d.) That kind. The kind that gets jaws flapping in the organization. The kind that can rob a person of integrity and credibility because for some reason it just is not right.

Here are some reasons why office affairs are bad ideas:

- No matter how hard they try, couples cannot hide the fact that they are lovers. Lovers deal with each other in many transparently obvious ways. They speak to each other, they look at each other, and they do things for each other in ways that scream, We are lovers! The most interesting, and the most amusing, thing about this is that they actually think they are fooling anyone. Listen up, lovebirds, it's on the bulletin board. Everybody knows! No one doesn't know. You are busted!

- Eventually the people who wish you ill and can do you harm, will.

- Going to the boss and saying, "Boss, Chris and I are seeing each other, and we want you to know from us, not the grapevine," does not work. First of all you and Chris are probably not supposed to be fooling around. Second, informing the boss offers you little protection if the union you are engaging in is forbidden. Alerting the boss may not maneuver him or her into condoning your congress; it may only trigger early retaliation.

- Falling in love is a nice thing. If it happens, one of you probably will have to leave the shop. Some organizations welcome husband and wife or partner teams, but others may not tolerate such arrangements in the same department. Check the corporate culture.

- Sweetness can go sour. This can also disrupt the working arrangements.

- Falling in love or in lust is not a *thinking* thing. Nevertheless, most observers hold that people are responsible for their actions. Deciding to act upon one's feelings *is* a thinking thing. Insofar as having sex with a coworker is concerned, your authors advise, "Think." Those may be errors, not arrows, that Eros is slinging.

Why You Did Not Get That Managerial Post You Interviewed For

1. You are not as ready as you think you are.
2. You interviewed poorly.
3. Your appearance did you in.
4. Other candidates made better impressions.
5. They did not like you.
6. You have promise, but not for that particular job.
7. Somebody else already has been selected; your interview was pro forma.
8. The employer is sleeping with—or wants to sleep with—the manager who gets the job instead of you .

(Baldwin and Malone 2001, 171).

Our experience teaches us that the people who make employment decisions often use mysterious criteria, and sometimes they make curious choices. This means that good people sometimes do not get hired or promoted. Not getting hired happens. So does getting hired. The best advice we can muster for aspiring managers is this: Work on the things over which you have some control; worry less about those things over which you have no control; and keep stroking.

An examination of the eight reasons listed above should reveal a few over which an aspiring manager has some control. One who seeks a managerial post should study the new post and the organization as much as possible. Read the organization's mission statement and its annual reports. Carefully scour the job announcement. Study their Web page. Prepare to convince an interviewer that you have what the agency says it wants. Read between the lines. If a position statement uses words such as *team*, *team captain*, or *work group*, how will you prepare to display yourself as having the qualities needed for these kinds of responsibilities? What will you say when an interviewer asks, "Tell me about your group skills and give me some examples." Will you be prepared, or will you use the "I am a quick learner" line?

Be careful about proclaiming that the agency you aspire to join sets the industry standard for knowledge sharing and you want to participate in those notable ventures. Find subtler ways to let them know you know what goes on in the organization. If you can produce portfolio evidence that you know how to manage information, you will be well prepared to demonstrate your fit.

Wear appropriate clothing to an interview. If the shop is a ponytail and jeans shop, you may get away with informal attire. If the shop is a coat and tie shop, your t-shirt and sandals may disqualify you. An observation—a previsit—can supply good intelligence about the corporate culture. You may also seek second and third opinions about your attire, especially if your fashion sense is shaky. Like it or not, accept it or not, your clothing makes a statement about you that your interviewers will translate—not you.

Arrive on time.

Prepare to ask questions. They will ask you if you have any. "No, I think you have covered just about everything" leads the league in wrong responses to their request. If you have done your homework, you will have good questions to ask.

Your interviewers are looking for some spark, some indication that you have initiative and can think on your feet. Prepare to demonstrate this.

If you are turned down, you have every right to inquire of your interviewers how well you performed and why they determined that you were not ready. The honest ones will share this information with you, and you may use it to shore up your interviewing skills.

So, you can determine and prepare to show your qualifications for a given managerial post. You can display some verve, and you can dress for the occasion. You can get there on time. You can inquire about how well you did.

If other candidates possess better credentials and/or better interviewing skills, you may lose out. You have little control over the pure chemistry of like/dislike and none over the fact that the post may already be locked up by an inside candidate.

So, work on the things you can influence: get good training, acquire marketable skills, study the agency you wish to join, and learn how to present yourself in a favorable light.

Sometimes Things Do Not Work Out

There will be times, managers, when best efforts fail, when people will not cooperate. Perhaps the issue will be a routine or procedure which several employees consistently refuse to observe. When the failure of a few torpedoes an initiative, or when foot-dragging by some erodes staff morale, a manager may have to act. Recently, on orders from above, a manager instituted an electronic sign-in/whereabouts procedure designed to alert the organization as to who had reported for work, who was where, and who was not available. Some workers viewed this as an imposition, an unprofessional requirement. A few did not comply. Management noticed and issued warnings to two consistent offenders. They persisted with noncompliance. Administration came down hard on management, so management fired the two biggest offenders. The next day, and from then on, folks signed in each day.

Sometimes managers will have to resort to a power move when other tactics like compromise or persuasion do not work. In the case above, the firing sent shock waves through the department and served notice on people who wanted to stay employed. Some workers get great satisfaction from simply obeying rules; others require a boot in the pants occasionally. Experience and/or a good mentor can teach a new manager the best times to use positive or negative reinforcement.

Foot-dragging may be curtailed when the draggers are excised, but there are other causes for things not to work out. If managers do not explain or teach well, especially the details of new planning processes or new projects, workers may mount excuses based upon the manager's failings. We once heard a worker claim, "Oh, we tried that MBO. It doesn't work." Upon questioning, the worker admitted that the organization really had not established numerical objectives to shoot for, and that only a few people in the organization had understood MBO and had participated in the experiment. No wonder it did not work! Managers who expect new things to work out had better remember their crucial teaching responsibilities.

Cliques

In any work group people who perform similar or related jobs may congregate and form alliances. Little pockets of friends will gravitate toward each other and bond. They will spend time together, often go to lunch together, and most important of all, they will share information and look out for each other. Sometimes these groups—these cliques—will exclude others or will be perceived as doing so.

The invitation to join a clique is seldom embossed on fine linen stock; and though it is issued in a subtler manner, it does require an R.S.V.P. That cliques exist is a given. What is not a given is the wisdom of the decision to join or not join with a group of people who band together for a variety of purposes: social, informational, psychological, and business. A new manager may decline such an invitation at his or her peril. To refuse to join may have the effect of systematically excluding one from information flow, a power base, or a source of organizational support. On the other hand, joining may signal to rival cliques or to the nonaligned that one has taken sides with a powerful in-group.

What do cliques look like and do? They may exist geographically in the same unit, perhaps at adjacent workstations. They may consist of supervisory and nonsupervisory personnel, professional and staff employees. They spend time together. They may work closely together, lunch together, and socialize during off-work hours. They get along. They help each other. They share information within the group, and they support each other's projects.

Are Cliques Okay?

In that cliques help get the organization's job done by providing a social structure for acquiring organizational intelligence and putting it to use, cliques are okay. In that cliques are powerful and have the juice to get things done, cliques can be good. In that cliques provide a support system for an employee who needs to learn the ropes and who benefits from team membership, cliques are fine. In that cliques can monopolize organizational intelligence gathering and deny information access to nonmembers, cliques are not okay. In that the very basis of knowledge management operations is the sharing of information, cliques which hoard information and refuse for whatever reasons to share it pose a threat to organizational health and are not okay. Cliques that sap organizational strength or injure morale are bad.

Cliques are not so good when they hog decision making, or when outsiders are denied organizational favors or given a disproportionately large share of organizational demerits.

It is not useful to pronounce all cliques either okay or not okay. It all depends. What do they accomplish? Are their activities benign or hurtful? Do they use their powers for good or evil? Do they exclude others and is this truly dysfunctional? Do they make the organization go, or do they drag it down? Can management marshal the power of cliques to good organizational ends? Putting them to work is wiser than attempting to eliminate them, for this can drive them underground and empower them even further.

Should I Join One?

If survival, or *thrival*, depends upon group membership, accepting membership in a clique may be a good decision. We know of skillful workers who retained membership in two cliques. They were able to move in both circles and benefit. In this case, of course, neither group was a rival group in the sense that it was at odds with the other, and neither forbade dual memberships. If it becomes clear to a manager that clique membership produces antipathies and actions harmful to organizational health, he or she should reconsider retaining membership in such a clique.

What about the lunch bunch? People who frequently lunch together may not form a clique, but they do associate and they do conduct business at lunch. They pass information. They test ideas. They drum up support. They influence each other. Opting out of the lunch bunch and choosing instead to do peanut butter and jelly in the break room may be in the long run bad economics, bad sociology, and bad business.

What about those people who are not part of a clique or who may be excluded from membership. Sometimes a job change is not available to these people and they must make the best of the work situation. The Internet carries some interesting questions and advice for the nonjoiner. Do you really want to hang out with these people? If they asked you to go fishing, would you like that? In other words, do you really want to spend time with these people? Does complaining about your situation help? If you cannot change the behavior of the clique, maybe you can change how you respond to them. They are exclusionary? You practice openness and friendliness to everyone, especially to others who may also be excluded from the in-group. Speak to everyone. Do not permit other people to influence your behaviors; you make the decision to be pleasant. Continue to get good training. Do not practice what you find so offensive in the clique; instead communicate with everyone, including the clique members. These things you do for yourself, to help you cope (Morem 1999-2002, 1-2).

Cliques often spring up in middle schools and junior high schools where students are desperate to fit in and fiercely contend to be accepted by peers. One elementary school involved its culture club in a table-hopping experiment wherein at lunch groups of two and three students sought to join students with whom they did not normally eat. The idea was to challenge the exclusivity practiced by the "others." It turned out that rejection was a regular occurrence and that those rejected had to learn to deal with the feelings that accompany the turndowns (Tam 2001). It appears that cliques are natural phenomena, that people begin at an early age to form them, and that one should not be surprised, therefore, to see them operating in organizations. Organizational leadership often stresses and encourages team approaches to project planning, project execution, and problem solving. Quality groups or empowerment teams can easily morph into cliques. Cliques can be outgrowths or extensions of team structures, or they can constitute the nuclei of teams charged with specific tasks.

We know of managers who have superior interpersonal skills and who are able to dart in and out of various groups and cliques. They will go out to lunch sometimes and sometimes they will brown-bag it in the break room with other *lunchbucketeers*. They have the skills to make most employees feel okay. They communicate. They do not exclude anyone when it comes time to seek organizational input. They may play poker with the boys, but the next day they might invite some nonboys to lunch. They often entertain the entire department in their homes.

Do Information Places Have Friends and Enemies?

Corporate information officers are on guard against industrial espionage. They are fully aware that competitors would love to know what their rival's research and development groups are up to. What new products are in the works? What is really in that secret sauce? What marketing techniques are in the offing? They believe in sharing but only in-house. They do not need scorecards to tell the players. Friends wear company colors and fund company enterprises. Friends are co-workers in product development and in sales. Friends buy company products and sell them to customers. Friends sing the praises of those products and demonstrate their loyalty and friendship by continuing to purchase them.

Knowledge managers know that employees who contribute to the intellectual capital of the organization by sharing and using information are friends. They know, on the other hand, that organizational researchers and developers, marketers and sales forces, and managers and technicians who do *not* share information are enemies of the cause.

What to Do about Friends and Enemies

Managers should court and encourage friends. Managers should try always to make new friends. The more support and the more customers, the better. Managers should try to win over the enemies, make friends of them in other words. Failing that, managers should at least neutralize the power of enemies to commit harmful acts against the organization.

Should Information Managers Call People Enemies? Is That Impolite?

We believe that information managers should court friends and neutralize enemies. There are people whose actions are harmful to the cause, and managers should seek ways to get such people to discontinue such behaviors. Ideally, the managers could influence the offenders to change their ways, maybe even adopt supportive behaviors. What are some examples of enemy behavior?

University and college presidents and holders of the purse strings who mouth platitudes such as, "The library is the heart of the . . ." but who underfund the information place are enemies. Managers must either convince these administrators, succeed in getting friendly faculty to do so, or neutralize the enemy by obtaining alternative sources of funding.

Politicians who brag about and point with pride to the new public library building but fail to fund the library for materials, facilities, and staff are enemies. Managers must win over these hard cases, convince the Friends of the Library and the board of trustees to use leverage, and deftly encourage citizen/voters to demonstrate their support of library-friendly candidates. Another way to demonstrate to politicians that the library serves a useful function is to regularly and systematically provide local political bodies the information they need for decision-making. To avoid partisan politics, the library managers should do this through contact with city or town managers who serve the whole town council, not just the Democrats or Republicans.

Employees who are rude to clients are enemies of the cause. Managers must retrain them or fire them. Managers work hard to plan and oversee the execution of services for clients, but such activities are dashed by employees who drive clients away with curt or unhelpful responses. Sometimes the most dangerous enemies reside within.

No information manager who rises in the faculty senate or at a county council meeting to denounce the provost or the county supervisor as an enemy is likely to alter the enemy's behavior in a favorable direction. If a disgruntled corporate librarian refers to the CEO as a cheapskate, or if a beleaguered school library media specialist uses the newsletter to call the principal an enemy of learning, neither is likely to find something extra in next year's fiscal allotment. Using the concept of enemy to slur or embarrass someone who appears unconvinced about the importance of the information place is not the intention here. What is important is that managers realize that some people support the cause and some do not. Managers should thank and encourage supporters. Managers should attempt to win over the nonsupporters. If these efforts fail, managers should find ways to soften the impact of non-support, perhaps by developing their own grant-writing capabilities.

In order to make the best use of the friends/enemies concept, a manager might ask staff to participate in an exercise. Each person would draw a line down the center of a legal page, label one column *Friends* and the other *Enemies*, and then list people or groups in a category.

Each listing should include a statement of why the person or group has been categorized. Then the group might brainstorm about efforts to continue to please friends, cultivate new friends, convert enemies, and blunt the efforts of enemies. By the way, one of us works in a town where the city manager was fired for composing an enemies list. So be careful not to give the impression that the list is a hit list. The object is more support and better service to more people, not mayhem. Managers will make this crystal clear to all participants and freedom of information inquirers.

It Is Okay to Be a Little Crazy

What is seductive about your information place? What is it about your organization that would influence people to trade their most valuable commodity—their time—for what you have to offer them? Creative approaches to responding to these questions often lead a manager to dream up ideas that are novel, even unusual. This is good. Inventive approaches to new services, for example, capture the attention of clients.

Finding out what people want and giving it to them is the essence of marketing, but many managers short-circuit the connection when they assume instead of assess. They promote their own values rather than cater to their clients'. They confuse public relations and advertising for marketing, which demands that managers find out what people want and need before they attempt to announce, persuade, and deliver.

It is good to be a little bit crazy, a little bit free and inventive, and a little bit right-brained when thinking about how to inquire of clients and how to deliver to clients. The moment we give in to adult impulses and question the value of dreaming, the moment we scold ourselves for allowing the child in us to wonder, the muse will abandon us and we will retreat to a business-as-usual approach to addressing client needs.

A manager who conducts a consumer needs survey and invites a staff to think up crazy ways to address those needs summons the muse and gets treated to some very innovative ideas, some of which will be in left field and a few of which will be quite seductive.

I Will Escape Management;
I Do Not Want to Be a Supervisor

Can't I just be a cataloger, a storyteller, or a master debugger of systems? I enjoy being responsible for myself and I abhor being in charge of others. I am naturally shy and am simply no good at telling others what to do.

The truth be told, there are still some jobs in the information business for people who work alone. There are some one-person shops. The vast majority of professional positions, however, call for manager/deciders, people who make decisions about the deployment of time, money, people, and things—even if that time, one person, a solitary manager, deploys money and material. No information organization is going to pay a professional salary to a hermit in residence. The advertisements for new hires these days are laced with terms such as *supervise, deploy, manage, direct, coordinate,* and *liaison.* New hires are expected to decide and interact on day one.

Managerial and supervisory skills are learnable. They can be acquired through study, identification, and practice. This does not apply, probably, to the pathologically shy. Mentors really help in situations where new managers can learn by shadowing and emulating their tutors.

Image

The way we dress, our mannerisms, our speaking ability are all image builders. Are these important considerations to a manager? You bet! The manager or would-be manager should be cognizant of the corporate culture of the information place and develop an image accordingly. She does not have to be lock-step with that culture, but she should be within the general parameters defined by it. That culture may permit casual dress, snapping her fingers on every third sentence, or youthful slang. It may stipulate a white shirt, coat and tie-type of place with formal titles and courtesies that, at most, permits business casual on Fridays. Whatever the culture, the manager will usually experience greater success if she projects an image that fits.

There are many other images a manager may wish to develop and project as well. What about the image of someone who gets the job done? Or the image of someone who really cares about the clients and will go the extra mile to ensure their satisfaction. It is likely to the manager's benefit to have the reputation of being a good budget manager or good in working with staff.

Whether we like it or not, image will be a part of our job as managers. We can ignore it and accept whatever image happens to develop. But it is far better to be proactive and to ensure that we cultivate a positive image.

It is interesting and instructive to note that this image issue floats to the top of library and information science manager concerns every few years when the more popular library literature has a go at it . . . and then lets go of it. Someone will claim the image of the information professional is poor. Another will express surprise at this claim and protest that no modern information professional displays the negative image of the fussy, misanthropic, "shushing" librarian anymore. A third party will assert that the image issue is a nonissue. Furthermore, third party has an excellent image of herself, and that is all that matters. A subsequent observer will claim that it is time to drop this discussion and get on with the real business of information transfer. Then the literature jettisons image and moves on until five years later when Hollywood or Madison Avenue portrays a nerdy librarian and triggers a firestorm of new complaints.

We do not subscribe to the nonissue thesis. We observe that society rewards persons substantially on the basis of their perception of those persons' contributions and value to the community. Library and information science practitioners should act to enhance those perceptions, for their good and for the good of the institutions they serve. How one is perceived matters!

How Do I Know if I Am a Good Manager?

Practically every other self-aware manager in history has wondered about whether he or she was doing the job well and being a good manager. Poorer ones do not ask! They assume one way or the other. But they may never really know, save for what is in the paycheck, what people think of them. They may not care. Our remarks are directed to the ones who care.

There is no definitive yardstick that one can use to determine the answer to the question, but other people issue some clues at regular intervals. These may come from your boss, your staff, and most importantly from your clients. Listen to and accept these clues. Males in particular seem to have a difficult time accepting praise.

One of the great maxims of interpersonal communication is this: "If you want to know what someone thinks about you or what you are doing, ask." Maintaining open channels of communication about personal performance can lead to authentic exchanges of information about good management and other important issues. This "ask" technique is not a formula; it will not work always, especially if one displays insecurity rather than inquisitiveness and a genuine interest in another's opinion. Asking every ten minutes is too often' asking once in a while, and then seriously considering the responses, may work.

This takes trust. The manager has to trust the boss or the supervisee. The boss or supervisee has to trust the inquirer. Managers build trust. They cannot demand it. It comes when people treat each other's authentic communication responsibly.

Okay, I Delegate!
But I Still Have to Hover (Micromanage)

Then you really have not delegated! "Delegate" and "hover" do not belong in the same sentence.

One of the keys to delegation is this: Work with your staff on outcomes rather than focusing on how they get the job done. What is it that you and they are trying to accomplish? Your focusing upon the end product will protect you, and them, from your having to stand over them and micromanage.

One of the hardest things to do is to let go! Delegation requires it. When one delegates, he does not let go completely and abandon all concern. What he abandons is having a hand in the execution of each detail. He entrusts the delegates with those details after both parties have negotiated and verified their understandings about what is supposed to happen—about what the end product is to be. The wise delegator makes himself available as a consultant on the project.

References

Baldwin, Paul, and John Malone. 2001. *The complete idiot's guide to acting.* Indianapolis: Alpha Books.

Morem, Sue. 1999-2002. *Ask Sue: Workplace cliques.* www.careerknow how.com/ask_sue/clique.htm (accessed on 12 May 2003).

Tam, Katherine. 2001. Table hoppers work to cross invisible barrier of cliques. www.appeal-democrat.com/archive/2001/121201/ykt12 culture (accessed on 12 May 2003).

Washington, Ned, and Dimitri Tiomkin. n.d. *Hajji Baba* (Persian Lament). Song recorded by Nat "King" Cole and Connie Stevens.

Index

About the Authors

Charles Curran received his master's and Ph.D. in library service from the School of Communication, Information, and Library Studies, Rutgers University, and his B.Ed. and M.Ed. from Duquesne University. He has served in the U.S. Army's ceremonial Third Infantry, coached high school basketball, and worked in school, public, and academic libraries. Curran has taught management and collection development at the School of Library and Information Science, University of South Carolina. He has served elected and appointed offices in ALA and the Association for Library and Information Science Education, most recently as president of the latter.

Lewis Miller received his M.L.S. from the University of South Carolina. He also holds an M.Ed. from the University of Georgia and an M.A. in English literature from Gonzaga University. He has more than twenty-five years experience as an academic library administrator and is currently dean of libraries at Butler University in Indianapolis. Throughout his career, he has been an advocate for and leader in a number of consortia. He has held various appointed offices in ACRL and sections of ACRL.